Just Compassion

Just Compassion

A Priest's Quest for Human Rights

Wally Dethlefs

Tafina Press

Brisbane

First published in Australia, 2017

Published by
Tafina Press
7 Drake Street,
West End, Q. 4101
Australia

ISBN: 978-0-9757658-6-9

Cover design: Danielle Long

Illustrations © Wally Dethlefs and Mick Porter. Used by permission.
Photograph of Wilson Youth Hospital from 'Find and Connect',
https://www.findandconnect.gov.au/ref/qld/objects/QD0000273.htm

Typeset in Warnock Pro
Printed and bound by Lightning Source

Dedication

Disadvantaged young people, who have taught and continue to teach me.

Youth workers, who stood and stand in solidarity with young people who are struggling for dignity.

My parents, who gave me the principles and values which formed the foundations of my life.

My siblings, who supported and encouraged me.

To all of you, please accept my undying gratitude.

Table of Contents

Table of Illustrations

Glossary

Absolution Forgiveness offered by the priest in God's name within the Sacrament of Reconciliation

(Lay) Apostolate Actions taken by non-clerical people to advance the work of Christ and the Church

Catechetics The act of imparting the teaching of Christ and his Church

Dean, Deanery A priest designated by the Bishop to coordinate and support Church work in a geographic region called a deanery

Ecumenism Refers to collaborative actions with other Christian denominations

Eucharist, -ic Literally means thanksgiving: denotes the principal form of worship in the Catholic Church, often called the Mass

Formation On-going and planned training, often using a commonly accepted methodology like see/judge/act

Grace The presence of God within a person

Homily A sermon or message delivered for spiritual growth

Holy Medal A small metal disk with an image of Jesus, Mary or another holy person depicted on it

Liturgy Public worship of the Church as opposed to private worship or prayer

Mass See **Eucharist**

Ministry Particular office or duty of service in the Church e.g. meeting the spiritual needs of prisoners and their families

Novenas Special prayers prayed over a period of nine days for special intentions

Novitiate Two years spent by religious sisters and brothers in intense preparation for a lifelong commitment to their chosen religious order

The Office Daily prayer based on the Book of Psalms and other biblical texts and recited by priests, brothers and nuns

Penance Prayers or actions making amends to God for transgressions of God's commandments

Penitents	People who present themselves for forgiveness in the confessional
Presbyteral, -ate	Means priestly, while presbyterate means those ordained as priests
Presbytery	The house where priests live. The administration of the parish is often located in the presbytery
Religious	A priest, brother or sister who belongs to a congregation like the Jesuits, Sisters of Mercy, etc.
Responsorial	An antiphon or refrain repeated by the congregation during Mass at the end of each verse of a psalm
Rosary Beads	String of beads used in a form of meditative prayer involving the repetition of common prayers, e.g. The Lord's Prayer and the Hail Mary
Sacrament, -al	The Catholic Church has seven Sacraments, including baptism and marriage, which mark special moments in life with their own solemn liturgical celebrations
Scapular	A small blessed piece of cloth worn around the neck and under the shirt as a devotional badge
Seminary	A tertiary institution like a monastery where men are trained to be priests

Foreword

WE OWE a debt of gratitude to Father Wally Dethlefs for sharing his life with us in this document of courage, faith, love, and perseverance. His story calls on us to reflect deeply as we examine our society's attitudes and behaviour towards its vulnerable young people "... *to whom mankind owes the best that we have to give*".[1]

My friendship with Wally began in the late 1970s in Brisbane. Across the decades it has been important and influential in my work with others to promote and protect the rights of children and young people. I have a store of memorable experiences with my esteemed colleague: enriching conversations, heart-to-heart chats about his engagement with deeply-disadvantaged kids living in deprivation, in despair, at risk. We have been involved in organisations dedicated to juvenile justice, that bring together inspiring, skilled, purposeful activists committed to social and legal reform.

Wally has always been at the forefront of these movements. In *Just Compassion*, he relates the history and development of a community movement born of fine principles. He does so with unique insight, searing honesty, and distinctive candour, uplifting our spirits and our confidence in our shared humanity. The dry gullies, the tough times, the political conflicts are there beside the resolute conviction that change must be made and that hard work is required.

Wally pares back the layers of his relentless search for his own understanding of Christ's mission; a priest's spiritual and theological journey. I am always drawn to the early years of memoirs, to the times of childhood. Evidence continues to grow on the vital significance of those foundations in shaping characteristics, capacities, and personality. The little boy living beside the church and the convent was surrounded by intense struggles for justice and economic survival. His loving family was immersed in one battle after another. What strength was shown by those parents in their day-to-day living and in their belief in a loving God!

Wally went next door to school at the age of four. Too wild for the nuns, in Grade 3 he was sent to the Christian Brothers at St Laurence's for a steadying influence. Kindness, patience, sensitivity were scarce; rather, fear, temper, strappings, violence of some brothers and nuns, beltings were the norm. These

---

1   Preamble to the United Nations Declaration on Rights of the Child (1959).

matters were not to be spoken of at home. They make distressing reading: cruelty to children, harsh lives, strikes on the waterside and in the factories, political lines not to be questioned. However, amidst the masses, the prayers and the sport he loved, a questioning free spirit was growing in Wally.

At 17 he went to the seminary. Seven critical years of personal growth, of transition from boyhood to manhood, were spent in social isolation. Wally's first years as priest were confronting, as he looked for a ministry that would be authentic and useful. He put his best foot forward in visiting, getting to know the parish, listening, caring, making the most of opportunities to serve: experiences that would stand him in great stead, lessons that made lasting impressions. Determined to put a human face to his role, he immersed himself in issues of family life, conflict resolution, and communication with parents.

There was little guidance for the young man of conviction and conscience, yearning to be of support and comfort to parishioners in need. Instead there were years of serious physical and mental deprivation, when Wally was helped out by family and friends who provided basic needs. The 'Boys' Groups' and the 'Girls' Groups' that Wally organised and encouraged during these times set him up for his life's work, for his contribution to children and youth. They were key to his courageous leadership, to the inspiration he has given across generations. They are part of his legacy.

This memoir contains heart-breaking accounts of the treatment of young people, stories recorded in poetry and prose. Wally's voice brought attention to horrifying events at Wilson Youth Hospital: indeterminate sentencing, solitary confinement, institutionalised violence and a total lack of opportunities for education.

Our community heard and responded. Service clubs raised funds. Advocates lobbied vigorously. In June 1979 I was invited to launch *Justice for Juveniles*. This path-breaking publication set out the case for reform of the 1965 Children's Services Act. It represented an enormous body of research, what we now call the evidence base: years of groundwork by social workers, lawyers, and volunteers. I recall that occasion as a powerful demonstration of grassroots action, not to mention the hours burning the midnight oil in the company of a duplicating machine.

In 1981, the Youth Advocacy Centre (YAC) was founded by dedicated reformers and clever strategists who came together in the *Justice for Juveniles* collaboration. They built a service that has assisted thousands of young people with professional expertise, care and compassion. Its rationale is drawn from the UN Declaration on the Rights of the Child: the section pertaining to special protection, legal assistance, with the paramount consideration *the best interests of the child.*

The YAC is respected and admired by the legal profession, who from its earliest days have given generous, extensive and constant support. Young people have always been at the heart of the organisation, with specific focus on the legal rights of children. Wally has written with fascinating detail on this important aspect of Queensland's social history. He includes the remarkable efforts of Brisbane Youth Service, with accounts of children of tender age, obliged to navigate the perilous journey of finding themselves. No hope, nothing to live for, no future.

It is no surprise that from time to time Wally suffered from exhaustion. Political conflict with State and Church, constant anxieties about young people in desperate need, at serious risk, in despair, who sought his help, took their toll. Sometimes the burden became too heavy.

There are a few light-hearted moments that light up in this memoir. I have many recollections in my times with Wally, of laughter and great good humour.

Wally wisely recognised when he needed to get away from it all, and used his self-imposed breaks to study, to travel widely, to revive his spirit, questioning, looking for new ideas, sharing his own, recharging his physical, spiritual, and emotional batteries.

Whatever the role, whether as parish priest, as prison chaplain, at Catholic Education, or as a Commissioner on the Human Rights and Equal Opportunity Commission Inquiry into Homeless Children and Young People, Wally's commitment was total—deep and meaningful.

He has always relished intellectual challenge, faced unfairness and disappointment with equanimity, and taken risks with boldness and daring. *"I just wanted to be a good priest".*

This book explores and explains the true meaning of poverty, injustice, and the prayer:

> Dear God
> I want to go home
> To some parents who care
> About why I'm alone.

It is to be lauded for its timely recognition of the service, selflessness and accomplishment of Wally and of remarkable individuals who made outstanding contributions to legal and social reform for our children and young people. Their commitment and dedication to the dignity and worth of some of our most vulnerable citizens stands as a source of courage, support and inspiration.

Dame Quentin Bryce AC CVO

31 March 2016

Preface

THE PURPOSE of this book is to encourage others to critically reflect on their life and society, especially the issues of injustice facing disadvantaged people, in the light of the Bible and the teachings of Christ. My intention is to trace my spiritual and theological development as a priest living and working with those on the fringes of the Church and society. Through a chain of life-circumstances, conscious choices and moments of grace, I was led to deepen my faith and to develop my understanding of the Bible, especially the words and life of Jesus. This, in turn, sharpened my understanding of the mission of the Church. Circumstances led me to the fringes of Church and society, to the 'Fourth World' of the cast-offs of our First World country, Australia. Ordained in 1963, my seminary training was pre-Vatican II and did not equip me for this task. I needed to reappraise and deepen my faith in the light of what I was being called to do. I have attempted to trace my spiritual development: to identify the significant times in my life and the moments of grace, when the Spirit was calling me forth to unseen and unfamiliar places.

Three themes run through this book. The first is the use, or rather the misuse of power and authority. My process of questioning of authority, and conflict with authority, began at school, and deepened through seminary training, where I was forced to ask myself what Christianity was basically about. I felt bound in conscience to act on the fundamental answer I came up with. The questioning of myself, this critical reflection on my actions and those in authority, continued after ordination as I sought to be an authentic Christian both in word and action. Some years later, working with students where the education system set student against student in a super-competitive environment, and knowing that this was not the way of Christ, I came into conflict with Church authorities. As my analysis developed, complemented by my understanding of the socio-political dimension of the Bible, I also came into conflict with the authority of the State: tentatively through the action for political prisoners in South Vietnam, then through the anti-freeway movement, the Australia-East Timor Association, and the movement for Aboriginal land rights. Finally, my experience of working with and seeing the juvenile justice system through the eyes of homeless young people who had been wrongfully incarcerated by the State under the guise of "their best interests"[2] propelled me into permanent conflict with both Church and State authorities.

The second theme running through this narrative is my journey into Gospel justice. My understanding of Gospel justice was revealed through a gradual understanding of what Christ's mission was concerned with and, as a consequence, what the Church should be concerned with. I came to an understanding that the purpose of the Church is to respond to the signs of the times[3], expressed in practical concern for the poor and oppressed people of the world, and in a deliberate commitment to making the big systems in our society just and humane. Practical concern and deliberate commitment have given me direction and energy—in other words, a passion for Gospel justice.

The third theme is the methodologies I have used in my work. The first was the Cardijnian methodology of see/judge/act, and the writings of liberation theologians, especially Gustavo Gutiérrez from Peru. This methodology catapulted me into social analysis and later into global analysis. The second methodology was the Twelve-Step program of Alcoholics Anonymous. The Twelve-Step program gave me a consistent way of working with people who were addicted, or whom I suspected of having an addiction to alcohol or drugs.

I have changed some of the names, places and identifying details of some of the people I have mentioned. My concern is with the use and misuse of authority, not with the personalities who exercised this authority. In some chapters I have relied on material obtained under the Freedom of Information Act. This material was not available at the time the events described were taking place, as the Act only came into force in the early 1990s.

Acknowledgments

This book would not have been possible without the assistance and encouragement of many friends. Archbishop Bathursby and Betty Roberts assisted me in the purchase of my first computer.

Family and friends welcomed me into their homes so that I could write in peaceful surroundings and without interruption. I am grateful to Vishwa and Maria Pillai, Bill and Noela Dethlefs, John and Jenny Dethlefs, Moira Andersen, John and Majorie Anderson, Paul and Debbie Shears, Dennis and Mary Harvey, John and Monica Birchley and Barry Copley.

2   Children's Services Act (1965)
3   The 'signs of the times' is a term I first encountered in the Documents of Vatican II and subsequent documents emanating from Rome. They refer to the major social issues which a nation or the world is facing e.g. the arms race, refugees and asylum seekers, or nuclear disarmament. Another example of the 'signs of the times' would be feeling the weather becoming hotter, deducing that humans are the cause, and rather than buying more air conditioners, thereby increasing global warming, we change our sources of energy and become more reliant on renewable energy.

Dave Andrews kindly read through an earlier manuscript and offered helpful advice and encouragement. Anne McMillan, with whom I worked closely for many years, checked the work on Justice for Juveniles and the Youth Advocacy Centre for accuracy. Ro Andersen did the same with the chapter on the Young Christian Students movement.

Ian O'Connor and Tony Kelly also offered encouragement and practical advice in the early stages.

Sandra Sewell did two complete edits of an early version of the manuscript. Having given her two chapters initially, I fully expected her to tell me she had shredded the work! Her helpful suggestions, comments and criticisms, sensitively offered, kept me at it, when at times I had thought of abandoning the project. Her professionalism and later that of Caroline Woods has made the manuscript what it is today. Mark Young undertook publishing editing responsibilities.

Mick Porter generously offered his services as a professional photographer for the photographs on the jacket of the book. Children and young people of friends of mine kindly agreed to pose for the front cover picture. Thank you Eva, Gabriella, Joseph and Roberto and their parents.

Danielle Long, from Brisbane Catholic Education, kindly designed the front and back covers.

Dave Andrews, Paul Toon, Steve Capelin and Sorcha Twomey formed a reference group which encouraged me in many ways and assisted me with the launch.

I am grateful also to Roland Lubett, my publisher, for his patience and painstaking work in bringing the work to completion.

"Not wild, just boisterous"

I WAS BORN in June 1939, just prior to the beginning of the Second World War, an event which was to have a major impact on my childhood.

My parents were Claus (Bill) Dethlefs, born in Hamburg, Germany, and Maria (Mary) Koch, born in Lucerne, Switzerland. Mum came to Australia with her family when she was seven years old. Dad, a sailor in the merchant navy, came after World War I, jumping ship in Adelaide. Dad and Mum met in Surat in western Queensland, and they were married in Saint Joseph's Church, Kangaroo Point, in 1934. They raised five children. I have two older brothers and an older sister, and one younger brother.

During our childhood my father worked as a labourer in the stevedoring industry, and was an active member of the Waterside Workers' Union. Dad supplemented the family income with a small carrying business, driving a 1929 Rugby utility truck which was also used for family picnics and outings. My mother worked at home, managing the house and its finances, raising the children, and taking in a boarder or two (mostly a young person) from time to time.

In February 1942 my father, a naturalised British citizen, was arrested on his way to work. Within a few days he was detained in an internment camp at Tatura in Victoria, and classified as an undesirable alien. He was charged with spying for Germany. There were no social security benefits in the 1940s, so our family had no income. The family survived on the charity of a number of people including the local Irish priest, Monsignor James Prout, and the corner store shopkeeper, Mrs. Hanlon, who allowed us credit over a very long period of time.

My mother was not in good health but she fought tirelessly for Dad's release. She visited many influential people, obtained character references, and was given some legal help through a solicitor, Mr. King. Eventually when the matter came to court in September 1942, Dad was acquitted of all charges. However the judge said that he could not come within 20 miles (32 kilometres) of the mouth of the Brisbane River. The military representative at the hearing added this stipulation, as Brisbane was being set up as the front line against a possible invasion by Japan.

Dad got a job at the Dinmore abattoir near Ipswich. Regularly Mum would pack up all of us kids, and a picnic lunch, and we would visit Dad for the day. I can remember some of this, though only vaguely. I can recall Dad being away for a reason either unknown or incomprehensible to me. I have a recollection of playing up badly while he was away, so much so that my mother explained to me what was happening. I understood it was serious, but not much more than that, except that it would help enormously if I behaved better.

I can also remember something of the trips to Dinmore—being hugged and clinging to my father, and begging him to return home. Dad's wrongful and unjust incarceration and Mum's fight for justice for Dad and our family were significant experiences in my childhood, a time that brought prayer and action together.

My mother was a woman of great faith, who prayed every day and encouraged her family not only to pray as a unit, but also as individuals. She encouraged us to take part in the local faith community in all its forms. We lived next to the Catholic church and convent school at Kangaroo Point. I witnessed a woman whose strong and active faith propelled her into action on behalf of her husband and family. She passionately believed in her husband's innocence and was prepared to take on the government of the day to have her

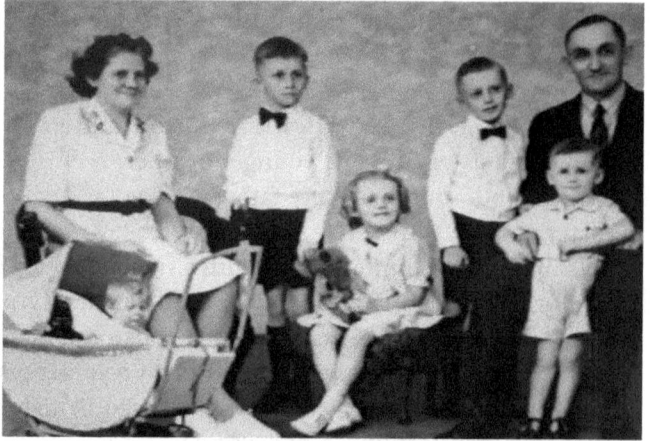

John (in the pram), Bill, Rosemary, Claude and Wally

husband and the father of her children returned to his rightful place in the home.

My mother did not have any resources to call upon, except her belief in a loving God, and the guidance and strength which God alone could offer. She did not know if she would be successful in her efforts, but that did not deter her. To fight for the innocent, for truth and justice, was important—the outcome was in God's hands.

After Dad had spent a number of months in Dinmore, the authorities decided that Kangaroo Point was the required distance from the mouth of the river and gave him permission to return home. They were desperately short of able-bodied men to work on the waterfront as stevedores.

My mother taught us to read at a very young age. I went to school at four years of age, a year earlier than I should have. I had told my parents that I was going to school, so when school began in 1944, I went. Later that morning my mother went to the school to talk to the nun, who told her that I was no trouble and that I could stay.

I enjoyed my first two years at school and Sister Mary Columkill was a good teacher. I remember being surprised by the examination results. They seemed to indicate the person who came top of the class was in some way a better person than the other students in the class. This puzzled me. Although placed in the top ten, I was uncomfortable with a method which seemed to assess a person's worth by the results of an examination. The message I received was: *what I am able to achieve is an indication of what I am worth.*

In Grade 3, I moved school to the Christian Brothers at Saint Laurence's College, South Brisbane. I was considered to be too wild for the nuns, and my parents felt the Brothers would have a steadying influence on me. In the first half of Grade 3 we were taught by two Brothers who also taught the Senior Grades. One was a real tyrant, the other quite gentle; one taught in the morning and the other in the afternoon. Fear reigned supreme for half the day, while during the other half the tension drained away as the teacher went about his responsibilities in a competent but not unkind manner. Unfortunately he died that year when he blew himself up in a chemistry experiment which went horribly wrong.

In the second half of that year, we were assigned a young teacher, Brother Sharp, who was a very just and good teacher. At times he would get upset with the class, but he never hit anyone in temper with the leather strap. He was a great consolation to my parents: when they had not heard any bad conduct reports about me for six months or more, they decided to approach him. His consoling words about me were: "He's not wild, just boisterous." Brother Sharp was a born diplomat and he has my undying gratitude.

In religion classes, Brother Sharp emphasised the practice of religion in daily life. Most of us were taken by surprise when in the examination we were asked:

> *Do you have your Rosary Beads in your pocket?*
> *Are you wearing a Scapular or a Holy Medal?*
> *Did you say your Morning Prayers this morning?*
> *Did you attend Mass last Sunday?*

Since these questions attracted more than 50% of the marks, if we missed most of them we were unlikely to pass the examination. What impressed me was the emphasis on the practice of religion, not merely the knowledge.

For the next two years we had another teacher, 'Basher', who was often pleasant but who had incredible mood swings and a fierce temper. I used to think he took his daily exercise by strapping as many boys as he could for as long as he had the energy. He was young and strong, and did not tire quickly. At the end of Grade 4, Basher asked those students who had not received the strap from him during the year to stand up. Several boys stood up. He then gave each one "four of the best", saying that they must have done something wrong, which he had not seen. A rather nervous and shy friend of mine, 'Barry', was a recipient and cried for the injustice of it as much as for the pain.

I had a very bad temper which could get out of control. About once a year, in a fit of anger, I would smash my glasses. Of course this meant I had to pay for new ones out of my meagre savings. I remember a priest helped me with my temper problem by telling me in Confession that anger was a great gift: it meant I had lots of energy which I could channel into positive things such as patience, kindness, firmness and perseverance. I began to work on that.

During this period, there was a lot of action on the waterfront where my father worked—stop-work meetings and strike action. Sometimes, during school holidays, I would accompany my father to the 'shed', as it was called, where meetings would take place. All workers were casual and had to report to the shed at 7 o'clock in the morning, when they might or might not be allocated a job on a ship. If they were allocated, they worked on that ship until it left port—unloading and then loading it.

The workers were divided into gangs of about 20. 'Floaters' were those who were placed individually on jobs when men were needed to make up the numbers. All who were not working turned up to the shed each morning, and were paid nothing for their attendance. Conditions were bad, safety standards were minimal, and there were no paid sick days or holidays. The strikes were mostly about wages and conditions, but also about social issues, for example Australia's involvement in the Korean War, when the waterside workers refused to load ships bound for Korea. There was always the cry that these strikes were communist-led, inspired and manipulated. Certainly, Communists were active in the Waterside Workers' Union. The media and the politicians of the day gave prominence to this point.

There were lots of discussions at home about what was happening on the wharf. Strikes meant no money coming in. Strikes made it difficult to pay off the debts accruing from Dad's incarceration and to keep the family afloat with five children, all by then attending private Catholic schools. I was always interested in my father's work. I would ask him about his workmates in Gang 48. Even though I had met few of the men, I knew most of their names. I would ask Dad about the ship he was working on, its size, the nationality of its crew, what cargo was being unloaded or loaded, where the ship came from and where it was going.

It was difficult for me to understand the local, national and international issues that were confronting Dad, his fellow-workers and their Union. On the one hand, our local assistant priest, Father Shine, became an Army chaplain and embarked for South Korea, hailed by all in the parish as a hero. On the other hand, the Waterside Workers around Australia refused to load ships bearing provisions or armaments for South Korea, and my father was a member of that Union.

I knew that my Dad was a good man, that Father Shine was a good priest, that Communists were all bad, that there were some Communists in the Waterside Workers' Union, that Russia and China were Communist countries and were supporting North Korea; but how all that could be reconciled was beyond me. Sometimes I would try to puzzle out these things, but mostly I had to put them in the too-hard basket.

In our family we were expected to say our morning and evening prayers. The family Rosary was recited most evenings after dinner, and a prayer was offered before and after meals. I attended Catholic Schools and, since we lived next door to a Church and I was an early riser, I attended morning Mass. Devotions to Our Lady were popular, plus novenas and prayers to the saints. I often read stories about saints and was inspired by them.

But the Church at that time had a ghetto mentality; for example, mixed marriages between Catholics and Christians from other denominations were not encouraged, and it was a mortal sin to attend a non-Catholic church service. It was said the Catholic Church, school, and community provided for Catholics in a complete way—spiritually, socially, and every other way. While I went along with most of this, I was puzzled by the violence of some of the brothers and nuns. We were not allowed to discuss this at home, where the policy was: "We do not want you bringing home tales from school," and "We are sure that the Brothers had every right in doing what they did."

Our teachers in Grade 9 at St Laurence's College South Brisbane were Brother Ryan, a huge man with a fierce temper; Brother 'Jack' Davey, the Principal, who taught Latin; and Brother McEllicot, who taught religion. Grade 9 was a reasonably pleasant experience. Brother Ryan, despite his temper, was a good man and a competent teacher. All of us were disciplined with the strap but this was normal practice. We disliked it, but had to accept it.

In Grade 10 we had Brother Rogan and again Brother Jack, plus 'Lieutenant' Len for religion. Brother Rogan was a reasonable and approachable man, a hard worker, but not a gifted teacher. We had Brother Jack in the morning for English, French and Latin. In Jack's view, there was a section in the class which he designated 'the wood-heap' and 'the goats.' These were the people who would leave school at the end of Year 10 and "end up as a sparky (an electrician) with a screwdriver in their back pocket." During my years at Saint Laurence's, such people—honest workers like my father—were spoken of in a derogatory way. Manual workers, labourers, and even some skilled workers such as electricians, were scorned and ridiculed. Interestingly enough, there were 64 students in our Grade 10 class, only 23 of whom went on to Grade 11. The rest went to work in banks, the public service and trades, as well as in labouring jobs, having been told repeatedly that the jobs they were undertaking were, at best, second-class.

The school rated sport highly, and I particularly enjoyed Rugby Union. School sport, image and dress were of vital importance, as were the externals of religion. Truth and justice did not seem to rate at all, except in insignificant and narrow ways. Mysteriously, truth only seemed to regain its importance when we did something wrong.

Our religion books for Years 11 and 12 were pathetic. The Church History book was written for 11 and 12-year-olds. The Gospel according to John was the only really decent book we used. Unfortunately this was often read without comment or discussion. *The Christian Gentleman*, written by a brother of the Principal who took us for these classes, was read to us from time to time, and commented upon.

In Grade 12, about one month after school recommenced, the 'Lieutenant' suffered another heart attack and died. Although we attended his funeral, we

Senior Class, St. Laurence's, 1956: Wally is top right

were not sorry to see him go. A statue of Our Lady was erected in his honour in the grounds of the school. I could not understand why they did that; they must have known what kind of person he had been and what terror he had caused students.

I attended Mass most mornings and prayed each day, mostly set prayers, but I do not remember meditating. I was also doing some spiritual reading, including Thomas à Kempis (*The Imitation of Christ*) and Saint Thérèse of Lisieux. I tried to read Thomas Merton's *Waters of Silence*, as well as his *Elected Silence*, but his books were incomprehensible to me.

For a long time I had thought about trying for the priesthood, and had discussed this with several people. I had explored two religious orders, the Redemptorists and the Missionaries of the Sacred Heart, and had decided there was scope for mission apostolate in Australia, even in Brisbane, but I conceived mission in very simplistic terms as conversion to the one true Church, which had a monopoly on salvation.

I was not keen to enter seminary straight from school. I thought a year at work would be a good and necessary experience. I needed to mature, and I wanted to experience life in the real world. I had grown up largely within the confines of the Catholic community, in parish, school and family, and I wanted to sample life beyond those borders. However most people advised me differently, and I ended up going straight into seminary from high school.

In the Christmas holidays of 1955 I worked for five weeks in a small factory which made floor polish. The conditions were terrible; the factory was always extremely hot as well as filthy. Slippery floors made the carrying of heavy cartons quite dangerous. I saw the biggest cockroaches I was ever to see until I worked in the Boggo Road prison some decades later. As I was the youngest and still at school, I was made to do the dirtiest work and subjected to verbal abuse. On one occasion I was held from behind while some guy punched me a few times. Despite this, I got on reasonably well with most of the workers.

Factory work was a valuable experience. It made me conscious of the working conditions many people had to put up with. It also made me conscious of the importance of the education I had received. I realised that being educated in a private school made me different: I spoke differently and some of my values were different. I was intent on doing a good job and being accepted by my fellow-workers. Above all, because I would only be in the factory for five weeks, I knew I could stick it out—one can put up with anything for a short period if one has to.

As an immature young person searching for a practical spirituality, I entered seminary in February 1957 to begin training for the priesthood. We began the year with a three-day retreat, almost before we knew our way around the place—even before some of us knew where to find the toilets!

When I was in third year, a fellow-student asked me what was the basis of Catholicism, for me personally. I replied: "Where I am at, at this moment, is hanging on to the words of Jesus, 'You must love the Lord thy God with all thy heart and strength, with all your heart and your neighbour as yourself'.[4]" He was not very happy with an answer which appeared to contain no specific Catholic content. I further scandalised and disturbed him by saying that specific Catholic content was not important to me at that particular time.

On the whole, the training we received for our ministry was very poor, even if the Rector boasted that if it was not the best training in the world, then it was certainly equal to the best. For myself, I could see injustice happening everywhere but, after trying to do something about it and not succeeding, I felt powerless. I decided to continue with my studies, and do the little I could in the meantime.

4   Luke 10:27-28.

In my second year, I was accepted into the advanced Latin class which was taught by an Irishman, Dave Hawe, or 'the Celt' as we called him. There is no doubt about the Celt's love and appreciation for the Latin classics, but for me it was sheer hard work and drudgery. The Celt would abuse the living daylights out of 'ignorant people' like me. "Why don't you go and get a harmless job, Mr Dethlefs," he shouted at me in my first class, "where you would do not harm to the Church, yourself or anybody else?"

I was quite depressed after that class, but one of the older students told me to play basketball after Latin classes "to get the Celt out of your system." I took the advice and played a hard game of basketball every Tuesday and Friday afternoon, which was a great help.

I suppose I might have been considered a sports freak, but I found it a great release for my pent-up energies. Many weekends I would play rugby league on Saturday afternoon, basketball on Sunday morning, and soccer on Sunday afternoon. The activity helped me face up to the next week of study. I had to work hard at the studies, because I found most of them quite difficult. Many of our textbooks were written in Latin, and some of our lecturers left much to be desired in their methods of teaching. Our seminary training was doctrinal in method. Doctrines stood by themselves and could be proven by reason, tradition, and from Scripture. They had no relationship to life. The priest was to labour in the world, but not be of the world. The priesthood was a closed club. Priests alone could understand priests.

I enjoyed a number of things at the seminary: the companionship, the sport, and some of the study such as the Scripture courses and Church History. But the bulk of the study we were required to undertake seemed useless for the job of working pastorally with people.

'The Principles of Catholic Action' was an exciting course we did for 30 minutes each week in the last four months of our seven years of training. Interestingly enough, it was the Celt, Dave Hawe, who lectured. He called the lectures 'gatherings'. They differed from other lectures because there was no textbook or examinations, but they involved reflections on how to help laypeople live a full Christian life.

The Celt's sense of humour shone through these gatherings. "Some people you will find as you go about your work, are hoping for the resurrection, others for their next glass of beer. Many people are skeptical of the claims of the Church. The world is not convinced by our grandiose claims any longer. The Church boasts about money and numbers which is what the world boasts about."

He told us that the danger after seven years in the seminary was that we could be self-satisfied with our Church and our training: "The seminary gives only basic training on which you must build, by studying not from textbooks but of everything that concerns your work. Your job is to bring the life of

Jesus to people. The sons of Zebedee, James and John, in asking Jesus for a place at his right and left hands, were boys anxious for an ecclesiastical career; that is, to be made Monsignors."

"What Peter said to the cripple was of great value, 'Silver and gold I have none. But what I have I give thee. In the name of Jesus Christ of Nazareth arise and walk.' Saint Peter knew nothing about Canon Law."

Dave stressed that priest and lay-people should not be separated, for "we are all baptised with the same baptism." Lay-people expect to be taken seriously. "We have a mission to be living Christians and the lay-people have the same obligation. Making lay-people genuine re-incarnations of Christ and preaching the word of God are our jobs." For Dave, the distinction between the hierarchy of the Church and lay-people was a distinction of service only, for "the Son of Man came not to be served but to serve others." The action of the lay apostle is to make Christ present in the life of the world.

Dave told us that when we left the seminary we must advance in wisdom, knowledge and grace. "We can be compared to Dorothy Dix (a woman who gave advice in a popular woman's magazine), except her advice is better." Catholic Action, he said, was for an elite, a chosen few with zeal. "Not everybody is called to be a lay apostle, so do not concentrate on building up numbers." Dave, in these gatherings, often spoke of the Young Catholic Workers, the Young Catholic Students and the Catholic Family movements, and had great praise for Joseph Cardijn, the founder of these movements.

In my last year I realised that our studies had ill equipped us for the tasks we were to undertake. I resolved to work hard to try to make up for these deficiencies once I was appointed to a parish. The social isolation of the seminary and its institutional framework meant that people like me had missed out on seven years of normal living—of growing up, of making decisions, being responsible, and therefore of maturing. I wondered if the deficiency could ever be overcome; but I resolved to listen and to learn, the best method I knew.

While at the seminary I studied privately the writings of Joseph Cardijn, the founder of the Young Christian Workers movement (YCW), as well as anything I could get hold of on the lay apostolate. During my time at the seminary Cardinal Cardijn visited and lectured us, as did the National YCW Chaplain. These inputs were usually met with scepticism, and even with derision by some

students. We as student-priests were convinced of our own God-given mission and of nobody else's, especially not of the young laity. Eyebrows were raised if you said anything to indicate that you considered that lay-people had a God-given mission in their own right.

Cardijn wrote that he believed a person cannot be successfully trained for pastoral ministry in a four-walled situation:

> People must be careful not to misinterpret the allusion I made ... to a 'lay seminary'. It goes without saying that I would have no part of a formation that takes place behind closed doors, between the walls of some institution or other, however orientated towards the world its teaching programme might be. This seminary must find its fulfilment in everyday reality; not in a room, but outside, in the open air! ... It is through permanent contact with life that we will strive to transform it, in order to integrate or reintegrate it totally in the divine plan.[5]

As well as Cardijn, I studied very closely the techniques and spirituality of Alcoholics Anonymous (AA). I had read somewhere that one out of every four Australians had a drinking problem, and had decided it would be important for me to know something useful about this area. I found that the spirituality of AA was basic, sound and helpful to me personally. The book I studied was *Alcoholics Anonymous*, or the Big Book as it is called by those who attend AA meetings. The first 160 pages of this book contain the theory of AA flowing from the practical experience of its founders. It isn't airy-fairy stuff but the distilled wisdom of people who have suffered from alcoholic sickness and who have struggled through to sobriety, stability and faith. To quote the first two steps: "We realised that we were powerless over alcohol and that our lives had become unmanageable. We gave ourselves over to a power that was greater than ourselves who could restore us to sanity."

I studied the book closely for a number of years and tried to apply some of its principles to my own life.

5   *Laymen into Action*, Joseph Cardijn YCW Melbourne (1964) p. 149.

The parish: teamwork and partnership?

Ekibin, 1963–67

ON THE day of my arrival at St Elizabeth's Ekibin, in December 1963, the parish priest, Father Basil, told me that teamwork and partnership would be the way we would work together. In a short time I realised the teamwork he envisioned was: "I give the orders and you carry them out." He boasted that he had not read a book on theology in 20 years, and that the only theology he read was the page on religion in TIME magazine. During the three years I was with him, we had no more than three or four good discussions together. At meal time, for example, he would always listen to the radio or watch TV, or have both going at the same time, and he was a little deaf as well. I knew I had a lot to learn and was keen to learn as much as I could from an experienced pastor; so I was both disappointed and disillusioned by our inability to communicate.

During the first few weeks I would tell Basil over the noise of the radio or during a TV commercial break about the families I had visited that day. His response would invariably be: "They are mad," or "They are crackers," or "They are liars, no-hopers." At first I thought I must be quite gullible to not pick up a hint or suggestion of these things, but then I realised that it was Basil himself who was the problem.

I was assigned an area to visit. I was to visit every house in that area, Catholics as well as non-Catholics. At first I found visiting very difficult. I did not know what I was really doing there—what I should be saying, what I had to offer.

In my first few months I happened upon a working-class family. To my amazement I could not talk with them. I wondered what was wrong with me, as these were the kind of people I should have been able to relate to with ease. One of their children was quite sickly. I used that as an excuse to visit frequently, which the boy and his family appreciated. I realised I needed them more than they needed me. I used to sit at their kitchen table, listening to the conversations taking place and trying to understand what was meaningful to these people, what was significant in their lives. I often found my efforts at making conversation were inadequate. That family helped me more than they will ever know.

My visiting was slow; I needed to listen and learn. Basil often criticised me: ten minutes per house was all that was required, he used to say. To demonstrate, he visited all 220 Catholic homes at one end of the parish in three weeks. Some of the people he visited told me he was gone almost before he arrived.

If I was to continue in the priesthood, I hoped my ministry would be authentic and useful, not just for myself but for those in my parish. Towards the end of my first year in parish ministry, I realised I was directionless. I had achieved ordination but had no new goals. I thought and prayed about this for a long time. To discover that I was directionless was a revelation for me, possibly a moment of grace. What to do about the situation was not clear.

As a result of prayerful reflection I was able to set myself a question. Achieving priesthood was a good thing, but what constituted being 'a good priest?' What was authentic priesthood in this day and age, in this situation and parish? Most mornings as part of my prayer I would reflect on the work of the previous day to try to discover what I was doing in my ministry that was good, what could be improved upon, what was relevant to the lives of people, and what was irrelevant or useless. I was trying to discover what might be an indication of 'the mind of Christ'.

I was put in charge of the Young Christian Workers (YCW) groups as their chaplain. We ended up with a girls' group at both ends of the parish and a boys' group attached to the main church. I attended most meetings. Through listening to these young people talk about their lives, reflecting on the Gospel, and praying together, I began to see Jesus as a real person and my prayer life became real again. Something that I seemed to have lost in the seminary was being restored.

One of the doctrines that had enthused us as seminarians was the 'Mystical Body of Christ'. For one meeting I delivered a short address on the doctrine. I was satisfied with what I had put across and certain that the young people would now have a clear understanding of this important and relevant teaching. I was taken aback when during my chaplain's talk at the next meeting I asked questions about their understanding of this vital tenet of our faith, and was greeted with sincere but blank faces. I reiterated what I had said at the previous meeting.

After several meetings it dawned on me that something was radically wrong, not with the young people, but with me. My approach and my method were both wrong. Here I was, trying to teach doctrine as an entity all on its own—apart from life. I was trying to do to these young people what had been done to us in the seminary. I had to change my approach. How could I do this when I knew no other way? That question exercised my mind for some time. I went back to Cardijn, I spoke with other chaplains, and continued to listen to the young people as they reflected on their lives as young apostles.

There was a lad in the boys' group, 'Joe', who worked in a large abattoir. He was 16 years old, semi-literate, not very articulate, of small stature, and shy. At

YCW meetings he said very little. What he said was said slowly and with great hesitation. When the secretary of the group resigned, Joe offered to take on the responsibility. The minutes he took were often not comprehensible even to himself.

Joe and the junior boys at the abattoir were often made to do men's work, but not paid for it. Some were injured doing heavy work which was too much for them. Obviously Joe had been listening closely at our meetings. YCW had encouraged him to mix with his fellow-workers, and Joe and his fellow-juniors were able to set up a table-tennis table for their own use during the tea breaks and at lunch time.

I had read a short report in the newspaper about a strike at the abattoir, and asked Joe about it before we started one meeting. Slowly and painfully the story emerged. Joe had been speaking to the other boys about the work they were having to do and not being paid for. They approached the bosses and were told in no uncertain terms to mind their own business. After discussing the rebuff the boys decided to go out on strike. The other workers at the abattoir wanted to know what was going on and when they found out, they too went out on strike. The whole place closed down, with several hundred workers on strike.

The boys elected a strike committee, and Joe was elected secretary. They drew up a log of six claims to be negotiated with the management. The boys were successful with most of their claims: no boys could be compelled to do men's work and, if boys did men's work, they were to be paid men's wages. Joe's actions rammed home to me the empowering formation of the Cardijnian method of action and reflection. Even the seemingly most ungifted and powerless of God's people could not only absorb it, but act it out in a spectacular and radical way. I realised of course that such actions were very rare in the humdrum lives of many young workers, and that many young workers would not be aware of such a situation or, if aware, would feel powerless to do anything.

As a Christian group we tried to reflect together on Joe's actions in the light of the Gospel: God calling Joe to "let his light shine before others" (Matthew 5:16), to uphold their dignity, and to put right something that was not only harmful to the health of some of Joe's fellow-workers, but also unjust.

I saw the abattoir workers' action as a classic example of what Cardijn was talking about (echoed in the Document on the Laity of Vatican II) when he said that young workers are the prime and direct apostles of other young workers in and through their lives:

Theological faith and life, deeply incarnate in everyday realities, must be revealed as the only positive, dynamic, victorious answer to secularisation. They can be applied to life in manifold ways: in the apostolic value of work, love, and family, professional and civic life ... What driving force, what conviction and pride this conception will inspire in the soul of the simplest and most ordinary Christian![6]

In the parish, the YCW groups conducted an inquiry into various aspects of family life: communication with parents, conflict resolution, and sibling relationships. The inquiry lasted several weeks and was carried out as thoroughly as possible. It culminated in an open meeting, where the findings were discussed by young people and parents together, and then by parents in groups by themselves.

The night went well. The parents in particular were very happy with the depth of the discussions. They were keen to form a group of parents who could meet regularly, support each other, and deepen their faith. One parent canvassed other parents. At least ten parents indicated their interest and one of them approached me. After I expressed my keenness to work with them, a parent approached Basil for his support. He turned them down flat: there were ample opportunities for parents to meet, he said, in the Legion of Mary group or the Saint Vincent de Paul group.

I felt powerless to pursue the matter any further. Basil was the authority on what would happen, when it would happen, and with whom. I was disappointed that we had lost an opportunity to engage with a group of adults in Christian formation—reflection and action—especially when the adults had requested it themselves. It seemed to me one of the essential responsibilities of the priest was to form people according to the mind of Christ. What better way to do this than for people to be meeting, praying, discussing their lives together, and reflecting on all of this in the light of the Gospel?

I used to enjoy hearing confessions in those days. I read a book in my last year in the seminary, *The Good Confessor*, which stressed the human face of the confessional. It spoke of the four duties of the confessor: father, physician, teacher, and judge. As spiritual father the confessor should deal kindly with his penitents; as teacher he should give some instruction; as physician the confessor tries to cure bad habits and assist in the acquiring of good habits; and finally as a judge in the place of Christ, the confessor authoritatively grants or refuses absolution.[7]

After a penitent had finished their usual routine I would ask them how they were keeping, and listen closely to what they said. If they said they had been fighting with someone, I would ask them who and what the fight was about. If they said they were having distractions during their prayer time, I would ask them about their prayer life and their relationship with God. Slowly people responded and began to want to follow up on issues they had raised in the confessional.

6   Ibid., p 139.
7   *The Good Confessor*, Gerald Kelly S.J., Clonmore & Reynolds Ltd, (1959) pp 53-54.

Many of the younger priests used to meet once a month at Ave Maria Retreat House for an afternoon of recollection, and I was one of the people who helped to organise the event. Twenty to thirty of the younger priests met, prayed together, and held a time of silence. It came as a surprise when some of the older priests were critical of us for doing this. Their point was that we had no senior priest to guide us, and we were like the blind leading the blind. Such criticism called into question our professionalism, the quality of our training, and the level of trust within the ranks of the clergy.

Bardon, 1967–1968

At the beginning of 1967 I was transferred to Bardon, where Ray Lyons was parish priest. I moved in on a Saturday; Ray, a shy man, welcomed me as did the housekeeper. I was to look after Saint Bernard's at Kennedy Terrace, and the surrounding area, made up mainly of poor and working-class people. I had responsibility for the YCW girls' and boys' groups, as well as a social club for young people. There was a branch of the Christian Family Movement in the parish, as well as Sunday morning catechetics offered to the children attending State schools.

On that first Saturday night, between sessions of confessions, Ray and I ate together. I thought I would find out right from the start what the parish priest was like. I began by talking about what Cardijn had said about promoting the lay apostolate through the confessional. Ray responded positively and with enthusiasm. I then told him what I had been doing at Ekibin, and he replied by telling me that he had been doing that for years; in fact he had chairs in his confessional so that people could sit and talk in a little comfort. This was the first of many conversations which I enjoyed with Ray. He was a very intelligent man who taught me a lot, in a pronounced Australian drawl.

Ray was progressive in his ideas and his pastoral practice. He often spoke about his own spirituality and his love of the Gospels. He was positive about people and their potential, his interests were wide, and his competence seemingly unlimited. He undertook an enormous amount of marriage counselling. He also had a following of people who had been classified as 'hopeless' by psychiatrists. With each one he worked out a plan, based on an agreement they had reached. He believed that everybody could be helped to help themselves, and he acted accordingly.

Ray could be very direct, would confront when appropriate, and would never tolerate hypocrisy from anybody, especially bishops. "Vatican II," he often said, "proved that bishops were not necessary. They left their dioceses for three months each year for three or four years and their dioceses flourished without them." I remember him saying that if the bishops really wanted peace in Vietnam, then they should go there and get between the protagonists. "They need to put their money where their mouth is." He taught me many things, including marriage counselling. I would have one session with the couple, and then I would have a session with him, and so on. He conducted his own marriage preparation courses. These were excellent, far superior at that time to what was being offered in Brisbane town.

Ray was always very encouraging. He backed up his encouragement with practical advice, and had empathy with the poor as well as a strong sense of justice. He seemed fearless when standing up for somebody who had been treated unjustly.

The finances for each Church in the parish were kept separately. Each community was encouraged to respond to the needs they identified in the way they thought fit. There was a Convent School attached to the main Church, and each section of the parish shared in the maintenance and other costs of that facility. Ray, with some of the parishioners, established the Bardon Parish Credit Union. The idea of the Credit Union was to make money available for the needs of the parish, and that through the provision of low-interest loans, those who were financially well off could assist those who were struggling. When the school required a new bus, the money was available in the Credit Union. When I met a poor family on visitation who were snowed under because of a hire-purchase arrangement with exorbitant interest rates, I would suggest they approach the Credit Union to pay off their debts and pay what they owed to the Credit Union at lower interest rates.

Being at Bardon for two years, working closely with the local community and with Ray, was a great grace. Ray would never tell a person to keep trying without giving that person something practical to try. He did not believe in spiritual 'Band-Aids', but in his own life and ministry, prayer and action were irrevocably fused. In his prayer life, he would try to be quiet so as to let the voice of Jesus speak. He mentioned on many occasions that God speaks to us through the voice of Jesus and the words of the Gospel. For me they were two great years; I had learnt much in many different areas.

During my two years at Bardon, Peter Callanan was the Archdiocesan YCW Chaplain, and he and I worked well together. About half way through my second year with Ray, Peter approached me about taking on the job of Archdiocesan Chaplain for the Young Christian Students Movement (YCS). Even though I told him I was not interested in students, but keen to put energy into young workers, he recommended me to the Archbishop. A phone call from the Archbishop appointed me as Archdiocesan YCS Chaplain, on a part-time basis.

It was not possible for me to stay at Bardon. It was a very busy place with three Churches, the Mercy Novitiate, and with Ray devoting most of his time to counselling. So I reluctantly requested a transfer to a smaller parish where I could combine parish duties with the student work. It was decided that I should be transferred to Moorooka Parish to assist the parish priest. My responsibilities were to look after the catechetics programs at the State Primary and High Schools, take care of the youth, and help out with Masses and Sacramental work. It appeared to be a reasonable arrangement and so, in January 1969, I moved my gear across town to Moorooka.

My years in Bardon had completely changed my attitude to parish work; I was sorry and reluctant to be moving away from it. I had enjoyed the variety of parish work, dealing with people of all ages, responding to a plethora of needs, identifying with a geographical community, and trying to respond to the many challenges. Now I was concerned about being in contact with mainly one age group, and potentially losing my ability to relate to people of all ages. Another concern was about working in an unstructured situation. Parish work had a set framework and routine which was a safeguard, a comfort, and a type of security. Working with students meant that I might not have a clear routine. The new responsibilities meant launching out into the deep, creating my own priorities, and establishing my own framework, and I was apprehensive about my ability to do that successfully.

Saint Brendan's Moorooka, 1969–1970

Upon moving to Moorooka, I quickly discovered that the parish priest, while a very intelligent man, was an alcoholic. During my time with him he hardly did a stroke of work except the occasional weekday Mass and, of course, Sunday Masses. He was an incredibly articulate person who could cut people to pieces in a few short sentences. I admit that I was scared of him, especially when I had to stand up to him.

There were often drinking and gambling parties at the presbytery which rarely broke up before 5 a.m. Some time after midnight there would be an argument which would go on for hours. The arguments were often about trivial things like whether a bet was for 50 or 60 cents. I found sleeping impossible when a party was in full swing. I was supposed to be the drink waiter, but I deliberately made a mess of it on my first night so I was summarily dismissed as useless and incompetent—which suited me fine.

The parish priest did not pay me for the first five months I was with him, which made life very difficult, as I was paying off my car and needed money for petrol as well. After five months he began to pay me something, but he kept little food in the house, so I was forced either to go home to my parents' place or arrange to have meals with friends, neither of which was satisfactory.

Towards the end of January of the second year, he announced that he would not be paying me my stipend any more, and that I would have to fend for myself. I saw the assistant bishop who did not believe my story, but who nevertheless suggested I seek an appointment with the Archbishop, which I did. The Archbishop told me: "You cannot teach an old dog new tricks." He gave me $200 after another five months without pay. A couple of my friends helped me from time to time with some money. Mass Stipends assisted also. Finally a neighbouring parish priest got to hear of the situation and went raging to the Archbishop on my behalf. He made arrangements for me to be paid regularly from headquarters. To my knowledge the Archbishop said nothing to my parish priest.

My ongoing study of AA was of great assistance in my current situation at St Brendan's. I had attended many meetings of Al-Anon, the support groups for family and friends of alcoholics, and knew at least some of the things that I ought to be practising. Despite this support, I still found the situation both difficult and stressful. Confronting an alcoholic with reality is good in theory, but not so easy in practice, especially with a strong and articulate person like my parish priest.

In the middle of my second year at Moorooka, the priest was transferred to a neighbouring parish. A new parish priest was appointed, who turned out to be an even heavier drinker. While his predecessor rarely drank before 10 a.m., the new parish priest regularly had a whisky for breakfast. As far as I was concerned, the situation was hopeless. I found myself becoming more and more depressed. I told the bishop I would be taking holidays and would not be returning to live at the Moorooka presbytery, although I was happy to continue working in the parish. When I returned from holidays I received a letter transferring me to the parish of Yeronga.

Having to live with ongoing conflict without the basic necessities of food and money proved to be a great trial to which I was not equal. My faith was a great support. My routine of meditation and Mass was a stabilising influence. I got a real boost from priests who invited me to talk over my situation. Family, friends and parishioners who offered hospitality helped to nourish me physically and emotionally. There was the temptation to become embittered, but thankfully I realised such bitterness would simply eat at my heart and prevent me from living the way God intended. Besides, bitterness would have done nothing to alter the situation.

Young Christian Students

Aﬀer serving at Yeronga parish from October 1970 to April 1972, I decided I had had enough of being pushed from pillar to post, and requested to be appointed as full-time Archdiocesan chaplain to the Young Christian Students (YCS) movement, a request approved after intense negotiation with the Archbishop.

My original, part-time appointment as chaplain had been made in November 1968. In the late 1960s and early 1970s the YCS movement operated in most Catholic secondary schools, as well as some State high schools and parishes, and boasted of a membership of about 4,000 students. The YCS executive often met without its twelve student members, which gave a free hand to the other twelve members, priests, brothers and nuns, to dominate the movement.

This, to my mind, was not lay apostolate. Authentic lay apostolate meant that lay people took responsibility for both organisation and action. Soon after I was appointed to YCS, I insisted that student members of the executive always be notified of meetings. We also reduced the number of religious on the executive—priests and those in holy orders—from twelve to four adults: one priest, one brother, one nun, and myself as diocesan chaplain.

Joseph Cardijn had said in 1948 that the YCS movement should be a student-run movement. Furthermore Vatican II had stated:

> The young should become the first apostles of the young, in direct contact with them, exercising the apostolate by themselves among themselves, taking account of their social environment.[8]

A student lay apostolate meant that students would take responsibility, with advice and assistance from their religious assistants. Because of their age, students needed help from adults; but my experience in YCW had taught me that 14, 15 and 16-year-old young people were already capable of making responsible and mature decisions.

My first year as chaplain showed me there were some very capable and dynamic students in the movement, as well as many dedicated adult religious assistants. However the movement seemed too respectable; it rarely got its hands dirty. It seemed to have little direction or Cardijnian methodology. The Review of Life (a fundamental of the Cardijnian method) was often a topic

---

8   Vatican II: *The Document on the Laity*: Young People at no. 12 p 780.

at training days and weekly meetings, but it was a review in name only. Students were given little responsibility, except to chair a meeting or take notes as secretary.

What I encountered in that first year resembled the YCS I had had some brief contact with when I was at school. For example, groups would have a discussion on discrimination in South Africa, and seemed content just to have an interesting discussion. They didn't contemplate how they could actually support black people in South Africa as part of their Christian duty. Nor did they consider confronting racism and isolation in their own schools, as experienced by Greek, Italian and Aboriginal students.

While each school elected its own YCS president and executive, the school authorities often kept a stranglehold on the group. For example it was not unusual for discussion topics to be chosen by the religious assistant, or to come from a National YCS program, which had little relevance to what was happening in the students' lives. Again, it was called 'review of life', but the lived faith-life was not being reviewed. Consequently I trained people in the Review of Life method. Rather than lecture on the topic, I gave a short introduction and placed students in a review group with a trained and experienced leader, so that the students learned the review by actually doing it. Central to the Cardijnian method is: do it yourself, get others to do it with you, get others to do it by themselves, and finally, encourage the others to do it with others.

In 1969 I initiated Review of Life groups for those religious who were interested. The groups met fortnightly, initially at All Hallows, a secondary school in central Brisbane. I wanted the religious assistants to train the students in the methodology of the movement. The meetings began with a reading from the Bible, and then incidents would be mentioned involving young people or others we lived with. We posed the question: "What do you think Christ is asking of us in this situation?" Initially we found it difficult to speak about things which were happening; however, given time and mutual encouragement, we managed to build trust.

The highlights of these review meetings were the times when people mentioned specific events. When in 1973 I moved into Kedron Lodge, which we initially used as a training centre for YCS and YCW members, many religious came there for various reasons: for example, to attend and participate in weekend training sessions. Because at the Lodge we were trying to live as a Christian community, it made all of us, especially those living in religious communities, look at the meaning of the word 'community' as well as 'openness' and 'welcome'. These visits helped all of us, not just the young people living at the Lodge.

At our meetings we stressed the principle of involvement; namely, that we cannot ask others to take a stand in their situations unless we do likewise in our own situation. We drew inspiration from many authors, but especially from

Gustavo Gutiérrez's *A Theology of Liberation*. The challenges we faced were many and varied, not least of which was the placement of some students from Catholic schools, in Wilson Youth Hospital.

Wilson, as it was known, was a particularly violent juvenile detention centre situated in Windsor, a suburb of Brisbane. The set-up was inhumane, with all children being incarcerated and treated psychiatrically, but the schools were reluctant to become involved in what was happening to their students at Wilson. My struggles with the conditions and injustices prevalent at Wilson became a pivotal experience in my ministry, which I tell in more detail below, starting on page 38 and continuing through the next few chapters.

Another challenge was the plight of people experiencing injustice and poverty in Cribb Island, a small island connected to Brisbane by a causeway. 'Cribby', as we affectionately called it, was inhabited mostly by disadvantaged people. We who lived at the Lodge, some concerned citizens as well as some Josephite nuns, helped to support the people who lived there, especially in the struggle for justice when the island was later purchased by the Federal Government for extensions to the Brisbane Airport. On page 31, in the chapter called *Speaking out for the 'least of these'*, I tell the story of our involvement with Cribby.

YCW members, including the Diocesan chaplain, also became involved in the work to free YCW political prisoners in what was then South Vietnam. Some South Vietnamese YCW members who were opposed to the war were being imprisoned and tortured by their government. YCW groups in Australia and in other parts of the world alerted people in their own countries of their plight and did all in their power to obtain their freedom.

The Radford System and student action

Working closely with students and religious assistants, listening to their concerns, and taking them seriously, led YCS—and, of course, me—into uncharted waters. With many of the emerging issues I had no previous experience and did not know what to do. All I could do was to trust the experience of the people involved, the process we were using, and my belief in God.

In 1969 the Queensland Government conducted an inquiry into secondary education under the chairmanship of Professor William Radford. As a result of his findings, what became known as the Radford System of Education was introduced into Grade 11 in 1971. Radford did away with public examinations at the end of the third and fifth years of secondary education, replacing these exams with internal assessment within schools. Unfortunately the universities demanded a very complex entrance assessment, diametrically opposed to many of Radford's proposals. The universities won the day. The Board of Secondary School Studies (BOSS) was established to implement the (much interfered with) Radford recommendations.

In 1971 the YCS Diocesan executive met to discuss the new system. Several students spoke about the impact Radford was having on Grade 11 students. They described the unfairness of standard marking, increased competition, and decreasing co-operation among students. They were even concerned about some students 'cracking up'. The executive decided to conduct a Diocesan inquiry into Radford.

The report of the Inquiry confirmed the concerns of the executive about Radford's impact on students. We contacted Brother Levander, a Christian Brother and a member of BOSSS, to discuss the results of the Inquiry. Brother Levander listened to the students' concerns. When the students had finished, he congratulated them on the good job they had done. The students were shocked by the Brother's patronising attitude and his clear lack of concern about the issues raised. His response angered them and disappointed me.

About that time I had begun reading Paulo Freire's *Pedagogy of the Oppressed*.[9] Freire and Cardijn had a lot in common. Both believed in the dignity of each person, that the individual could improve their own lot as well as the situation of others, and in the vital importance of *praxis*, the cycle of reflection and action. Both Freire and Cardijn were educators who believed in working with people at the grassroots. Freire believed that there was no such thing as a 'neutral education process'. For him, education was either an instrument used to make the younger generation conform to the system, or a means by which people dealt critically and creatively with reality and discovered how to participate in the transformation of their world.[10]

Despite my disappointment, I knew the students had already achieved a great deal. They had examined the system and reflected deeply on it. They had looked critically at the society they were living in and, at the same time, they had tried to look through the eyes of faith at the effects the Radford System was having on their fellow-students.

The documents of Vatican II challenged and encouraged me, as they did the students and their religious assistants. On many occasions I was accused of being radical. I thought to myself: *would that I were as radical as Jesus*. As far as the teachings of the Church were concerned, I felt that in some respects I was rather conservative, while in others, I was just carrying out the teachings of the Church. For example I saw the work on Radford as part and parcel of the Christian role of working with young people, as the following quote from the Document on the Church in the Modern World directs:

> Above all we must undertake the training of youth from all social backgrounds if we are to produce the kind of men and women so desperately

9   Paulo Freire. *Pedagogy of the Oppressed*. Angus & Robertson. 1970.

10   Ibid. in Chapter 2, pages 57ff.

needed by our age—men and women not only of high culture but of great personality as well.[11]

My involvement with students' rights brought me the tag of radical, even subversive. I understood 'subversive' as a compliment, although not meant as such. A radical subversive works with people on the ground and works for change from below. Students, like everybody else, were created in the image and likeness of God and therefore should be listened to. It was just this that we were trying to do, in all sincerity, in YCS. We were trying to understand the mind of the Church, live in the spirit of Jesus, and denounce injustice, but at the same time work constructively with all people to make things better.

As early as 1972 I could see that the aims of YCS, the student apostolate, Vatican II, and the Gospel were diametrically opposed to those of the education system, including the Catholic education system. The education system was focused on control rather than participation and co-operation. If those in the system promoted participation or co-operation, they did so strictly on their own terms and within narrow defined limits.

Many priests and some bishops were convinced that their role was simply to preach the Word of God and to celebrate the sacraments, to offer Mass and to perform baptisms, marriages and administer the Sacrament of Reconciliation. To question the *status quo* in Church and society was alien to their thinking. Doing justice and working with people who were poor, oppressed or alienated in any way was not a central part of their role.

Added to the above, I was not living in a presbytery. I was living with lay people and working with them to 'renew the face of the earth.' Even at social gatherings of priests, I was semi-publicly ridiculed to the point where I decided not to attend these functions for a few years.

I continued to study Cardijn, Freire, and the Documents of Vatican II, as well as to re-read the Bible from the viewpoint of the poor and the oppressed. I could see that YCS and myself were in for a stack of trouble. The odds were stacked against us: we had no power (nor did we want it), and we were not influential. I could see that the job we had to do was difficult, nearly impossible, but nevertheless vital in terms of Gospel integrity. We had to follow the dictates of our consciences and our Christian principles, come what may.

11   Vatican II: *The Church in the Modern World*: Responsibility and participation: no 31

A trip to the Netherlands[12]

I N December 1973, I was nominated to attend the International YCS Conference at Maastricht in the Netherlands, to be held in July and August 1974. The month-long conference was a real shot in the arm—certainly a moment of grace. We spent one full week on societal and global analysis, followed by a week on faith-reflection with Gustavo Gutiérrez, whose book I had read.

The societal and global analysis was done in small groups, with a minimum of seven nationalities to each group. We began by examining an action that we or students in our own country were taking, to see what it revealed about our nation's various social structures. I was the only Australian in my group of fourteen people, all from different nations: French-speakers and English-speakers, some from the global North, most from the South. There was a priest from Madagascar, where there had been a revolution just prior to the conference. (The YCS students had participated in this revolution, and some had been killed.) He had a clear understanding of the destructive effects of capitalism, especially on the poor, as well as the corruption which he believed was an integral part of capitalism.

The social analysis helped us to understand the functioning of the capitalist system and to identify the most recent phases of its development. The work was intense and demanding. By the end of the week, we had assembled, both from small groups and plenary sessions, a global analysis. On the last day of this segment of the conference, we again looked at the action we had mentioned on the first day, to see if we were acting for change or merely putting on a Band-Aid.

I spent much time with Joseph, a university student from Kenya. Joseph told me much about his country, his people, and the work his YCS was engaged in. He spoke about the endemic corruption in his society, especially in government. We discussed at length the actions he and his colleagues were engaged in, and the personal risks they took in trying to bring about a more just and humane society. He had been chased many times by police when they broke up demonstrations. Joseph had had to run and hide, in fear of a severe beating, arrest or worse. He said to me, laughing: "I can run very fast. On one occa-

---

12 Most of the material in this chapter is drawn from the reports I wrote on the Conference in the latter half of 1974, from hand-outs from the Conference itself, and from a document entitled *Report on the VII World Study Session of the International Young Christian Students Movement*, Cadier en Keer 1974.

sion, I ran for nearly 24 hours." (I wondered aloud if this was the reason Kenya produced so many world-class marathon runners!) Our discussions had a profound effect on me. I tried to keep in contact with Joseph after the conference by letter; I received just one reply, and then heard no more from him.

Corruption was something I had not thought much about at that time. I suppose I had focused more on the dishonesty of individual people, rather than systemic corruption. Dishonesty, in the sense of fraud and deception, is a strong word; but corruption with its connotations of evil, iniquity and depravity was something I had not considered as common in my own country.

Collectively, conference members saw YCS as participating in the transformation of history. More precisely, we saw ourselves promoting Gospel justice and the dignity of all people, with an option for the exploited and marginalised people of the world. History was 'open', a constant process of building up humanity towards law and justice, ultimately to the realisation of the sisterhood and brotherhood of all peoples. History, in this sense, was the history of salvation.

Gustavo Gutiérrez

The second week of the study session was led by the Peruvian priest, Gustavo Gutiérrez, who has rightly been called the father of liberation theology. Gustavo was a small man who walked with a limp. He arrived at the conference in time to be present for the last sessions on global analysis, because, as he said, his work on faith-reflection followed on from the intense study of our reality, of society, of student action and social conflicts, of the nature and effects of capitalism, imperialism and colonialism.

On the first day of our faith-reflection session, Gutiérrez lectured for an hour or two and then sent us into discussion groups to consider some questions which he had prepared. That night, he met individually with the leaders and secretaries from all groups, so as to understand clearly where we were at and where we were coming from theologically. He was so disgusted with what he found out that he lectured for nearly four hours the next morning!

It seemed to me that the South Americans, some of the people from Canada and some from isolated areas of Africa were working for change and reflecting on society through the eyes of faith. However most of the people from Africa, especially in those places where white missionaries worked, were very conservative, indeed reactionary. They obviously had not studied the documents of Vatican II, and they had little or no understanding of biblical or Gospel justice. There was a Dutch missionary in our group who was working in Ghana. He was openly racist and patronising. Indigenous Africans tried to talk to him about his racist attitudes and actions but to no avail. He would rarely listen and, if he did, he would not agree that he was exploiting the local people.

Gutiérrez challenged us with the big questions:

Is it possible to be a Christian and not be involved with the oppressed and the marginalised people of the world?

How do we announce God in an adult world, a world that is becoming mature?

How do we announce to the 'non-person' (the one who is hungry, badly dressed and who smells) the fact that God is his/her Father (when there is inequality) and the other person is his/her brother/sister (when one is exploiting the other)?

Gutiérrez told us that theological reflection needs to question the world which creates the non-person. I had never met someone who was fluent in many languages. One morning Gutiérrez was lecturing us in Spanish, which was simultaneously translated into French and English through headphones. Suddenly there was an eruption in the conference. For some reason the French speakers were not receiving their translation. The technical people tried in vain to find the fault. After ten minutes Gutiérrez asked if it would be of assistance if he lectured in French, which would be simultaneously translated into Spanish. The lines were tested and, yes, this could be done. So he then began lecturing in French, from his notes which were in Spanish, while he wrote on the blackboard in English.

With international friends, Netherlands

Gutiérrez spent some time talking about 'neighbour', in the context of the story of the Good Samaritan (Luke 10:25-37). Neighbour, in the Biblical sense, is not the person who lives near us or is near to us, but the person who is 'away from us'. Since neighbour literally means 'one near to us', how can we say neighbour means the one who is away from us? Luke's Gospel gives the answer in the story of the Samaritan.

Christ asks the question: who among these three was neighbour to the wounded man? Who now is my neighbour in the world?

For Gutiérrez the starting point was *the other*. If I do not place myself in the world of the other, then I do not understand the Gospel. The Gospel emphasises conversion—to 'convert' is to go from one's own world to the world of the other. Or, put differently, to be a neighbour is the result of an *activity*—I become a neighbour as I get nearer to a faraway person. The Samaritan went out of his own way and into the wounded man's way, which meant going into another world, another cultural class.

To be poor is to be part of a social group of races, cultures, peoples and classes. The poor person is a product of our society, and to come into the world of the poor is to come into the action of history. Gutiérrez concluded that to be a Christian is to come into the world of the poor and to know real conversion.

The World Conference of International YCS profoundly affected and influenced my ministry. Although I had previously been aware of and involved with the poor and marginalised of our society, the week with Gutiérrez in particular, and the conference as a whole, confirmed the direction that my ministry was taking.

Back home in Australia, I had been living with homeless and disadvantaged young people, and was beginning to look at the systems which dehumanised them. I also had some involvement with an anti-freeway protest group. When freeways were being planned and built on the south and north sides of Brisbane, residents living in the pathways of the proposed freeways were given inadequate compensation for their homes. Some families with whom Pat Tynan and I were associated, requested we assist them in their endeavours to receive just compensation. I had been trying to encourage students to make connections between the Jesus of the Gospel (who opted for the poor) and marginalised people in their own schools, the people at Cribb Island, and Aboriginal people. For this, I had been ostracised by my brother priests and placed in conflict with the bishops. What was happening to me? All I had ever wanted was to be a good priest, and here I was being alienated by many good priests.

The conference gave me direction and renewed hope. Gutiérrez taught us that theology must come from life, from reflecting on the actions and the lives of the poor. This theology, he said, must then be useful when you are working with the poor. If it is not useful, then it should be discarded. His theology was deductive, not inductive. In fact, he talked about a theology of verification. By this he meant that, on reflecting with Jesus in the Gospel on action with the poor and for justice, one then moved back into the world of the poor to see how relevant the theological reflections were. If they proved to be helpful, they were valid and therefore authentic. If not, they were to be discarded as useless.

I had tentatively been doing this with Pat Tynan, the YCW chaplain with whom I had moved into Kedron Lodge (see page 37 below). The theological training that we had received at Banyo was almost completely useless in our engagement with the young people from Wilson Youth Hospital, in the work to free YCW political prisoners in what was then South Vietnam, and in the efforts, initially to gain fair compensation for those living in the path of the freeway, and later to halt the building of freeways completely.

Pat and I would pray the Office together. Rightly or wrongly, we felt we were under siege. Priests we consulted, told us we should not be involved in what we were doing, especially our work with the poor and for justice. But then we would come across something like this in the Office of Readings:

> Wash yourselves; make yourselves clean; remove the evil of your doings from before my eyes; cease to do evil, learn to do good; seek justice, rescue the oppressed, defend the orphan, plead for the widow. Come now, let us argue it out, says the LORD: though your sins are like scarlet, they shall be like snow; though they are red like crimson, they shall become like wool. *Isaiah 1:16-18*

After we had finished, or sometimes even in the middle of the Office, I would say to Pat:

"Did you notice that bit about defending the orphan? Do you think that is what we are trying to do?" Then we would discuss the text in the light of what was happening at the Lodge.

On another occasion, when Pat was involved in the anti-freeway movement and getting into trouble with bishops and friends alike, we were praying the Office of Readings when we came across:

> Alas for those who devise wickedness and evil deeds on their beds! When the morning dawns, they perform it, because it is in their power. They covet fields, and seize them; houses, and take them away; they oppress householder and house, people and their inheritance. *Micah 2:1-2*

At that time we were witnessing people's homes being literally taken away or destroyed to make way for the South-East Freeway, the owners paid insufficient compensation to purchase a comparable home. The same thing was beginning to happen in the Bowen Hills area with the proposed northern freeway. People were suffering. Those in authority were not listening.

The passage in Micah seemed to be speaking to us about this situation. Houses were being coveted, seized and taken away. Householders were being oppressed. People were being uprooted and losing significant parts of their inheritance. Gutiérrez said to us: "You should be reflecting on the words of the Bible in the light of your involvement with and on behalf of the poor, the oppressed, the dispossessed and the marginalised." I was determined to do more theological reflection when I returned home.

For my work with YCS students, the implications were enormous. The conference strongly encouraged me to continue with the formation of students through the Review of Life method. It impelled me to identify injustice and work with 'all men and women of good will'[13], to ask the hard questions, to continually do structural analysis, and to engage in theological reflection. However in the light of the experiences of the Brisbane YCS movement, I could see that if I put into practice the conference's conclusions, there would be suffering, misunderstanding and further conflict with authority: a daunting thought.

Gutiérrez told us that to find God in the poor is demanding and conflictual. Spirituality does not run away from these conflicts. For him, relationship with the poor was the core message of the Old Testament prophets and the core message of Christ. I wanted to have a relationship with Jesus who loved the poor. I even wanted to be, in some real way, one with the poor. As far as criticising the rich and the powerful was concerned, I did not want to do that. Somebody else more capable, more articulate than I, could do that. I just wanted to be a good priest.

13 Vatican II: *The Church in the Modern World*, paragraph 22; *Populorum Progressio* at para 83.

Speaking out for the 'least of these'

O N MY RETURN from overseas at the end of 1974, I observed that the Diocese seemed to be systematically undermining Young Christian Workers, sacking the Archdiocesan Chaplain, Pat Tynan, and leaving the position vacant. I could see Young Christian Students going down a similar road without explicit support from those in authority, especially from the bishops who should have known the mind of the Church.

I had been aware for some time that we were on a collision course with both school and church authorities. In our YCS work we tried to emphasise such things as respect for all people and a continuing search for truth and justice. We knew we often failed, and we could be hypocritical ourselves, but we were determined to be people of integrity, and less hypocritical.

By January 1977, YCS in the Brisbane Archdiocese had been reduced to 16 groups, eight in parishes and eight in schools. Since 1968 YCS membership had dropped from 4,000 to 400 students. The movement was being marginalised and I was banned from entering several Catholic secondary schools and parishes. (The principal of one school even phoned parents and told them if their daughters had anything to do with me they would be suspended. Some of these parents phoned me and told me I was always welcome in their homes, and that they had strongly objected to the principal's actions).

As students and adults associated with YCS, we continued with formation through the Review of Life. We conducted student live-ins and days at the Lodge for members of YCS, as well as other students interested in serious Christian discussion and action. Students were asked to reflect on important personal matters in their lives, such as sibling, parental and peer relationships. Then they might be asked what assignments they were working on. In economics, history and English, they were often doing work which was of interest to their fellow-students as well as to their Christian formation. For example if a student said they were doing an assignment on Aboriginals, the topic would be discussed and the student would be asked if they had met any Aboriginal people or read anything written by an Aboriginal. Most students had done neither. As the Lodge had some contacts within the Aboriginal community, as well as other relevant resources, these would be made available. Many students took up this opportunity and used these firsthand sources in their assignments. The response from some teachers was (and I quote): "If you use any of this information from the Lodge in your assignments I will give you a zero mark. Confine yourself to the information in the school library."

Through our regular YCS training sessions at the Lodge, the students came into contact with homeless young people as well as young people who had been locked up in Wilson. They were introduced to a world they could scarcely believe existed. At the training weekends held at the Lodge, students would often request a session on Wilson, because they had met young people from Wilson who were welcome to attend or participate in meetings. The students were horrified at what they heard, and wanted to have a part in any planned action. For example, they participated in the Wilson Protest Group campaign (and later the Justice for Juveniles Group) by writing letters in support of a better deal for incarcerated youth. We also encouraged students to talk about the young people in trouble at their own schools or from their own areas. Mostly they knew of these young people but did not associate with them. We encouraged them to meet and befriend these troubled young people, making certain they had appropriate support, as they were engaged in what was in effect preventative work.

I often wondered why YCS lost the support of the Bishops. In YCS we tried to be faithful to the teachings and example of Christ as well as to the teachings of Vatican II and the social encyclicals which followed. I was puzzled by the fact that while Brisbane YCS could be regarded as 'radical' by Church authorities, YCS groups in other dioceses were not tagged as such. My conclusion was that maybe the Australian Conference of Bishops had made a decision to abandon its support for the student movement.

Cribby

Cribb Island is about 15 minutes by car from Kedron, in the north-eastern suburbs of Brisbane. The island was then connected to the mainland by a causeway. During the depression of the 1930s, 60 acres of land on the northern end of the island (which became known as Jackson's Estate) were opened up to people in desperate circumstances. Little cottages and shanties were built from whatever materials were to hand. In the early 1970s many of these dwellings were still inhabited. The remainder of the island, which was the greater part, contained a variety of homes—some of brick construction, others substantial wooden houses, while the rest were small workers' cottages.

Two of the people who had been part of our community at the Lodge, married and purchased a shack on Jackson's Estate for not much more than $1000. When they moved in, the shack had some dirt floors and the front wall waved in the breeze. Many people helped Carmel and Terry make their place more livable, and they in turn, as part of the Cribb Island community, did some wonderful work with their neighbours.

Some 800 residents lived on the island, mainly people who were socio-economically disadvantaged. We supported them from the Lodge as much as we could; this sometimes involved providing shelter for people fleeing domestic violence. At a later stage two Josephite Sisters, Mary and Angela, moved there to work with the people. I had had previous contact with the place, supervising seminarians on placement, occasionally helping out with Sunday Mass, and following up with young people and their families, especially when a young person returned home from Wilson.

In December 1971 the Federal Government decided to purchase Cribb Island to extend Brisbane Airport. The residents responded by forming the Cribb Island and Districts Preservation Committee in January 1972, in an attempt to try to change the redevelopment proposal and, when that failed, to seek a just deal from the government. The acquisition, like most others in Australia—and we had seen it all before in the destruction of homes and communities for freeways in Brisbane—was done as cheaply as possible and with little regard for the people affected.

When the protest and compensation group formed, the Catholic Church, the Methodist, Presbyterian and Congregational churches (soon to join in the Uniting Church), as well as a few multi-property owners, were its backbone. The government paid each of these groups adequate compensation for their properties, whereupon they resigned from the group. For the rest, the sole criterion for compensation was the value of their land. Values were already depressed because of the threat of resumption for redevelopment. Therefore the government paid very little compensation for the properties. Since alternative low-cost housing was unavailable, many former home owners went into debt in order to buy another home.

As some of the older residents sold up and moved out, the government rented their dwellings to tenants, mostly poor and destitute families. These poor people, some of whom were barely literate, were left to fend for themselves. As tenants of the government, they were responsible for all maintenance on their houses. They also had to pay insurance on the house on behalf of the government, and pay rent and rates. From time to time they were subject to house inspections by government officials, to ensure the houses were being maintained, or to carry out a review of rents.

After August 1976, whenever people got behind in their rent, the government issued them with an eviction notice. Immediately the roof of their house was torn off, even if it was raining, or if the residents had not been able to remove their meagre but essential possessions, like bedding and clothing.

Often as part of our training, we would take students on a tour of Cribb Island. We would show the students what was happening. After the tour, we would drop in to speak with some of the people we knew, so that the students could ask questions and receive fuller explanations from the locals. For instance we visited Alice, an Aboriginal woman, whose home was a refuge for young people who were experiencing violence at home. Sometimes we would have a cuppa with the nuns who lived down there, or chat with some of the other people we knew, and listen to their stories and ask questions. Mostly we would end up at Carmel and Terry's little house, where we were always made welcome.

The students were shocked by what was happening in their own country, almost in their own back yard. We spent time reflecting on this experience, trying to encourage them to begin to make some sort of initial social analysis. We also reflected on Jesus and his relationship with the poor and disadvantaged groups of his time, as well as his socio-political actions.

Early one morning I received a telephone call from the bishop. He wanted to see me that day. I had a busy day ahead of me, with many appointments.

"Is it urgent?" I inquired.

Yes, it was.

"The only time I have available is now."

It was 7:30. I hopped in the car and drove to his place.

Sitting me in his office, he began by accusing me: "You've been involved in political activity."

"Yes. Which particular activity are you referring to?"

"You organised a demonstration down at Cribb Island."

"No, I didn't," I replied. "However, if it was necessary to do something for those powerless people down there, I would not have hesitated."

"You organised a sit-in and obstructed the police."

"I told you, I didn't. When is this supposed to have taken place?"

"Recently."

"Well, I have no knowledge of it." I again pointed out to him the plight of the people on Cribb Island, but I was wasting my breath.

The interview was going nowhere, and he terminated it. I was left wondering if I was suffering from early-onset amnesia. At the first opportunity, later that day, I asked people at the Lodge if there had been a demonstration at Cribb Island recently. There had indeed been one. Alice had phoned up a week earlier to say that she and her children were to be evicted that day and asked if some people could come down from the Lodge and be with her when the Federal Police and government officials arrived. A few of our people were able to go, and they went in my car. I was out of town for a few days that week.

The Federal Police arrived with guns drawn, to be confronted by Alice, some of her children, some other local residents, and 'our' people sitting on her front porch, which was really the pavement, as her house had been the bakery. The people refused to move, and tried but failed to negotiate with the police and the government officials. A stalemate ensued, and the official visitors departed, obviously having taken note of the registration number of my car: hence the accusation by the bishop.

In one school in 1977, several years after their YCS had been disbanded, the new principal asked me to conduct a retreat for her Year 10 students. Following the retreat, I visited the school to follow up some of the issues which had arisen. The principal wanted to see me in her office. I was told to sit down. She told me a complaint had been made about the way I had conducted the retreat. In fact, she said, two gentlemen from the Special Branch of the Queensland Police had been to see her about me. They had been to see the Archbishop and told her that the Archbishop did not want me in parish work, that I was a subversive—that word again—and that my priesthood was just a front for political activities.

I tried to speak with the principal to put my point of view, but each time I tried she held up her hand, indicating she did not want to be interrupted.

Here we go again, I thought. *I bet this is the last visit I'll be making to this school.*

She finished by saying: "I wouldn't have listened to them if one of them had not been the father of one of the Year 10 students. In fact if that had not been the case, I would have asked them to leave this office."

"I'd like to say this to you," she continued. "Anyone who professes to be a Christian and who doesn't work for the poor and for justice is some kind of schizophrenic."

I could not believe my ears. Here was a person in authority who agreed with my approach to formation and the Gospel! I could have hugged her.

At the beginning of 1979 I resigned my position as YCS Archdiocesan Chaplain. The number of students involved had decreased to about a hundred. I was saddened by the demise of YCS in Brisbane. I knew its potential and capabilities to form students according to the mind of Christ and the Church, and had seen it do some difficult but excellent work.

I left YCS with many unanswered questions. What if we had done things differently? What if we had not taken so seriously the teachings of Jesus and of the Church? What if the hierarchy and the school authorities had given us the backing we needed? I noticed that Diocesan YCS movements in other parts of Australia, which had not gone down the same track as we had in Brisbane, were also disappearing. Was this guilt by association, or was it that other activities like the Catholic Lay Activities Group (CLAG) and Antioch, which were much less demanding and less questioning of the *status quo*, were being encouraged from on high?

YCS groups at tertiary institutions in Brisbane did not exist when I was given responsibility for YCS in the diocese. I had sought and obtained permission from the Archbishop to establish groups in tertiary institutions. In 1969 Tertiary Christian Students (TCS) groups were established in the universities, teacher training colleges, and the then Queensland Institute of Technology (that later joined with other colleges to form the Queensland University of

Technology). The group at the University of Queensland flourished under its first president, Jim O'Donovan. These groups were involved in issues on campus as well as the wider society, such as conscription, the war in Vietnam and the erosion of civil liberties in Queensland.

We campaigned on behalf of Young Christian Students imprisoned and tortured in Vietnam. At the same time we were trying to find out exactly what the war was about, and why the United States and Australia were involved in it. A right-wing Church organisation, the National Civic Council (NCC), was monitoring our activities and possibly—I feel sure, but of course I have no evidence—reporting to the Bishops.

I had had some contact with the NCC in the past. I joined some university students to request and obtain an appointment with their Queensland President. At the meeting the NCC argument went like this: if there are Communists involved in any social issue then the Church should not be involved; if Church people do become involved, then they will be manipulated by the Communists. In my view their argument ran as follows: if, in a matter of justice or peace, a Communist is involved, then a Christian should run away from this issue for fear they be manipulated by evil people. It did not seem to enter their heads that Christians could exercise an influence over the Communists.

After the meeting with the NCC, the students and I had another meeting to debrief. We rejected the logic of the arguments and decided against further association with the NCC. For me to have no more contact with the NCC was a significant decision. I had had great respect for Mr. Santamaria, the founder of the NCC, and those who worked for his movement, but it was obvious that I could no longer accept their analysis, let alone their reasoning.

At this time I was also teaching a weekly class with final-year students at Banyo Seminary. I was finding it easier to work with secondary and tertiary students than with students for the priesthood. The non-clerical students were keen to live out their Christianity in their daily lives. By contrast, many of the students at Banyo suffered from inflated egos and were wrongly convinced of their own and nobody else's apostolate.

Under a new rector, Bill O'Shea, this situation changed dramatically. Bill made pastoral work compulsory—any student who did not take the work seriously was asked to show cause as to why he should stay on in the seminary. Second-year students did an excellent telephone counselling course with Lifeline, as well as six months of hands-on telephone counselling. Third-year students worked with the poor and the underprivileged. Fourth-year students undertook hospital work, while fifth-year students engaged in youth work. Sixth-year students had general parish responsibilities with parish organisations. It was certainly a much better system.

In 1980 the fourth-year students began spending most of the year in parishes. While I supported this innovation, it meant in practice they spent little or no time working with the poor and the underprivileged and reflecting on that work. I regarded working with the poor and the underprivileged—and the consequent obligation to work for justice—to be of the essence of the Gospel. With this emphasis in their training lost, I felt it was time for me to finish my responsibilities at the seminary. By this time, I was deeply involved in ministering to, and advocating for, young people in Brisbane and Queensland who had fallen on hard times.

Kedron Lodge

I N 1973 PAT TYNAN AND I were needing to support each other during the troubled times of YCS and YCW. We decided to live together in the same house, initially trying to become the priests of several small inner-city parishes. Pat even approached some incumbent priests, but they expressed no interest in resigning their parishes!

Then Kedron Lodge became vacant. The Lodge was a huge old sandstone house at Kalinga, built in 1860 for Justice Lutwyche, the first Judge of the Supreme Court in Queensland. St Anne's Catholic Church was on its western side, Kedron Brook at the rear, while the closest houses on the eastern side

were 50 metres away. After several meetings we prevailed upon the bishop to allow us to move into the Lodge, despite his concern about the dampness in the building, which could have been a health hazard.

We moved in at the end of January 1973, with Michael, a sixth-year student from Banyo who was on two years' leave of absence from the seminary. The

Lodge had 19 rooms and was almost totally unfurnished. We scrounged furniture from anywhere and everywhere.

Because the Lodge had loads of space, we were able to make it into a YCS-YCW training centre, a decision more or less forced upon us by the fact that the city training centres for these Catholic lay youth organisations had either closed down or raised their tariffs beyond the reach of most students and young workers.

In the early days at the Lodge, the young people with whom we were working were welcome to stay for a few hours, a night or a weekend, as a break from the tension in their own homes. We used to say to them: "Don't wander around the streets at night waiting for the perpetrator of the violence to go to sleep. Come over, or phone us and we will pick you up." During their stay, we would spend time with them and help them work through their experiences.

Michael was working at the drive-in bottle shop of Chardon's Hotel at Annerley. One night, he phoned from work, saying he had met an elderly man who was homeless and who had run away from a violent situation where he was being exploited and beaten regularly. Mike wanted to know if he could stay with us.

That was how Tom came to stay. All he had were the clothes on his back. Tom had been a soldier in the Second World War and suffered from a nervous condition as a result. At the end of the war, he lived with his mother at Wynnum. After she died, he couldn't afford the rent, so he moved into a place run by three brothers (family, not Christian brothers!). Each week, he and the other elderly people were belted until they signed and handed over their pension cheques. They were made to work hard and were often physically and verbally abused.

We had no end of trouble trying to get Tom's gear out of that place. On one occasion Peter Callanan and a friend went down in a truck to pick it up. Peter was physically pushed around by one of the huge brothers and ordered off the property. He went to the local police who said that they knew of the situation but could do nothing. None of this helped poor old Tom. For a long time we phoned the brothers every day, and even had a solicitor send them a letter. Finally, one night around midnight, a huge furniture truck arrived in our back yard. I went down, to be confronted by a massive man who demanded fifty dollars for cartage before he would unload anything. I had only forty dollars on me, so he withheld Tom's bed. Tom stayed with us for several months until we were able to help him find more suitable accommodation.

Wilson Youth Hospital

In August 1973 Pat and I became involved in Wilson Youth Hospital, a remand, assessment and treatment centre for young people: in practice, a juvenile prison for young people between the ages of eight and 17 years for girls, and eight and 15 years for boys, in the nearby suburb of Windsor. It was to change my life dramatically.

A woman phoned the Lodge. Her 14-year old niece was in Wilson and wanted to see a Catholic priest. When Pat went to Wilson, he was told a Catholic priest had not visited for some six months. When he came home, he told me about his visit and asked if I would be prepared to share the chaplaincy with him.

Wilson Youth Hospital, before it was surrounded by high walls

From August 1973 until December 1974, Pat and I shared chaplaincy responsibilities at Wilson. On my first visits, I could not believe what I saw taking place. Most of the young inmates found their way into Wilson through the Children's Court. Many young people—and, in fact, most of the girls on their first admission—were placed in Wilson for non-criminal offences. These were called 'status offences', like running away from home, being uncontrollable, living in moral danger or likely to lapse into a life of vice or crime.[14] If these offences were proven—and hearsay evidence was sufficient—the young people often received a Care and Control Order, which meant they were placed under the care and control of the Director of Children's Services until they were 18 years of age. Under this Order, the Director could place his charges in secure custody.

I found many things which horrified me in Wilson. Indeterminate sentencing was one of them. Since most Care and Control orders were valid until the young person reached 18, they could in theory stay in custody until their eighteenth birthday. Indeterminate sentencing meant, in practice, that young people never knew when they were to be released. Their release depended on

14 Children's Services Act 1965: Sections 60 & 61.

a number of factors: the way they responded to the 'treatment' they received while incarcerated, the availability of accommodation 'on the outside', and the way they reacted to being locked up. Once they were placed on a Care and Control Order they could, after release, be placed back in Wilson without reference to the Children's Court.

There was solitary confinement either in Open Tantrum or, as it was often called, 'the fish bowl', a room with a glass wall, or in Closed Tantrum which was simply a cell with a bed base built into the floor and a small window high up on the wall. Regulations prescribed that young people should be placed in seclusion for one hour, and then only with a staff person in close attendance. However, these regulations were often contravened. In fact, many young people spent days at a time in solitary confinement. One 15-year-old girl, 'Antoinette'[15], spent more than three weeks in solitary before she was certified as being mentally unbalanced and transferred to Osler House at Wolston Park Mental Hospital, the lock-up section for adult women who were judged to be criminally insane.

There were no trained teachers in Wilson, and therefore no schooling—an obvious breach of the United Nations Declaration of the Rights of the Child, as well as of the State law requiring compulsory education to the age of 15.[16] Those children in Wilson who were illiterate were not helped to gain basic literacy-numeracy skills. A young person who had not been truanting (and had been coping well at school) ended up well behind their classmates when they returned to school, because they were unable to continue with schooling while in Wilson. Even if they spent only three months in Wilson, they fell so far behind their classmates that they effectively lost a year of schooling.

'Annie' was 14 years old when she went to Wilson. She was doing quite well at school in Grade Nine and wanted to continue her schooling while inside. At first she was refused. After six weeks of persistent requests, she was allowed to do her schooling by correspondence, which meant she had to sit in a room by herself all day without any assistance. She approached me to see if I could obtain a book she needed for her French studies. She also needed a tutor for maths. I was able to obtain the book she requested, and to enlist the voluntary

15 All names have been changed.
16 United Nations Declaration of the Rights of the Child states that the child is entitled to receive education which shall be free and compulsory (Principle 7). Section 28 of the Queensland Education Act (1964-1974) states that "every parent of a child being of the age of compulsory attendance shall, unless some reasonable excuse exists, cause such child to attend a State school on each school day." What applies to parents surely must apply to those acting in the name of parents (*in loco parentis*) and in the best interests of the child.

    A number of the young people who had been incarcerated in Wilson, and whose education had therefore ceased, have often remarked that this played a significant part in condemning them to a life of poverty.

services of a qualified teacher, who was prepared to tutor her in maths at the convenience of management and staff at Wilson. I approached the manager of Wilson, to arrange for the book to be handed over and to organise a tutor for Annie. The Manager said neither was possible—it would establish precedents. "Other children would be wanting books and tutors," he said, "and the whole thing could get out of hand very quickly."

Wilson institutionalised violence. Most children had not committed serious crimes, contrary to what the Minister for Children's Services, Mr John Herbert, often used to say: "Wilson is full of murderers, rapists and arsonists." In the three years I worked there, I met two arsonists but never a rapist or a murderer. Most of the young people had run away from violence at home, been deemed uncontrollable by the court, and then been incarcerated. A significant percentage of the young women I met in Wilson had been victims of sexual violence in their homes.

Many of the young people who were sent to Wilson were dehumanised, brutalised, victimised and criminalised. On a number of occasions, staff told me that their young charges were 'savages'. I saw young people with broken arms which they had received from staff who were supposedly 'restraining' them. One girl suffered a fractured skull when staff

The entrance to the 'solitary' wing in Wilson

dragged her upstairs by her legs. Her head bounced on the edge of the steps, and she was later admitted to the Royal Brisbane Hospital for treatment.

'Sandy', a very intelligent and courageous girl, told me about this incident. She was so enraged by the violence of some of the staff that she fully intended to report the incident to the visiting magistrate who appeared at Wilson every month. However, she was prevailed upon by staff not to take any further action. They told her: "Remember, you have to live here. Staff will not take kindly to you reporting them. Also, staff members have families, and your action could result in them losing their jobs and, if their families suffered, that would be your fault and on your conscience." When Sandy told me that she did not have the courage to write up a report for the magistrate, she broke down and cried.

There is no doubt in my mind that some of the staff were sexually abusing both boys and girls. I knew of several cases that came before the courts. When staff were charged with sexual offences, the courts were closed when minors were giving evidence, and in many instances I was unable to find out the determination of the court.

In my opinion, staff were also using drugs to control the young people. Young people were often injected with sedatives. If some staff wanted to have a quiet shift they were not above giving sedatives to their young charges. Some young people who did not have a drug problem when they entered Wilson certainly had a raging habit by the time they were discharged. I spoke publicly about what I termed the misuse of legal drugs in Wilson. On one occasion I was given a verbal warning, saying that I would be brought before the courts if ever I mentioned it again. That worried me for a short time, but then I reasoned that such a court case would be worth losing: the associated publicity would surely highlight the terrible things which were occurring in Wilson.

In Wilson all young people were 'treated' with incarceration, and seen by psychiatrists. If a young person was incarcerated for truanting, running away from a violent home situation, shoplifting or a serious criminal offence, they were treated psychiatrically, the result being that the young person regarded themselves as 'mad' because they had been treated by psychiatrists. And, because they had been incarcerated, most young people upon release were also convinced that they were 'bad'. So the result of their time in Wilson was the double stigma of being 'mad' and 'bad'. Years later, many young people were still struggling with this slur on their character and their consequent negative self-image.

I found it difficult to believe that our so-called civilised society could treat vulnerable young people in such a harrowing way. The only parallel situation which I had heard of was the psychiatric treatment of political prisoners in Siberia, by the government of the former Soviet Union. On many occasions I was all but reduced to tears by the stories I heard from young people in Wilson.

The following story, one of many similar cases, may illustrate the environment I have been describing. 'Glenn' was the eldest of four children. His father had left the family home soon after the youngest was born. His mother battled on alone. When Glenn was twelve years old, his mother had a nervous breakdown and could not get out of bed. Glenn assumed responsibility for his mother, his brothers and sister for the next few days. He cut lunches, got the children off to school, and did the cleaning and the cooking, but his mother seemed to be getting worse and Glenn did not know what to do.

He spoke to his class teacher, who couldn't assist him in any practical way. He spoke to the neighbours, who didn't want to become involved. There was no food in the house, so Glenn reluctantly decided to steal some fruit and vegetables from the local greengrocer. He told me three years later that he was not a thief, that he hated stealing, but did not know how else to feed his mum and the kids.

The greengrocer caught him stealing and called the police. 'The welfare' department was called in. Glenn's mum was placed in a psychiatric institution, his brothers and sister placed in children's institutions, and his sister later fostered out. Glenn, however, suffered a worse fate. He was charged with stealing and placed on remand in Wilson. He appeared in court, was legally unrepresented, and was placed under the Care and Control of the Director of Children's Services until he reached 18 years of age.

Two weeks later, he was placed in a church-run boys' home, which he told me he hated because of the violence of the staff who bashed the boys. The other thing he detested about the place was that when a boy infringed the rules, he was placed in a boxing ring with an older and bigger boy, whose job it was to punish the smaller boy in front of the other boys. Glenn loathed this violence. He coped in that place for three years by keeping his nose clean, his trap shut and learning to defend himself. He told me that when he was placed in the boxing ring with a smaller boy, he would not hurt him. He would rather incur the wrath of the staff and the ridicule of his peers than participate in organised and institutionally-sanctioned bullying.

Upon release from the boy's home, Glenn had nowhere to go. One night, he rang me at the Lodge. He had been living with two young men at Manly, a suburb on the eastern side of Brisbane. One of the men was working and paying the rent, but had decided to move on. Glenn said he needed accommodation, and needed it immediately. I told him we had a spare bed. It was then that he told me his mate needed a bed as well.

I arrived at the Manly house at about eight o'clock that evening. The electricity had been disconnected, and Glenn and his mate were sitting on the floor in total darkness. I chatted with them for a while and then asked them to get their gear together and come and stay with us at the Lodge. They had a small bag each, in which they carried all their possessions. They had no food. Glenn told me that he had asked the local shopkeeper for some food and was not only refused but threatened with calling the police. Glenn certainly did not want to steal, and absolutely did not want to have any involvement with the police. He had decided to ask for help.

Glenn was at the Lodge three days before he found out that I was a Catholic priest. He came to me and asked, "Are you a priest?"

"Yes," I said. "Why?"

"If I had known it when you picked us up the other night, I wouldn't have come with you. I hate priests and I hate Christians."

It was then that he told me about the treatment that was meted out to him and others in the church-run boys' home. I asked him if he wanted me to find another place for him and his mate to stay.

"You're all right," he answered. "I'd like to stay on here until I get a job and can set myself up."

Glenn stayed with us for six months. He kept on trying for work until he was taken on by a volunteer at the Lodge who ran his own business. Every Sunday he would get dressed up in his best gear, jeans and T-shirt, and catch a train to visit his mother, who was still in a psychiatric hospital, his brothers, and finally his sister who was living with a foster family on the north side of Brisbane. Glenn often said to me, "If only there had been help available, my family would not have needed to be split up."

Another story: 'Mary Anne' was still a baby when her mother sent her to be cared for by her grandmother. As Mary Anne grew up, she called her grandmother 'Mum' because her grandmother was a real mum to her, and the only mum she had, as far as she knew.

When Mary Anne was eight years old, her mother remarried and, on the wedding day, took Mary Anne from her grandmother to live with her and her step-father. The experience was traumatic. She tried hard to fit into the new situation, but could never bring herself to call her real mum 'Mum'. She called her mother by her first name, which her mother resented. Her real mum and her step-father both drank heavily, and prevented Mary Anne from seeing her grandmother, who lived on the western outskirts of Brisbane.

Mary Anne was a good student who caught onto things easily at school. However, as the home situation became worse, with her parents drinking and arguing most nights until the early hours of the morning, Mary Anne started skipping out of school and spending time with her friends, because as she said: "They are in a similar situation as me and because of that, everybody understands everybody else."

Her parents resented her spending time this way, and reported her to the police. She was charged with being uncontrollable, and because she continued to skip out of home, she appeared before the Children's Court and was committed to Wilson, where she stayed for six months. During her stay in Wilson, she was unable to continue her schoolwork and got further behind in her studies. She asked to be sent to her grandmother upon discharge, but her request was refused and she was sent home to her mother and her step-father. Of course she ran away again and, subsequently, was returned to Wilson. Her grandmother wrote to her while she was in Wilson, but the letters were withheld from Mary Anne. Mary Anne also wrote to her grandmother, but the institution did not forward the letters. Mary Anne often wondered why her grandmother never replied. When she turned 16, Mary Anne moved back in with her grandmother. She obtained a job in the supermarket in a neighbouring suburb, and never again came to the notice of the police.

Pat and I attended Wilson for one half-day each week, and we saw young people mostly one-on-one. When they were nearing release, we gave them slips of paper with our name, address and phone number, and encouraged them to make contact with us if necessary. We also went there on Sunday mornings to celebrate Mass. It was not too long afterwards that the young people who had been incarcerated in Wilson began turning up at the Lodge requesting shelter. We took them in, and tried to help them.

The first two young people who we accommodated at the Lodge were girls from Wilson. I was woken by the phone ringing very late one night. It was the Juvenile Aid Bureau at the Clayfield Police Station, asking if I would come over. They had two young women, 'Katie' and 'Kerry', whom Pat and I had met in Wilson. The police had contacted their parents: in fact, one of their mothers was at the police station. The girls were homeless, the police said. Their parents did not want them. Kerry's mother said that she was about to enter into a new relationship with an airline pilot. She tearfully told me that she did not want her daughter around to complicate things. The police said they were reluctant to return the girls to Wilson as they had not committed a crime, and they were unimpressed with the way Wilson dealt with young people. However they had no alternative except, as the girls had mentioned, maybe, the Lodge.

I knew enough about Wilson at that time to agree totally with them. I had never anticipated living with young people. Here was a genuine need. What else could I do but respond? I took the girls home and made up beds for them in one of the upstairs rooms.

The next morning at breakfast, I said to Pat, "Did you hear the phone go last night?" He hadn't. I said, "How do you feel about homeless young people living here?"

He was pleased that I had bought Katie and Kerry home rather than placed back in Wilson, but the questions remained: what would we do with them now that they were living at the Lodge? How would we deal with Children's Services? What would these young people do each day? We trusted in our God, and decided to get on with it, reflecting as we went, acknowledging our mistakes and limitations, and often asking for assistance from our friends and those who had more skills than we did.

East Timor

One day towards the end of 1974, three young men from East Timor visited the Lodge and requested accommodation for a few days. One of these men was Jose Ramos Horta who many years later became Prime Minister of East Timor. We listened and were appalled by their stories of murderous incursions by the Indonesian Army into their country. These young men were on their way to Canberra confident that the Australian Government would assist them, as they, the people of East Timor, had assisted the Australian commandos during the Second World War, to the extent that over 40,000 of their people were killed by the Japanese Army.

We, at the Lodge, hastily called together interested people from Brisbane to hear what these young men had to say. Out of these meetings, a large group was formed to educate the community and to lobby the Federal Government to support the people of East Timor.

David Larkin, who lived and worked at the Lodge, was employed full-time by this organisation for a lengthy period of time. During the first ten years of occupation by the Indonesian Army, more than 100,000 people died through murder, torture, starvation and general neglect.

In 1999 the people of East Timor voted in favour of independence and the Australian Government finally supported this oppressed people. I had the privilege of visiting East Timor on three occasions from 1999 to the Independence celebrations on 20 May 2002. I enjoyed and was deeply moved by being with the people as they celebrated the success of their struggles for independence.

Pat is sacked

When I returned to the Lodge in December 1974, after attending the International YCS Conference at Maastricht in Holland, I was greeted with the news that Pat had received a transfer to a country parish, where he was to be the assistant to a difficult or, should I say, quite eccentric parish priest. Pat was not to be replaced.

I felt angry, frustrated and alone. Pat and I had worked well together. We had tried to be authentic Christians. We had prayed, reflected and supported one another. We were intent on searching out 'the signs of the times' according to Vatican II,[17] but the very people who should have been encouraging us were stabbing us in the back. It was with a heavy heart that I took up my responsibilities at the Lodge in 1975. I felt as if my right arm had been cut off. Despite the distance involved, Pat and I continued to meet for mutual support once a fortnight, at a halfway point between Brisbane and the country parish to which he had been appointed.

17   See, for example, Paul VI: *Evangelisation in the Modern World*, para 76.

A small Christian community

Struggles and rejection

1975 PROVED TO BE a very hard year for me after Pat was transferred. We had become good friends. We prayed and reflected well together and complemented one another, even though our personalities were very different. I felt I was being rejected by my fellow-priests, and not being received very well by the new bishop. I thought he was being influenced by the National Civic Council. YCS was in big trouble in the schools, even though students were responding well in terms of formation and responsibility. And Wilson was breaking my heart because of the needless suffering it was inflicting on young people.

At the Lodge, we had some of these young people living with us, and we were trying to walk with them in whatever way we could. We entered into their world of violence, rejection, unemployment, incarceration, drugs, prostitution, and incest, as well as State and institutional abuse.

My routine was that I would get out of bed soon after 5:30am, no matter what sort of night I had had the night before. I was often called out as many as two or three times each night, several nights a week. Sometimes these calls came from young people within the Lodge, or from someone in crisis who was associated with the Lodge.

In the mornings I would meditate and pray the Office before the house awoke. For the previous two years, I had been working through the Gospel of Luke. I would take a passage and sit with it, sometimes for two or three mornings. Then I would move on to the next few sentences. I was looking at what was happening in my life, and in the lives of those around me, and reflecting on this in light of the passage.

In January 1975, I was at the beginning of the Passion narrative of Luke. I could identify with the rejection happening to Jesus, because I could see rejection all around me: of homeless young people, of the student movement, of Pat Tynan, of the people of Cribb Island, of the people of East Timor. I could see that those who spoke out were asking for trouble from Church authorities, the Federal and State authorities, and even from friends. I wrestled with the Passion narratives, wondering if I was deluding myself or indulging in self-pity. But I also knew that the suffering of others was real—as was mine. Finally I moved onto the Resurrection and the Emmaus episode: "Was it not necessary that the Messiah should suffer these things and then enter into his glory?" said

Jesus (Luke 24:26). I realised that there was purpose in suffering—in my suffering, in the pain of others. God could and would draw good out of evil.

I was also spending much time reflecting on the Exodus story: God hearing the cry of the poor and the oppressed, and using Moses and Aaron as the human instruments of liberation. I was happy for God to call Moses and Aaron but, in the present situation, I thought God could have done with somebody more capable, astute and articulate than me.

We tried to live at the Lodge as a Christian community. We prayed and reflected together, supported and challenged one another, and worked with young people whether they lived at the Lodge or had moved into independent living. At least twice each week we celebrated Eucharist. The Eucharist was open to everybody in the house as well to visitors. Those present would fully participate—or, at least, be invited to join—in the Penitential Rite, the reading and discussion which followed, the prayer of the faithful, and prayers of thanks. In some respects the Masses were simple in language and ritual as we tried to understand and respond to God's Word in our lives and our world.

We celebrated Eucharist each Sunday in Wilson, a practice that acquired a negative image when some staff used the Mass as a punishment, making some young people attend who did not wish to attend, or not allowing others to attend who sincerely wished to be there.

After Eucharist one Sunday, one of the young women, Annie (mentioned earlier, and now 15 years old) told me that many of the young people could not understand the words of the Eucharist. I was aware of this, even though I had tried to make sure what I was saying was simple and easy to understand. I asked Annie to re-write the Eucharistic Prayer in her own words. She said that she could not do it, but I knew that she could and encouraged her to try. She ended up re-writing the whole of the Eucharist from beginning to end—an excellent job, and we were so pleased that we printed multiple copies and used it every second week.

A constant problem for the girls at Wilson was coping with the violence which had been inflicted upon them by incest. For me, dealing with young women who were victims of incest was a totally new field. But because of the trust which Pat and I had built up, some of the young women could talk with us about prior incest. They felt shame, had never mentioned what had happened to anybody, and were experiencing extreme mental agony.

I encouraged the young women to speak with the professional staff in Wilson, but they flatly refused to do so, because they had no trust in them and because of the shame they felt. As I assisted some young women in Wilson, they would bring others who had similar problems. They would say to me, "She's got the same problem I talked to you about. I told her how you'd helped me to find some peace of mind and that she ought to talk to you." I would reply: "You know me and trust me, and she doesn't. I will see her but I'd like you to come in with her. That will make it easier for her and you will be able to continue to assist her as well, because you have worked through some of it yourself." At one period in 1975 I remember spending time with as many as 18 young women who were incest survivors. The work was an enormous pressure, listening to heart-rending stories of violence and the gross abuse of trust.

The Wilson Protest Group

By about the middle of 1975, the small gains that had been achieved in Wilson in the previous twelve months were slowly being eroded. Some tertiary students had been following up young people, one to each student, upon release from Wilson. They and I formed an organisation which we called the Wilson Protest Group.

The group aimed to bring about changes in Wilson through public education and action. The Wilson Protest Group did achieve some results. For example, as a result of publicising the abuse of solitary confinement, the Director of Children's Services stated:

> I have each month called for a list of people who were secluded and I have asked for a report as to why children have been secluded.... This has brought some control into the situation for the Director of Children's Services who is the legal Guardian of the people who are secluded.[18]

The fact that the Director was exercising his guardianship, regularly and responsibly, of these young people who were wards of the State was something he should have been doing all along. However, it would seem true from what former inmates were reporting, that some staff, while punishing children in solitary confinement for two to three days, were writing 'one hour' in that record book which the Director was so meticulous in reviewing.

Sacked

In January 1976 I was sacked as chaplain to Wilson on the grounds of "harbouring absconding children and interfering with the work of the psychiatrists." The memo, as I learned later, deplored the fact that:

> his interpretation of his role as a Pastoral Counsellor has brought him into conflict with the therapeutic regime conducted by the Psychiatrists at the Hospital, and it is for this reason that a change of chaplain has been asked for.[19]

---

18 Freedom of Information file. Memorandum for the Honourable the Minister from Mr R Plummer, Director on 9 February 1976 at p 4.

19 Ibid., p 2

Neither of the two charges was proven.[20] I was always at pains to make certain that I did not work at cross purposes with the psychiatrists. In fact, when requested and permitted by a young inmate, I regularly made appointments to see a young person's psychiatrist.

My removal from Wilson, and the manner of my removal, depressed me for weeks. I felt I had failed the young people and that I was a failure myself—as a chaplain and as a priest working for justice. My method of working seemed so inadequate that I was unable to attract the support of my superior, the bishop.

But then I realised that I was now free to speak out publicly about the injustices in Wilson. I was able to work for the much-needed changes to the juvenile justice system in Queensland. Here was an opportunity to turn my back on Wilson and all that went with it. But for some reason I could not do it. I just could not walk away, saying, "Well, I tried to do a few things, and now it's somebody else's turn." Was this another moment of grace, God impelling me to continue working for his 'little ones' (Matthew 25:40)? In retrospect, I am sure it was.

Taking young people into our home was not something we had planned to do. It had been thrust upon us by their circumstances. We accommodated young people who needed emergency shelter, and those who needed respite care or time out from a violent situation at home, as well as those who needed to stay for longer periods of time.

At that time, there was no emergency shelter available in Brisbane for young people. Certainly young men could go to the Saint Vincent de Paul shelter or Pindari, the shelter run by the Salvation Army. However, these two facilities did not specifically cater for young people, and were largely unsuitable for them. Suitable emergency accommodation for young women was almost non-existent.

With many of the young people, particularly those who had been incarcerated in Wilson or Westbrook[21], we knew that it would take a long time for them to get their acts together or, as they often put it, "to get our heads together." We realised early on that if a young person had been severely abused and rejected for a period of years, they were not going to turn it around in a short period of time. We knew our commitment would have to continue for years, whether or not the young people were living in the Lodge.

---

20 Memorandum for the Honourable the Minister from Mr R Plummer Director of Children's Services, 9 February 1976. "I indicated to Father Dethlefs that I was prepared to accept his explanation" [that I was not present and did not know of the instance of a particular girl who had stayed at the Lodge overnight].

21 Westbrook Youth Detention Centre, the detention centre for older boys near Toowoomba, west of Brisbane. It showed the same patterns of neglect and abuse as at Wilson.

The young people had many needs. Some had drug, gambling or alcohol addictions. Some suffered from mental illnesses. Some came from alcoholic families. Others were incest survivors or survivors of pack rape. Many were suicidal. Most had been in institutions like Wilson and had no security whatsoever. I could throw words around like "prostitute" or "delinquent," but the young people who arrived on our doorstep were special, unique, very hurt and very damaged. They exhibited incredible courage, generosity and simplicity in trying to make a go of life. If they often failed, who were we to judge? Our contact with these brave young people taught us so much about hope and trust in God, the Gospel, and of God's people.

From time to time, we met with social workers from Lowson House and the Department of Children's Services. We worked well with those who were competent, and we lived with the inept and the results of their broken promises. We spent much time in the casualty section at Royal Brisbane Hospital with young people who had overdosed, slashed their wrists, or who were just ill. Many of the young people had not had a significant adult person in their lives for any lengthy period of time. Many adults had told them that they loved them, that they would always be there for them, and many of these same adults had simply disappeared after a few short months. Some even abused the young people physically, emotionally or sexually. It did not come as a surprise that they did not trust adults.

Some of the young people we accommodated would ask, "How do I know you will be around in six months' time?"

"Just keep breathing and you'll see for yourself," I'd say.

Our method of working with the young people was to reflect with them on their actions, 'good' or 'bad'. Most young people act impulsively. The challenge we set ourselves was to break through this impulsive and reactive, often violent, behaviour. We would sit with them, either individually or in a group, often over a cuppa in the kitchen or around the dinner table. We mainly asked 'what' questions. Rarely would we ask 'why': such questions tended to force them to justify their behaviour, and this led nowhere. We hoped the sessions would, in time, assist the young person to understand what was acceptable behaviour. If a young person had been involved in socially unacceptable behaviour, we explored alternatives and encouraged them to try new ways of acting in the future.

We had rules, or guidelines as we preferred to call them. Respect was the first—and the key to what we were trying to do. We regarded respect for yourself and for the other people who lived in the house as the foundation of every relationship. Our young guests were encouraged, for example, to welcome anybody who came to the door and to offer them a cuppa. We hoped they would feel a sense of ownership and responsibility for the place. We wanted the young people to feel important and to learn to like, maybe in the future even love, themselves.

We had other house rules: for example, everybody should let the others know when and where they were going out and when they would return. We encouraged mutuality. We also asked people to pull their weight around the house and to clean up their own mess. For instance, if a person did not assist in the preparation of a meal, then they were expected to help with the dishes.

The Lodge was a drug and alcohol-free zone. We could not hope to control what people did when they were out or away, but we wanted them to respect our wishes while they were at the Lodge. Many did, some did not.

We encouraged everyone to be home for the evening meal, a time to catch up with what each had been doing during the day. At these meals we often reviewed what was happening with each person, in a very informal way. Many important discussions took place at dinner time, so much so that they often took the place of house meetings.

Many young people came to the Lodge locked into a destructive self-image, thinking that they were totally useless and unimportant. Those young people who had been locked up in Wilson thought they were of low intelligence and that the best they could hope for would be to graduate to Boggo Road, the adult prison. That many did not is a tribute to them.

One young woman, who had previously been with us, was arrested for breaking, entering and stealing. She was remanded to the Lodge by the Children's Court. Almost every day she would ask me if I was praying for the successful outcome of her court case. She had been in Wilson on a number of occasions and could not bear the thought she would end up there again. On the night before the court case, she asked if I had been praying for her. Even when I replied that I had, she insisted that I pray again. I suggested we find a quiet spot in one of the lounges. I also suggested that she should pray first. I was surprised when she said, "I don't pray any more."

"But you used to," I said.

She told me that God would not listen to her any more, because of all the wrong she had done. She said that the fundamentalist Christian group she had been with had convinced her that God saw everything that she did and noted it down. She told me that she had done so many bad things that God would not want to have anything more to do with her. I knew she had enjoyed a relationship with God which she had found comforting. So I prayed for her. Amazingly, in court the next day, although she was found guilty, she did not receive a custodial sentence.

When young people left the Lodge, we told them they could return if they wished to have a chat, do their washing, or celebrate their birthday. Many came back, either to stay or to use the facilities. Many felt a security in the place just being there, even when they were not living in. For some, it was the only roots they ever had—and they clung to them.

One of my favourite quotations at that time was from the writing of Helder Camara, Archbishop of Recife in Brazil who lived in one of the poorest parts of the world:

> Let us open, while there is still time, a bold and unlimited dialogue with youth, with full confidence, for the young do not accept a half-confidence. After all, and I address you, my adult listeners: the young are your offspring, are they not? You think they go too far? It is normal that there should be an exaggeration here and there. When the day comes that our young people are moderate, prudent, and cold, like old people, then the country will die of disgust.[22]

As the numbers in our community increased, so did our difficulties in paying our bills. For a long time we were forced to live on damaged tins of baked beans and spaghetti, kindly supplied by a friend who was a sales representative for Heinz. Other friends also helped out. As we were going broke and hardly able to pay our bills, let alone feed an increasing number of homeless and disadvantaged young people, I increased my efforts to obtain secure funding.

I tried service clubs, and some did assist us with money, which helped to keep us going. Most of these groups were only able to sponsor a project for a year. I began to think that God might not want us to continue with the work, although I couldn't fathom why. However, as I did not pretend to know the mind of God, all I could do was listen to what God might be trying to say to me. Having exhausted all the avenues I knew, it seemed to me that closing down the Lodge was the only alternative.

Then in March 1978 our fortunes changed. The Archbishop phoned one day to ask if we were having financial difficulties. He asked how much we would need to pay our bills and to keep us going for the next three months. When I said $2,500, he astounded me by saying that a cheque would be in the mail that afternoon. Who had been talking with him, or why his sudden change of mind, I was never to find out.

Some of the service clubs began inviting me to speak to their members, suggesting that the Lodge should apply to them for sponsorship. I spoke to the Brisbane Quota Club. They decided to fund-raise for us for one year, which did not meet with the approval of the Minister and his minions:

> It is particularly noted that Quota Members have adopted Kalinga [Kedron] Lodge as their project for 1978/79. Whilst it would not be the wish of the Department to influence any decision made by Quota, it must be said that officially it would have been preferable for that worthwhile organisation to have extended its support in other worthy directions in preference to Kalinga Lodge.[23]

22 *Dom Helder Camara: The Violence of the Peacemaker*, Jose de Broucker, 1970, p 19.
23 Letter from Mr Sam S Doumany, Minister for Welfare, to Mr. J.A.R. Lockwood Esq.,

The Zonta Club, a group of professional and business women, offered to raise funds and organise practical assistance such as a spring-clean of the Lodge. Zonta also advised us about forming a constitution and becoming registered as a charity with the State Government. Two Zonta members were part of our initial steering committee.

Then somebody arranged for an article to be printed in the newspaper, on the work which was taking place at the Lodge. The article, while somewhat exaggerated, did point out that we had lots of needs, especially financial.[24] The response to the article was overwhelming. People phoned up, telling us that they had this or that bit of furniture and asking if we needed it. Others volunteered their time to assist us in any way we thought they could. Still others sent money.

Next, I received a phone call from Betty Roberts, whom I had known from the parish of Yeronga. She had been talking to her husband and some friends, and they had decided that they would be prepared to raise money for us. They called themselves 'Friends of the Lodge'. They raised considerable amounts of money and offered practical advice, and best of all, understanding and friendship. The parish priest of Rosalie, Dennis Power, also phoned us, asking if we would be happy for his parish to contribute $200 each week from their Bingo night.

Finally, the Department of Children's Services had a change of heart:

Mr. Smith has also commented on the position of Kalinga Lodge as follows:

'Father Dethlefs has not been too popular with the Department in the past because generally, as I understand it, he has done virtually what is harbouring children in care without the Department having knowledge of their whereabouts. The need for services such as his Kalinga Lodge is so desperate that I think it is probably time that the Department endeavoured to co-operate with Father Dethlefs and perhaps a fresh approach to him for a co-operative stance may be beneficial...

I have therefore taken action to ensure that a low-key discussion be arranged with Father Dethlefs to ascertain his present activity and approach. Discussions are to include the possibility of the Department funding certain beds at Kalinga Lodge for use as emergency accommodation.'[25]

M.B., B.S., M.L.A. p 1.

24 *Courier-Mail*, 20 December 1978: "Kalinga Lodge and Brisbane Youth Service are both in desperate financial need."
25 Letter from Acting Director, Children's Services, to the Under Secretary, Department of Welfare Services, 23 January, 1979, p 2 and 3.

Desperation may have been their motivation, but it seemed at least that we were becoming acceptable. We began negotiations. They would fund two beds on a permanent basis, but we retained the right to decide whether these beds were to be occupied or not and by whom: we knew that if we were flat out working with those whom we had living in the Lodge already, then it was not sensible to take in others. We were also worried that if we were accommodating some so-called 'heavy' young people, we would not want non-street-wise young people to be influenced by them.

Mr. Sam Doumany became Minister for Welfare in 1978. Anne McMillan and myself, together with a 15-year-old lad who was living at the Lodge, made an appointment to see him. As well as discussing on-going matters, we suggested the Minister should meet with a number of homeless young people, to hear their point of view as clients of his services.

The Minister readily agreed to this, and the historic meeting took place at Kalinga Lodge on 1 June 1979. In the briefing notes for the Minister a few interesting points were made.

> ... Father Dethlefs has been a critic of Wilson Youth Hospital though of recent times he has been involved in this in a more organised manner through the Justice for Juveniles group.

> ... Some of Father Dethlefs' criticisms of the Wilson Youth Hospital are valid enough. However, he organised his facts poorly and often exaggerated truths, leaving them easily denied. Had he been better organised, he would have been a more formidable critic. The fact that he went to the media, plus the out of context statements and exaggerations, led to some staff becoming antagonistic towards him, and publicly we were forced to be defensive. This seems however to have cooled down and Father Dethlefs has been less public, relying as far as I can see on contributing to the Justice for Juveniles lobby.

> Father Dethlefs does seem to have a commitment to helping youth in need. The Lodge accommodates some very difficult and hard to place young people, probably because they sense his care and acceptance. We need to utilise whatever reasonable accommodation is available.[26]

On the appointed afternoon there were 15 to 20 young people waiting to talk with the Minister. I was standing at the front of the Lodge, talking with a couple of the young people, when a police car pulled up. The two young people ran inside, and they and most of the young people raced out the back door of the

26 Briefing Notes for Honourable the Minister for Visit to Kedron Lodge, 119 Nelson Street, Kalinga, on 1 June 1979 by D.A.C. Smith, Principal Child Care Officer Residential Care Services, 30 May 1979, p 1.

Lodge and, as I found out later, hid down by the creek. I thought: "What's gone wrong now?" The policeman came over. I introduced myself and asked how I could be of assistance.

"You have a Minister of the Crown visiting your establishment this afternoon. When this happens, the local police station is notified and we must come down and check the place out for possible assassins."

"All of our resident assassins have been given the day off today," I assured him.

"I believe you," he said. "I won't even bother coming in to have a look around."

I asked him if he would excuse me for a moment. I went inside, found someone, and told them to tell the people down the creek to come back.

The Minister duly arrived with his minders. At first he was defensive about the Department, until I reminded him that he had not come to defend his Department; there was not time for that. Rather, he had come to listen to the young people. That seemed to relax him. He listened well and had someone take notes on what the young people said. I know he was impressed by the exercise, as he referred to this meeting subsequently in public addresses. What a pity that more of this type of dialogue does not take place.

It was obvious that attitudes to the Lodge were changing, and our financial situation was less precarious. In fact we were now able to offer some wages to full-time staff. My situation with the bishop also seemed to have taken a turn for the better. I am still at a loss, even today, to understand why attitudes changed at that time. Some said that the hierarchy realised I was not just "doing my thing" but doing authentic work of the Church.

At its Annual General Meeting on 18 November 1979, the new constitution of the Lodge was accepted and the name, Kedron Lodge Youth Support Service, formally adopted. A Management Committee was elected, charged with the responsibility of applying to the government for registration as a charity and of attending to the business side of running of the Lodge. On that first committee was a young woman who had spent a number of years in Nudgee Orphanage, and also a current and a former resident of the Lodge.

Staffing the Lodge was always difficult. Experienced people were hard to come by. Many recent graduates, while qualified, lacked the experience to cope with our deeply troubled young people. Living in and making a commitment to a Christian community and lifestyle was a huge ask, and an obstacle for some. Sometimes we made mistakes in the selection of suitable staff. We were always on the lookout for people who would assist us in the work, either to live in as part of the community, or to attend the place on a regular basis. That people came forward is a tribute to their generosity and to the health of our society.

From welfare to protest

Bound by conscience

IN EARLY 1976, Pat resumed duties as chaplain to Wilson. After I had recovered from the depression of being sacked, I realised I could not turn my back on Wilson, especially the powerless young people incarcerated within. I knew I had done a reasonable job on a one-to-one level, while failing to bring about much needed changes in the larger systems of the institution. Even so, I could not wipe my hands of the place. Ex-Wilson inmates were constantly saying to me upon their release, "You must do something about that place."

I could not forget young people like 'Joe', a 15-year-old Aboriginal boy from far western Queensland. Each week when I visited Wilson, Joe would come to see me. He was a quiet lad, and I had to listen intently in order to understand what he was saying. He had been working on a cattle station. He enjoyed the work. He said he had not been in trouble with the police and had not broken the law. It was obvious to me that he was suffering enormously from being incarcerated, after being used to wide open spaces. Like so many others, he did not know when he was going to be released, or if he could cope with the place much longer. He asked me if I would see the manager for him.

On my next visit, I approached the manager. I asked him what was happening to Joe, and why he had been put in Wilson. He said that Joe was suffering from a medical condition, and he had been placed in Wilson so that he could be given tablets three times a day. Astounded, I responded: "Surely somebody responsible on the station where he worked could have seen to that? I am concerned about Joe being kept in here. What arrangements are being made to release him?"

"I've written a letter," he replied.

With that, he pulled out two huge clipboards of letters and proceeded to go through them. He could not find the letter.

"I must not have written it yet. Anyway, it is doing Joe a lot of good being in here. He is too quiet, and he is learning to socialise."

Unbelievable! I thought, *Now, we're locking up young people to give them social skills.*

Aloud, I asked, "Would it be in order if I came to see you about Joe next week? I am concerned about him."

"That would be in order."

When I turned up in his office the following week, and the week after, the manager went through the same pantomime with the clipboards saying, "I'm certain I wrote a letter to somebody about Joe."

Finally, Joe was released. However, he was not sent back to where he had come from, but was released to a hostel in South Brisbane. The injustice of it all! Later on, I found out that while Joe was in Wilson, his mother had died. Who told him of his mother's death, and in what manner he was told, I shudder to think, but was never able to find out. What I do know was that he was not allowed to attend his mother's funeral.

I was burdened with the issues, both of individual abuse, and, more importantly, the institutional and systemic abuse. Any person with a conscience, especially a person with a knowledge of Gospel justice, could not walk away from such situations.

Demolished and discharged

In 1976, two specialist sections of the police force were dealing with young people, the Juvenile Aid Bureau (JAB) and the Education Liaison Unit. At the JAB, plain-clothes police mostly cautioned and counselled young people, while arresting and charging very few. At this time the JAB was under a cloud. The Police Minister and his Commissioner wanted the unit abolished. The JAB police were called the 'kiddies' cops', and were regarded by their peers as not being real police—this despite the fact that their procedures and practices were producing excellent results in terms of diverting young people from the juvenile justice system. Many of us believed that the JAB was doing excellent preventative work, and we were active in pressing for the continuance of the unit. The campaign was successful in preventing its disbandment, but it was transferred to the Department of Family Services.

The policy of the Education Liaison Unit was to arrest and charge (as they did) for such minor offences as stealing a chocolate bar. The unit would visit a primary school principal and ask who the bad guys were in the school. A child would be called up and told by the police, "We know what you've been up to, and we know who you've been doing it with. It will go easier for you if you tell us yourself what you've been up to and who you've been doing it with." After a day, or sometimes two days, the unit would walk out of the school having charged as many as thirty children with such offences as receiving a stolen ruler. Much of what the unit was doing, and how it operated, was formally documented by the 1977 Commission of Inquiry into the Enforcement of Criminal Law in Queensland. The inquiry, known as the Lucas Inquiry, looked into the use and abuse of police powers in Queensland. The Lucas Inquiry confirmed what many people suspected about the Education Liaison Unit.

The processes of the Children's Court were a travesty of justice. The magistrate normally heard as many as thirty cases in three hours—on average, one case every six minutes. The court was often called 'kiddies' court' by lawyers and police, and portrayed as very lenient, especially by the police. However, young people as young as eight were being locked up for non-criminal or minor criminal offences. So, in reality, serious determinations were being made which had long-term consequences and devastating effects on many young people. Very few children were legally represented in court. Those who appeared in court usually came from socio-economically deprived backgrounds. Children's rights were neither explained nor respected. Many young people and their parents, especially those from non-English-speaking backgrounds, did not understand the procedures, let alone the terminology, used in court.

I would ask young people, "How did you go in court?"

"The judge admired and discharged me," or "The judge demolished and discharged me," they would say, which meant that the magistrate had done nothing more than 'admonish and discharge' the young person.

I would ask intelligent young people, "Did you understand what was being said in court? Did you get to say anything in court?"

They would invariably say 'no' to both questions. The police or the court officer would often tell them to say nothing, or to say 'yes', when asked if they pleaded guilty. Many told me that they knew to stand under the clock in the court, and that was all.

'Annie', the same 15-year-old young person I mentioned earlier, lived on the north side of Brisbane. Her father had left home, and her mother was working from home as a prostitute. Night after night, Annie would be forced to leave home while her mother was working. She met up with other young people who were roaming the streets at night. Her school work was suffering. For a while she enjoyed the companionship of the other young people because they understood her predicament, and that made her feel good.

However, they were into anti-social and sometimes criminal behaviour, like smashing street lights and throwing bricks through shop windows. She had never been in any trouble with the police, and did not want to begin. So, sick of being kicked out onto the streets night after night, scared of breaking the law, and wanting to do something constructive with her life, she approached the local police and told them her story. Her request was that they find a foster-family for her. They told her she would have to go to court—but not to worry about that. She would then be placed in an institution for a few days, and then in a foster home. She agreed to these procedures. She went to court. Many charges were read out. She did as she was told and said nothing. She was asked not one question. She ended up in Wilson, spending over six months there, until I arranged her release and a foster placement.

Wilson and Westbrook were inhuman places. They were, in the main, characterised by violence and abuse, dehumanisation and degradation. Most of the staff who had contact with these troubled young people were untrained and recruited from the streets. Many lacked basic communication skills. Some were very violent. I often wondered about the kind of society we were living in, which 'treated' its poorest and most powerless young citizens by putting them behind bars, stopping their education, and arresting and charging instead of rehabilitating.

The young people at Wilson were viewed by many people as hopeless—savages, delinquents, drop-outs. Indeed, many young people further dehumanised themselves by calling *themselves* sluts, criminals, derelicts and junkies. Many were without hope or ambition. These young people were numbered among the despised of our society. They were poor in a material, spiritual and emotional sense: captives in the sense that they spent time in secure institutions or prisons, blind because they saw no alternative lifestyle for themselves, often oppressed by society, police and the welfare system. The only salvation they knew was that of alcohol, drugs and sex.

The young people, the Jesus of the Gospels, and the teaching authority of the Church were saying some explicit things to me that seemed to coalesce with what was happening to disadvantaged youth. I felt obliged to listen, heed and act. I knew what was happening to the young people in the justice and welfare systems. I felt compelled, in conscience, to work with "men and women of good will"[27] to try to bring about change. I did not see myself as a crusader or campaigner. I just knew that I should lend whatever support I could.

I did not have long to wait. In March 1976, only two months after I had been relieved of my duties in Wilson, I was invited by the secretary of the Queensland Council of Social Service (QCOSS) to a meeting of interested people to discuss Wilson and to help formulate a public statement.

We met several times, and decided to widen our focus by examining the juvenile justice system in Queensland. We would study the police, courts, the welfare system, Wilson, and the alternatives. We identified and allocated tasks, and set a time frame to complete the work and meet again. I was given the task of writing up the section on Wilson: the selection, training and monitoring of staff, the treatment and education of young people, the use of solitary confinement and the consequences of the medical model of treatment. QCOSS staff undertook to research the Children's Courts.

I worked with Cathy Humphries and Michelle Daly, two social work students who had worked with the Wilson Protest Group and who were associated with the Lodge. We completed our tasks in the given time, but unfortunately nobody else did. QCOSS had its own problems at that time, and did not or would not convene any more meetings, even though I phoned them on a number of occasions. Finally, nine months later, QCOSS gave me access to the work they had done on the Children's Courts. They had produced a very long draft report which was full of inaccuracies. They refused to give me a full copy

27   Vatican II: *Constitution of the Church in the Modern World*, para 92.

of their report, but instead provided me with a one and a half page summary, which was totally inadequate.

In the meantime, I had undertaken some research on the police and the Children's Court, as well as obtaining some information on alternatives. I ended up writing the bulk of the document, which we called *The Juvenile Justice System, Secure Institutional Care and Alternatives in Queensland.*

Stencils were typed up and we ran off five hundred copies on our ancient Gestetner. Our strategy was as follows:

- To disseminate the document privately to individual people;
- To educate the community about the situation as we saw it in Queensland, and to invite people to submit their names and addresses, so that if we were forced to conduct a public campaign to bring about change, we would have a list of people to call upon;
- To work through established channels in an effort to bring about change, that is, to seek meetings with senior public servants and the Health and Welfare Ministers;
- If and when this approach failed to produce change, to conduct a public campaign to bring about the much needed changes;
- To do all that we could, according to our circumstances and means as private citizens, to help individual children at risk and their families.

The above aims and strategy were adopted by the Justice for Juveniles group when it was formed in mid-1977, a development of the Wilson Protest Group. We sought and welcomed criticism of our document. We wanted it to be truthful and accurate. In the light of the feedback we received from police, staff in Wilson and from the Departments of Health and Children's Services, we revised and updated our document and produced a second edition.

Meanwhile, we sought meetings with the Health and Welfare Ministers—waiting 18 months for the latter appointment—but these meetings proved to be a waste of time. While we were waiting for the appointments, we gave public lectures, and noted the names and addresses of interested people.

The Establishment reacts[28]

The Head of the Division of Youth, Welfare and Guidance (The Head of the Division) from the Department of Health notified the Department of Children's Services: "The Wilson Youth Hospital Action Committee has struck

28 The Freedom of Information Act came in under a State Labour Government in 1990 which was years after the events described here took place. Consequently, we attended meetings with Ministers and senior bureaucrats completely ignorant of what was being said about us, and who and how many people were bad-mouthing us. We were never given the opportunity to counter any accusations.

again. They have addressed a lengthy communication to Dr Edwards (Minister for Health) in which they have attacked the administration of the Wilson Youth Hospital."[29]

The Head of the Division followed up this phone call with a letter to the Director General of Health and Medical Services, under the heading *The Wilson Hospital Action Committee*, in which he states:

> This committee (if the same people as originally) consists mainly of a group of people, who, as individuals, have been active in other action groups, i.e. criticising the Premier on civil liberties, etc. Some are Social Workers who seem to be anti-medicine and anti-psychiatry. Most of the attack on Wilson Hospital (about two years ago now) was easily answered by Mr. Herbert and most of the activists have become quiet until now...

> ...The present attack in the paper submitted by Father Dethlefs seems to have come out as "Anti-Psychiatry and Anti-Welfare and Guidance". This may be due to the above personal reasons [my sacking from Wilson] or from the alleged fact that some Social Workers of the Children's Services department go round apologising for Wilson Hospital pointing out that they do not control it and can't clean up the mess etc. In the paper all of the attack is on Psychiatry, Welfare and Guidance, the Police, the Court, and the Establishment. The solution offered seems to be to turn things over to Social Workers.

> The recommendations (submitted elsewhere) for the Division of Youth Welfare and Guidance to take over Warilda building as a Youth Guidance Hospital would solve most problems and silence most critics.[30]

Apart from the usual claptrap of stigmatising so-called social activists, the Head of the Division seems here to be agreeing with two of our major recommendations: namely, that all children entering Wilson should not be treated psychiatrically, and that one Department—the Department of Children's Services—not two, should be responsible for Wilson.

The Head of the Division enclosed with his letter a nine-page response entitled *Comments on the Wilson Hospital Action Committee Report*. Suffice to reproduce some of his more salient points.

Under the title "Philosophical Concepts", the Head of the Division has this to say, in part:

29 Memorandum to the Director of Children's Services from his Deputy Director L. L. McAllister, 23 May 1977.
30 Senior Medical Director to Director-General, Health and Medical Services, 29 June 1977.

The population of delinquents in Wilson Hospital has a high percentage of emotional disturbance. This group of inpatients consists of about 5% of the children going before the Children's Court and are mainly recidivists or those with serious offences.[31]

In fact, most of the inmates of Wilson suffered from emotional disturbance because they had been treated unjustly by the police and the Children's Court, and because they were reacting to the environment and the regime in Wilson. Certainly, there were many recidivists in Wilson; most were the victims of neglect by the Department of Children's Services, who undertook no planning or active follow-up upon their release. Many children were returned to abusive situations, from which they naturally ran away once again. It would be interesting to find out the exact figures of young people entering Wilson for the first time on serious offences. In my opinion and from my experience, the figure would be extremely low.

Of those going into Wilson Hospital some 80% of the girls and about 70% of the boys need child guidance treatment. There is an organic aspect as some 35% have a history of abnormal birth and about 25% have confirmed brain dysfunction. About 65% have abnormal E.E.G.s. On the whole then about 65% to 75% have a psychiatric disorder using the American Psychiatric Association classification and/or the G.A.P. classification (American).[32]

The Justice for Juveniles group disputed the above diagnostic figures, but of course didn't have the medical expertise to dispute them publicly. However, even accepting the above diagnoses, detention seemed an inappropriate method of treatment.

Under the heading, "Physical Aspects of Wilson Youth Hospital", the Head of the Division makes a number of points, including the following:

The recreation and exercise area for the girls (mostly they don't like exercise anyway) is a bit small but they have a heated swimming pool which is very good and popular. They also have trampolines etc. There is no question of lack of physical exercise.[33]

In reality, the girls, especially those in remand and treatment, stayed in their sections 23 hours a day, seven days a week. Adjacent to their cells, they had

31 Comments on the Wilson Hospital Action Committee Report marked "Confidential" by the Senior Medical Director Wilson Youth Hospital, dated 29th June 1977 p 1.
32 Ibid., p 1.
33 Ibid., p 2.

their meals, did their therapy and watched TV. Their one hour downstairs each day in the recreation area was their only relief from the four-walled section.

The Head of the Division continues:

> The Boys section is larger because of more boys. The Boys section seems to meet with general approval as far as play areas are concerned, but criticisms of the recreation rooms, dormitories etc. is fairly accurate. They are rather drab perhaps because they are under male control. The girls' section is very nice.[34]

> It is agreed that the institution is not 'homely" but it is a closed detention centre which the law requires.[35]

The Head of the Division then moves into the realm of theology:

> They (the social workers) are also confused about behaviour modification. Treatment and punishment is anathema to them. Some confuse 'permissive' handling of delinquents with 'forgiveness' from the Chirstain [sic] ethics and so let the child "get a way [sic] with it again and again" thus condoning and reinforcing his delinquency. They forget that in the Christain [sic] ethic "go and sin no more" is part of the deal in forgiveness."[36]

In our report, we mentioned neither forgiveness nor Christian ethics, and we didn't advocate letting the child "get away with it again and again."

Under the next heading, "Number of Functions the Institution is Trying to Fulfil", the Head of the Division qualifies his agreement that the court should be situated elsewhere:

> (a) *The Court*: It is agreed that the court could be elsewhere and I have heard that some people consider it not a good idea to have a punitive agency i.e. the court with a therapeutic agency i.e. a treatment centre. The court and the court Clinic being together is a common set-up. There are advantages.[37]

In the next section, "Treating and assessing in the one institution", the Head of the Division makes another qualified concession to the Justice for Juveniles group:

---

34 Ibid., p 3.
35 Ibid., p 2 and 3.
36 Ibid., p 3.
37 Ibid., p 3.

It is desirable that the psychiatric aspects of Wilson Youth Hospital be removed but not for the reasons put forward by the Committee.[38]

At least we could agree upon the separation of the psychiatric services from detention.

In a long section entitled, "Education", the Head of the Division is at pains to justify why education is "contra-indicated". He begins by explaining that

it is somewhat difficult to explain to people who are "anti" Wilson Hospital and Psychiatry, that the prime need of the children taken into treatment at Wilson Hospital is psychotherapy not education.[39]

This, maybe, is why others, especially Justice for Juveniles, could not understand what he meant by "education in Wilson is contra-indicated"! It seems that Dr. R. J. Andrews, Reader in Special Education at the University of Queensland, did not understand either, so we were in good company.

Later, the Head of the Division says:

Most delinquency seems to occur while the delinquent is still at school, but failing. If schooling is *forced* [his emphasis] on them in an institution, this can only exacerbate the problems which, through school failure, led to delinquency in the first place. If, on the other hand, the delinquent is motivated to satisfy his own curiosity and achievement needs via psychotherapy, it then becomes the task of the remedial educator to provide adequate instruction outside the institution following discharge.[40]

The arguments get worse. Take this little bit of wisdom, for example:

It can be stated with confidence that the children in Wilson Youth Hospital do not suffer educationally by being there. Indeed, under the system devised at the Hospital they receive an education which is not available anywhere else in the State. Furthermore, the psychotherapy and remedial help which they receive there motivates them towards adapting more efficiently to the classroom on leaving the Hospital.

It might be pointed out that most of these children are extremely negatively disposed towards schools, school teachers and classrooms and a remedial teacher would get nowhere with them. The children need to be desensitised by psychotherapeutic means before they are agreeable even to listen to a teacher.[41]

38 Ibid., p 4.
39 Ibid., p 4.
40 Ibid., p 8 and 9.
41 Ibid., p 5.

And finally, this little gem, still under the heading of education:

> The girls in Wilson Youth Hospital who have their liberty removed and are also cut off from smokes, sex and in some cases alcohol and drugs, no doubt find Wilson Hospital not exactly to their taste. Many of them would find all work boring. If the members of the Committee [Justice for Juveniles] care to go round any Hospital, School, Church or other Institutions, they will certainly find a number of disgruntled people complaining about the way the institution is run.[42]

An interesting comment, in view of the fact that most, if not all, of the young women in Wilson Youth Hospital had been victims of sexual abuse. As I have previously mentioned, most, if not all of them, had been incarcerated initially for running away from a violent and often sexually abusive situation.

In our report, we included a chapter which we called "Women's Issues". The Head of the Division dismisses our concerns in four short paragraphs:

> The girls are placed in Wilson Hospital by a legal procedure and no doubt the Magistrate sees they get a fair trial.

> Their offence is not really our concern except in that it may be connected with their psychiatric condition.

> Wilson Hospital is quite suitable for the treatment of emotional disturbances and its rehabilitative facilities are suitable for a short stay.

> Rehabilitation after leaving Wilson Hospital is the responsibility of the Children's Services Department.[43]

While the Head of the Division did agree with quite a number of our criticisms and recommendations, he did not of course convey that to us. There was, apparently, no room for government to heed its critics.

We learnt that the Department of Children's Services also pored over our document. Their response post-dated the Head of the Division's by over six months. Again, there is substantial agreement between the Department and the major thrusts in our submission, as Mr Herbert, the Minister, writes:

> The issues about which the Committee is concerned are all legitimate and are issues about which I personally am greatly concerned.[44]

---

42 Ibid., p 6.
43 Ibid., p 6 and 7.
44 Letter from the Hon. John Herbert, Minister for Welfare to the Hon. L.R. Edwards, Minister for Health, dated 10 January 1978, p 1.

The Minister cited a Cabinet Decision which related to breaking the nexus between the Department of Children's Services and the Health Department in Wilson.[45] Already our work was having an impact.

Mr Herbert continued:

> The section on the Philosophical Concepts of Treatment, especially that which raises issues concerning Labelling Theory and psychiatric treatment are matters of concern.

> The conclusion at the end of the fifth paragraph 'that inmates of Wilson are therefore forced into perceiving themselves as mentally insane' is related to Labelling Theory. A percentage would indeed be psychiatrically disturbed. It is unfortunate that those who are not psychiatrically disturbed have to remain at Wilson Youth Hospital because of a lack of alternate facilities which presently exist.[46]

Stigmatising the young inmates as 'mad and bad' was a matter which concerned us greatly. The Head of the Division did not consider this to be an issue.

> Regarding the 'labels', the children should receive only a 'child guidance label'. The 'insane label' seems to come only from the Action Committee.[47]

Mr Herbert believed that at least some formal education should be possible in Wilson:

> The Director, Department of Children's Services was employed as a Psychologist at Wilson Youth Hospital when it was decided to close the school. The decision at the time appeared to him to be legitimate, but a great deal turned on personalities. The Director has stated that while he cannot speak about the training of the Child Guidance Therapists presently employed, those employed during his period at Wilson Youth Hospital were well integrated into a therapeutic team, but had no formal training in teaching or on the curriculum.

> The Director has commented that it should surely be possible to integrate some formal instruction into the therapeutic endeavour because when children are discharged from Wilson Youth Hospital, they do have the additional burden to carry of having had no formal teaching during the period that they were in treatment at Wilson Youth Hospital.[48]

---

45 See Cabinet Decision No.27192 of 17 October 1977.
46 Ibid., p 2 and 3.
47 Comments on the Wilson Hospital Action Committee Report by Senior Medical Director, Wilson Youth Hospital, 29 June 1977, p 1.
48 Ibid., p 2 and 3.

So much for the Head of the Division's argument that education is contra-indi-cated.[49] It is interesting to note that the Minister did not remember that educa-tion is compulsory for children up to the age of 15, nor did he seem to be aware of the statement on education in the United Nations Declaration on the Rights of the Child.

In his final remarks, Mr Herbert speaks to the dual control operating in Wilson and the lack of power of the Director, as the legal guardian of the children:

> The Director of Children's Services acknowledges as being correct the first sentence of the fourth paragraph (on Page 31):
>
> 'The Director of Children's Services has very little influence in the func-tioning of Wilson Youth Hospital.'
>
> There have been continual difficulties of the dual control of Wilson Youth Hospital... which have caused a great deal of conflict. It is to be hoped that when the matter is finally resolved ... the best interests of the children in the legal guardianship of the Director, Department of Chil-dren's Services, will be protected.[50]

49   See, for instance, the letter from the Hon. Mr Herbert, Minister for Welfare, to the Hon. Mr Knox, Deputy Premier and Treasurer, undated (but I would estimate to be written in March or April 1978). Mr Herbert states on page 2: *"The children who are undergoing psycho-therapy under the control of Officers of the Division of Youth Welfare and Guid-ance do not [receive education] because on the advice of the Senior Medical Director, Division of Youth Welfare and Guidance, **remedial teaching is contra-indicated** [my emphasis] for these children."*
50   Ibid., p 3.

Justice for Juveniles
flexes its muscles

JUSTICE FOR JUVENILES had a core group of six to eight people, including Anne McMillan, a lawyer. Anne and I were appointed the spokespeople for the group. We had a list of as many as four hundred people who were prepared to write letters or make phone calls. We conducted several campaigns on such issues as solitary confinement, education, the medical model, and lack of legal representation for young people in the Children's Courts, and organised a particularly successful seminar, *Locking up Girls: is it the answer?*

A major difficulty Justice for Juveniles faced in their work, was the dual control of Wilson. When we approached the Minister of either Department, or senior bureaucrats, each one would blame the other, and tell us that their hands were tied. We argued that, since the Director of Children's Services was the legal guardian of the children, he and his Department should be running Wilson and taking complete responsibility for what happened there. (We did not think for one moment that the Department would do a quality job, and history has proven this to be true.) The cat-and-mouse game being played out by the two departments had to stop, and responsibility sheeted home where it belonged, with the Department of Children's Services.

Our group, and especially Anne McMillan, used every opportunity to spread the message about what was happening to the vulnerable young people in Wilson. Wherever possible, we invited ex-clients of the juvenile justice and welfare systems to share the platform with us. As they were the recipients of the services, and had experienced the systems, they were in a unique position to speak to the injustices they had experienced. The young people were quite capable of speaking at the universities, in schools, and at public meetings.

They would often ask me, "What do you want me to say?" I would tell them what the meeting was about and say, "You have your own experiences and you know what they are. As well as that, you have your own reflections on these experiences. Whenever you are ready, just interrupt me and speak away."

And that is what usually happened. I would give an introduction. Then the young person would speak. After that, we would answer questions together. They would often give anecdotal testimony, while I would fill in the background information and the bigger picture.

The Justice for Juveniles Group made submissions about the proposed new family welfare legislation, and submissions to the Parliamentary Committee set up to look at education in Queensland. Representatives of the Group gave talks, ran seminars, were interviewed by newspaper, radio and television reporters, and had a number of interviews with government Ministers and senior departmental officials.

The actions of the Justice for Juveniles core group and members certainly had results. We wrote to Members of Parliament and Ministers of the Crown. We sent deputations. Justice for Juveniles was making a name for itself. In some circles we were regarded as doing an important and necessary job; others, for example, Mr Herbert, thought differently:

> I am considering meeting some more responsible elements in the community to discuss the Juvenile Justice System and with them meeting representatives of the Justice for Juveniles Group.[51]

The meeting took place on 11 April 1978. Justice for Juveniles had been requesting a meeting with the Minister for Welfare for nigh on 18 months. The meeting was to be attended by "The Right Reverend Ralph Wicks, Anglican Assistant Bishop of Brisbane, the Right Reverend John Gerry, Roman Catholic Assistant Bishop of Brisbane, the Reverend Father W. Dethlefs, the Reverend Father Leo Wright and Ms Ann (sic) McMillan. It was suggested that the two Bishops attend to bring some degree of decorum to the discussions, but it is hard to see the group reaching consensus on any particular issue."[52]

The meeting was unsatisfactory, as Anne McMillan raised in a follow-up letter to the Minister for Welfare:

> It seemed to me that you were not prepared to concede that there was any deficiency in the present approach to children who come within the ambit of the Children's Services Act, and that where certain limitations might exist in the form of facilities and personnel, you were powerless to improve the situation.[53]

Justice for Juveniles had argued for increased numbers of facilities for young people. On this point, Anne continued:

---

51 Undated letter (approximately March or April 1978) from the Minister for Welfare, Mr John Herbert, to the Deputy Premier and Treasurer, Mr Knox p 4.

52 Briefing paper for the meeting to be held on the 11th April 1978 with the Minister for Welfare from the Director of Children's Services. This is obviously not a briefing paper at all, but a character attack on Anne McMillan and myself.

53 Letter from the Justice for Juveniles Group to the Minister for Welfare, dated 24th May 1978 and signed by Anne McMillan p 1.

If Western Australia can provide separate facilities for the care and treatment of children at risk, then there is surely no reason why Queensland can't. We live in a prosperous State, and some of that prosperity must be channelled into helping our young people who could develop into productive members of society if they are given a chance at this crucial stage of their development. To show you what is actually happening to them under the present system, I should like to quote verbatim from a letter from an inmate of Wilson Youth Hospital:

> The difference in reasons for admission is incredible. Some girls are in for reasons absolutely beyond their control, like sexually suggestive fathers or men out to beat them up. Some are in for running away from home, some for "moral danger" charges (living with men etc.), some for under-age drinking, or stealing, drugs, prostitution, violence and so on, up to arson, attempted murder etc. With such a variety, it is easy to see why relatively innocent kids start getting deeper and deeper into trouble after being there. They learn all they need to about crime and vice there, then go out and get into serious trouble. Then they wind up back in Wilson, then learn more and hate authority more and get into more trouble.

> The ages of Wilson Girls is 12 years to 17 years. There is quite a difference between a 12 or 13-year-old in for absconding, and a 16 to 17-year-old in for violence or stealing or a more serious charge. The younger and more innocent learn from the older ones with more experience.

> Psychiatrists run Wilson Youth Hospital, yet it could just as well be a prison. Quite a few Wilson girls I know were transferred to Wolston Park [the adult Psychiatric Hospital at Wacol] from Wilson. But why, when a girl is supposed to need psychiatric treatment, is she transferred to Wolston Park when there are trained psychiatrists working at Wilson Youth Hospital?

> Wilson Youth Hospital is not working. That's obvious from the number of girls who keep returning time after time. I have experienced Wilson Youth Hospital. I know the negative effects it has on girls, and I know the system does not work.

> I think it's about time someone showed concern for the conditions in Wilson.

> So, thanks.

That, Mr Herbert, is a cry from the heart from an adolescent girl caught up in the present system. It is an indictment on our whole society if we cannot find funds to respond to that appeal.[54]

The letter Anne quoted was written by a 14 or 15-year-old girl. Many of the young people in Wilson were quite capable of reflecting upon their experiences in the system, and were articulate in expressing their concerns. They were the people who knew first-hand what the system was like. They often guided us. We listened to them, and if they wished, used their words.

Other things were changing as a result of the work of Justice for Juveniles. The group targeted the lack of legal representation in the Children's Courts. As a result, a Duty Solicitor scheme became operational at the Brisbane Children's Court. The scheme was established and maintained by the Queensland Law Society. It was working so well that the acting Director of Children's Services was able to report:

My previous memorandum dated 29th November 1978 attached a table outlining appearances, representation and result since the introduction of the scheme. Most children appearing in Brisbane are represented. All have the choice. However, the situation is quite different in other metropolitan areas or country areas where in some situations aboriginal [sic] children appear to be more able to arrange representation.[55]

Other community organisations, some specifically concerned about the plight of children, supported the thrust of Justice for Juveniles. The Government had commissioned an inquiry into the needs of children and youth in Queensland in 1974. The inquiry was chaired by Justice Demack. A substantial part of his final report and recommendations was devoted to youth at risk, the Children's Courts, and Wilson Youth Hospital. Justice for Juveniles relied heavily on his work and often quoted from it. We were often frustrated by Government inaction on an Inquiry which they themselves had commissioned:

As most of the recommendations put forward in this submission [by Justice for Juveniles] are based on the findings of Justice A.G. Demack, and considered urgent in 1975, it seems incredible that so much time has already been wasted. We trust the Government will take immediate action to bring about this much needed reform before more valuable young lives are ruined because of the lack of help and the correct guidance.[56]

54 Ibid., p 2.
55 Letter from the Acting Director to the Under Secretary, Department of Welfare Services, dated 23rd January, 1979, p 3.
56 Letter from the Hon. Secretary of Aid to Children Everywhere to The Hon. Mr. S. Doumany, M.L.A., dated 9th August, 1979.

In 1979, Ian McCol, a tertiary student, revised, updated, and rewrote the whole document. Its new title was *Justice for Juveniles in Queensland??* Having received some Federal money to publish the edition, we were able to produce a very respectable and presentable document, which we formally launched at the Catholic Centre in June 1979. The document was launched by Ms Quentin Bryce, a member of Justice for Juveniles and a lecturer in law at the University of Queensland.

So successful was the launch that the document received maximum media coverage. Deputations from Zonta and other organisations met with the Minister; others wrote detailed submissions; some also penned letters of support for our work. All of this prompted the following admissions from the Director of Children's Services:

> I have previously commented verbally and in the brief referred to above, that I have little disagreement with the April 1979 report of the Justice for Juveniles Group.

> What these organisations are really saying is that the Demack Report recommendations should be implemented and something should be done about Wilson Youth Hospital. With these comments I agree.

> The Justice for Juveniles Group's report referred to is attached, and although some of it is factually incorrect, I think what is more important is that it is a reasonable documentation and echoes all the relevant Demack Report recommendations.

> ... The whole matter hinges around the two issues of the implementation of the Demack Report recommendations and in particular, making some significant changes at the Wilson Youth Hospital.[57]

They had known what had needed to be done for five years, but had done nothing!

* * *

I gave the following address at the Albert Street Methodist Church in Brisbane City, on December 17, 1976. The occasion was the dedication ceremony for the first street worker at the Brisbane Youth Service, an ecumenical venture of the inner-city churches to respond to youth on the streets. It was my privilege to be the Catholic Church's representative on the committee which worked to have the project established. I served on the management committee until June 1979.

---

57 From the Director of Children's Services to the Under Secretary, Department of Welfare Services, dated 4 December 1979, p 1.

THE CHALLENGE OF CHRISTMAS

I have worked, been involved with and had the privilege of living with so-called 'delinquent' children over the past three years.

Tonight, I would like to tell you about one of these young people. We'll call her Jenny. Even though this story is fictitious, nevertheless many of the elements which go to make it up were often repeated to me by young people over the years.

Jenny is fourteen years old. She comes from a far western Queensland town. Her parents are not very well off. In fact, her parents split up and her father left the family years ago. Her mother's boy-friend now lives with Jenny's family. They both drink to excess and often fight.

Jenny doesn't cope well at school. She doesn't do her homework and she plays up in class. She regularly doesn't turn up at school.

She ran away from home on a couple of occasions and was picked up by the police. On the last occasion, she was brought before the Children's Court, charged with being uncontrollable, and sent to Wilson Youth Hospital in Brisbane. The Children's Court Judge was very kind and asked her why she had run away, but she was scared of the police and the court and found it difficult to understand what she was being asked. Certainly, she could not tell the judge that her step-father had assaulted her sexually on several occasions, particularly since he was in the court and had threatened to kill her if she breathed a word to anyone about it.

She was flown to Brisbane. She'd never been in a plane before and never been to Brisbane. She knew nobody in Brisbane. In Wilson, she was locked in an institution, behind high walls. There were high steel gates, and bars and locked doors, and she was locked into her room at night. She felt homesick and lost. She cried a lot.

In Wilson, her formal schooling stopped completely. Instead, she learnt knitting and crocheting, and above all, she learnt to be tough. She received no visitors and had no leave, because she had no family in Brisbane. There were interviews with psychiatrists and therapists and chaplains. She spent three months in Wilson and, on discharge, was sent to a hostel in Brisbane. The very next day she began work in a textile factory, sewing buttons on shirts all day.

In our society, Jenny is termed a "delinquent," but who among us has not at some time indulged in so-called "delinquent" behaviour?

As Christ said: "Let anyone among you who is without sin be the first to throw a stone at her." (John 8:7)

These co-called "delinquent" young people are not delinquents at all, but normal children, who mostly are disadvantaged in so many ways.

- They are aged between seven and seventeen years.
- Many cannot cope well with education.
- They are emotionally deprived.
- They often have never had the continuing interest, love, and friendship of anybody, let alone an adult.
- They are poor materially.
- They are generally illiterate.
- They are often bitter and even self-destructive.

They are also wards of the State, that is, of the government. It is easy for us to say that the government should provide for these young people. The government does provide for them: for example, it provides

- Homes like Warilda at Wooloowin, which costs the government over three hundred dollars per child per week
- Subsidies for Church homes like Enoggera Boys Home, Kalimna—a home for girls run by the Salvation Army, Saint Vincent's Nudgee, where the subsidy is twenty-six dollars per child per week and is about to be increased to thirty-two dollars
- The Children's Courts, where over five thousand children appeared in Queensland for the year ending June 1976, while only one thousand children appeared in Children's Courts in Victoria in the year ending June 1975, yet Victoria has a much higher population than Queensland
- Institutions like Wilson Youth Hospital and Westbrook Training Centre.

What doesn't the government do?

- Look into the causes of delinquency;
- Carry out intensive research—it is difficult to obtain important facts and figures. (Several Boggo Road chaplains have told me that a high proportion of prisoners they interview are ex-inmates of Wilson and Westbrook);
- Provide adequate and suitable educational facilities for children in Wilson;
- Expand the Juvenile Aid Bureau, instead of scaling down its activities;
- Set up family type half-way houses and attendance centres throughout the State.

But the government isn't solely responsible, nor are the social workers, probation officers, therapists, the people who run Church homes, the psychiatrists.

Christ, applying to Himself words written by Isaiah, said He had come

> to preach the good news to the poor,
>
> to proclaim liberty to captives,
>
> recovery of sight to the blind, and
>
> to proclaim the year when the Lord will save His people

(Luke 4:16-18)

My point here is that "delinquent" young people are poor, oppressed, blind, captive, and in need of the salvation of the Lord, that is, [in need of] people to be faithful to them as God is faithful to us.

My point is also that, if this is how Christ saw his ministry, then we who wish to go by the name of Christian must also see our ministry in the same way as Christ—a concern and practical love for everyone, but a special love and concern for the outcast and the marginalised.

We Christians can't say, 'they ought to do this and they ought to do that.' Instead, we must say, "we ought to search out what we can do. We must look to all men and women of good will and work together with them." The Incarnation, Christ's coming, Christmas, surely means Christ putting flesh on the promise of God being faithful to His people, being faithful to His word.

If we wish to be faithful to God, to Christ and to His mission, if we are true Christians, then we too must put flesh on our words and make sure that our word and our action are one. Christ lived for, prayed for, worked for

> justice
> love
> unity
> reconciliation
> and peace.

We who opt for Christ must search out, work for, suffer for, sacrifice ourselves for this same

> justice
> love
> unity
> reconciliation
> and peace.

The address was published in the YCS (Brisbane) Newsletter of March 1977. The purpose of publishing it in a student newsletter was to broaden the focus of action and reflection in the lives of the students, because the Jenny's of this world were fellow-students. Lay apostolate meant identifying at-risk students and entering into a relationship of friendship and trust with them. The address attempted to alert students to the ways in which structures of society deal with their disadvantaged peers. It was a call to deepen their faith through their action.

Learning about juvenile justice

WITH ENCOURAGEMENT from friends, I applied to the Church for study leave to examine juvenile justice, both in Australia and overseas. I wanted firstly, to look at the alternatives to institutional care for young people at risk between the ages of 10 and 18; secondly, to study community groups working with young people at risk to bring about change in the juvenile justice system, especially in the areas of police, children's courts, government and non-government institutions, and government welfare departments. Finally, I wanted to look at institutional care for young offenders, both status and criminal offenders, and to make contact with people working in preventative ways and study their programs.[58]

I was exhausted from living and working at the Lodge for seven years. I needed time to regain energy and vision and to take on new and challenging ideas. At the beginning of July, I set off from Brisbane for Perth in an old VW Combi van belonging to friends of mine. A family friend, a retired carpenter and cabinet maker, had fitted out the van with bed, study desk, fridge, stove, and bins for clothes, books and food.

I had only been in Perth for one month when my father died. I flew back to Brisbane to be with my family and to conduct Dad's funeral. On my way to the funeral, I called into the Lodge to pick up my soutane. It was not where I had left it. When I had searched around and couldn't find it, I went down to the kitchen. Mick Tansky, one of the people who was looking after the Lodge in my absence, was having a cuppa with one of our young people.

"Have you seen my soutane, Mick?" I asked.

"What does it look like?"

"It's a long white robe."

"Does it have buttons all the way down the front?"

"Yes."

Mick began to laugh. In fact he couldn't stop laughing.

He told me that, the day before, he had seen one of the girls who was living at the Lodge wearing it in Fortitude Valley, an inner-city neighbourhood of Brisbane well known for its pubs, clubs and other dens. She was trying to pass herself off as a nun, and asking people for money. She was also eight months pregnant with twins. Needless to say, I never saw that soutane again.

---

58 Taken from a letter sent to key people in the United States, Canada, Great Britain and Europe and dated 31st January, 1979.

Back to Perth and on the road in the Combi van, I set out across the Nullar-bor Plain towards Adelaide. I had to do some mechanical work on the Combi in Albany prior to driving across the desert. A garage man allowed me the use of his tools and checked my work. In conversation he told me of two local pre-ventative programs. One was run by a smash repair operator who employed and trained Aboriginal young people who were at risk of ending up before the Children's Court. To assist these young people in their studies, he employed a part-time teacher and set aside a section of his workshop as a schoolroom. The other was in the form of local youth organisations which took a young person who was in trouble with the police and included them in their activities. For example, the local Scout group would take one of these young people on a camp and one of the Scout leaders would pal up with him and follow up at the conclusion of the camp.

I looked at juvenile justice systems, Children's Courts, secure institutional care, community and preventive programs in all States. I read literature and tapped into the limited research which had been undertaken in Australia. I reflected alone and with others on the work I had done, on the juvenile justice system and how to change it. I had few evening appointments, and almost none on weekends, so I was able to catch up on much needed rest.

I left for the USA on 13 January 1980. I spent three months in the US, two weeks in Canada, three weeks in Sweden, and five weeks in England. I lived frugally, often staying in the cheapest boarding houses, many in the big cities, especially in the US.

In San Francisco I was reintroduced to the work of Thomas Merton, the Trappist monk, by Sister Noelene, a nun who was working with pregnant and homeless young women. She told me I was a contemplative. I told her she was wrong: I had tried to read Merton when I was in my late teens and couldn't understand his writings. She lent me *Merton's Palace of Nowhere*,[59] a biography of Merton. I returned the book after a few days, remarking that the book had convinced me that I was not into contemplation in any shape or form. Noelene disagreed, and told me to read the book again. When I did, I began to see the possibilities of contemplation: sitting with God and letting God speak to me in silence, in the midst of the pain, suffering and injustice that I was trying to address in an inadequate way.

In Ilyria, Ohio, I worked with a man who had lived in Gethsemane Monas-tery with Merton. He was the director of a multi-faceted agency for homeless young people. As well as offering accommodation, his agency ran a restaurant where young people trained to be cooks and waitresses, and a small shop which sold arts and crafts as well as a number of Merton's books. I purchased *Conjec-*

---

59   *Merton's Palace of Nowhere: A Search for God through Awareness of the True Self,* James
     Finley, Ave Maria Press (1978).

tures of a Guilty Bystander[60] and, since then, I have profited from reading many of Merton's books, especially *Contemplative Prayer*.[61]

In Ontario, Canada, I visited Options Youth, a program for young people who had a prognosis of institutional living for the rest of their lives, oscillating between juvenile detention centres and mental institutions. The aim of the program was to facilitate young people's access to services which could assist them to live in the community, or if particular services did not exist, to create them.

Tom was a big and physically strong lad who had been incarcerated on a number of occasions and had also spent time in a mental institution. He had been a ward of the State since birth, and been placed unsuccessfully in numerous foster placements. The Options Youth staff convened a meeting of the significant people who had worked with Tom at different stages of his life, as many as they could get hold of. Many came to the meeting armed with mountains of files, but they were asked to forget what was written in the files and to speak to anything they had seen in Tom which was positive. One spoke of an interest he had in woodwork. Another mentioned Tom trying to play a guitar. After several meetings and some interviews with Tom, Options Youth staff developed a plan. A physically strong carpenter agreed to have Tom work with him on his jobs, and was reimbursed for his trouble. He also agreed that, if Tom responded to training, the reimbursement would slowly decrease and he would pay Tom a wage. Amazingly, he further agreed to accommodate Tom in his own home with his family.

A support worker was engaged to work flexibly with Tom up to a maximum of forty hours a week. If the carpenter's family needed time to themselves, the worker would look after Tom for a weekend. The worker accompanied Tom to guitar lessons and taught him to use the public transport system in Toronto. There was an arrangement with the local detention centre for Tom to be placed there for two or three days, but only if he became violent and out of control. During the incarceration, he could be visited at any time by the carpenter and the worker.

I sat in on Tom's case review. Tom had been in the program for six months. He was still working and living with the carpenter's family. His carpentry skills had improved considerably and the subsidy to the carpenter was minimal. The support worker's time had been scaled down to 30 hours a week, then to 20, and later again to ten. The worker had accompanied Tom to dances and helped Tom treat girls with respect (Tom tended to want to maul any female who came within arm's reach). The plan for Tom, while initially very expensive, became progressively less and less, and was never as expensive as incarcer-

60 *Conjectures of a Guilty Bystander*, Thomas Merton, Image Books (1968).
61 *Contemplative Prayer*, Thomas Merton. Darton, Longman and Todd (1973).

ation—a mere fraction of the cost it would have been to care for Tom in an institution for the rest of his life.

After 15 weeks in North America I flew to Sweden. I found Sweden a very enlightened country for many reasons. First of all, many people, including those I met on the street, spoke about the dignity of the human person, and nowhere did I come across the 'blaming the victim' attitude so prevalent in our own society.

I stayed in a youth hostel in inner-city Stockholm, arriving on a Sunday afternoon. The middle-aged couple who booked me in, asked if I had noticed people in a nearby park who were drunk, and told me that Alcoholics Anonymous met next door on a regular basis. They went on to tell me that Sweden has a problem with many people who are alcoholics, but who tragically did not want to use the shelters. The couple were very concerned, and asked me if Australia had solutions to the problem. "What else do you think we should be doing?" they asked.

While in Stockholm, I caught the bus out to a so-called detention centre for young people, on the outskirts of the city. I was walking down a lane with scrub on either side, when a woman appeared out of the scrub pushing a bicycle. Her name was Bridgette and she was the second-in-charge of the centre. She apologised for not being at the bus stop, and passed on apologies for her boss who had been suddenly called to the city for a meeting. We walked on through the bush together and to the detention centre.

There were no walls or security fences. In fact, the first thing we came across was a large boat on blocks. I thought to myself: *I bet the manager owns that.* Bridgette told me that most of the young people in the institution were there for drug or alcohol-related offences. Rather than punish the offence, their emphasis was on drug/alcohol treatment. There were four large houses, each with 16 young people, both males and females. Two of the houses were locked, the other two were open. The young people were required to work, either in a bicycle repair shop or a garage or somewhere else on the premises—and they were paid award wages. They had individual and group counselling sessions. They had to negotiate with their boss to attend these sessions, and make up the time or have the hours off deducted from their wages. The ethos of the place was work, with liberal doses of counselling.

I asked to be shown through one of the lock-up houses. Bridgette had the keys with her and we went in. There was nobody there. "Where is everybody?" I asked. Bridgette pointed out the windows: "They are on the oval practising football. We're in the finals of the local mixed soccer competition, which are on in a day or two." I looked out the window at the young people in soccer training. The oval was surrounded by a very low picket fence—so much for security. Bridgette told me that, if a young person ran away, they notified the police. The young people paid something towards board and paid for the things they needed. When they had saved an agreed amount of money, they were eligible for weekend leave. She also told me about the boat. In summer, each house spent two weeks sailing it, eight young people at a time. In winter, they went skiing in the mountains, in groups of eight, for one week.

When the young people came in from the oval, I was introduced. At first, they were shy, but gradually they opened up, and many were able to converse with me in English. After ten minutes or so, a young lad asked me if I wanted a cup of coffee. I said yes, and he then asked the others if they also would like one. Most did, so he went to the nearby kitchen to prepare it and brought it out, serving all of us. The young people were relaxed and obviously felt at home.

Bridgette asked me about Australia and the places I had worked in. When I told her about Wilson, she couldn't believe her ears and, in fact, was very close to tears. She commented, "When a human being has to be the custodian of another human being in the way you describe, both are dehumanised. Even animals should not be treated in such a way."

People think of Sweden as a highly-taxed society. Many told me this themselves, but added, "I think we should be paying even more taxes so that all can live properly."

I finished my study leave with five weeks in England. I returned to Australia with a wealth of information and, more importantly, with ideas to share with people who were committed to working in the juvenile justice area.

Integrating spirituality and life

Brisbane Youth Service

IN 1977 I had been involved in the setting up of Brisbane Youth Service, an ecumenical street-work program for homeless and disadvantaged young people in Brisbane city and nearby Fortitude Valley. After it was established, I supervised a worker for a year and was a member of the management committee until the middle of 1979.

On the occasion of its fifth anniversary in June 1982 I was invited by the management committee to give the homily at the liturgy. In the preparation of the homily, I asked one of the young people whom I was working with at the time, to comment on my draft and to write something herself which I could incorporate. The following is the text of the address:

On the day he was shot, Pope John Paul II had this to say: "The Church by its vocation is called to be the faithful protector of human dignity everywhere, the mother of the oppressed and those on the fringes of society, the Church of the weak and the poor."

All Churches—all Christians—all people of goodwill are called

- to uphold and protect the dignity of the human person,
- to stand with and support the oppressed and those on the fringes of society,
- to go out to and be with the weak and the poor.

But what of the Brisbane Youth Service—what is its mission? What is its job? What is it called to do?

Yes, it is called to uphold and protect the dignity of the human person

Yes, it is called to stand with and support the oppressed and those on the fringes of society

Yes, it is called to go out to and be with the weak and the poor.

But the vocation, the call, the brilliance of the Brisbane Youth Service is a very particular call, a very particular vocation. The detached youth workers of the Brisbane Youth Service are called to do this for a particular group of people; namely, young people in a defined geographical area—the streets of inner-city Brisbane. The Brisbane Youth Service—its workers, committee members and supporters—must never forget this: The Brisbane Youth Service's special mission and vocation is to uphold the dignity, stand with and support, go out to and be with the young people on the streets—the homeless, the sick, the confused, the rejected, the violated young people on the streets of inner-city Brisbane.

One evening recently, I dropped in to see a young friend of mine. She told me that, on that particular day, she saw a young girl sitting in the gutter crying. She went over to her, sat down beside her and asked her what was wrong. The young girl was fourteen years old and she had been severely beaten up and had run away that day. My friend, who is sixteen years old, said to me, "Who in this rotten society cares about her and those like her?" I said, "The youth workers from the Brisbane Youth Service." "Who are they?" she asked. I told her. "Where are they today?"

Later on she said: "Street workers should concentrate on the street. If they choose to follow through with someone, they must make sure it doesn't interfere with the street."

The detached youth worker always has to go out; he or she always has to make the first move to go onto the street, to go up to young people, to begin again the process of getting to know a young person, and to build up trust—a slow and difficult job.

This going out takes lots of will power, self-discipline and energy. It means that the detached youth worker must have his or her priorities worked out clearly:

- What am I employed to do?
- Where am I spending my time?
- How much time am I spending on the street?

Christ, in his own way, was a detached worker:

He came to seek out and save what was lost.

He came not to be served but to serve and to give his life as a ransom for many.

He came to preach the good news to the poor—and we know what his good news was: health to the sick, sight to the blind, life to the dead, freedom to the imprisoned, dignity, respect and justice for all, especially the outcasts and the marginalised.

In the first chapter of Isaiah, God says through the prophet,

> Yes, stop doing evil and learn to do right.
>
> See that justice is done.
>
> Help those who are oppressed.

Give orphans their rights and defend widows. (Isaiah 1:16-17)

"Give orphans their rights." I wonder what these rights would be? Would they be such rights as the right to

- food
- shelter
- clothing
- have a job
- be literate
- health care
- legal protection
- be treated with dignity
- be loved and respected
- receive a living allowance?

I asked a young woman who had been fending for herself since she was eleven years old to comment on these rights. Her comments I now pass on to you.

Food: "You get really hungry, and you can't afford food, and this leads to ill health." This week I met a girl who hadn't eaten for two days and two boys who were stealing for food and food only.

Shelter: On March 3rd this year six boys and three girls between the ages of 12 and 14 stayed at Pindari, the Salvation Army hostel for adults. These young people should not be in with older people, for obvious reasons. There is a need for special shelters for these younger people.

Clothing: "Winter clothes are harder to come by. Even warm underwear is very expensive and out of the range of a person on $36 per week (the dole), without thinking of work-boots, proper shoes and dresses for job interviews."

Health-care: "You wait around the hospital for hours. You are often not taken seriously, because you are young and on your own and because you have trouble explaining. You can see a private doctor, but then you can't afford the medication advised." I have been approached by girls and asked for money for personal hygiene items, simply because they could not afford to buy these things themselves. You can imagine the difficulties a young girl would have in approaching a male with such a request.

Legal protection: Young people are so vulnerable before authority, whether that authority be police, courts, the Department of Children's Services, staff of institutions, and even foster parents. Children are often treated as chattels, mere appendages, of no consequence, to be used and abused at will.

Dignity: "To be treated and respected like other people, not to be put down. We are normal and are part of this society just as much as you."

Loved and respected: "We need love just like you and your kids, not worse, just 'cause we got no parents. Not to be rejected once again," she said with emphasis, "that is the big point. We are fighting to survive as a person and when we are rejected it shakes us to our foundations."

A job: "Not to be turned away at job interviews 'cause we're not dressed as nice or 'cause we aren't living at home. We need jobs more so 'cause we got no parents to support us if our dole doesn't stretch far enough. We are not criminals and employers treat us like we are."

A living allowance: "For food, rent, for emergency modess, tampons, undies. $36 just isn't enough when you pay $20 per week for a room or a flatette."

Literate: "A chance to read and write. If you have difficulties then supply special help. You don't have parents to ask teachers for it, and you don't know how to ask for it yourself."

Our God says, "to give orphans their rights."

The Brisbane Youth Service, detached youth workers and committee take up this challenge as it links young people on the street with existing services. The Brisbane Youth Service has taken up this challenge over the past five years. Workers have gone on to the streets. Workers and committee have become aware of gaps in services, and have persistently and strenuously endeavoured to educate our society so that these gaps will be filled.

Much has been achieved: one youth worker to four youth workers; one and a half people working in the office; supervisors; a management committee constantly supporting the workers on the streets; a thrift shop; a drop-in centre; other detached youth work programs springing up throughout the State.

The Brisbane Youth Service, workers, supporters and committee must be congratulated. God must be thanked.

However, over the past five years the problems have worsened and our understanding of them has deepened. The need not only is still there, but is even greater.

My prayer for you is: that you will continue to love tenderly, act justly and walk humbly with your God. (Micah 6:8)

* * *

The Priests' Assembly

In the early 1970s I attended a seminar of about 50 priests who were working with young people. At the final session of the day many priests spoke about how they had lost direction, how they did not know where they were going, or what they were on about. Some of those who spoke had only been ordained two or three years, so it was quite an admission. Wishing to turn their admissions into something positive, I put a motion that we request that the Senate of Priests organise a live-in seminar on the current mission of the Church in the Archdiocese in the light of Vatican II. The motion was unanimously agreed.

In time the motion was put to the Senate which, in turn, gave it over to a committee to action, and I was invited to be a member of that committee. Unfortunately the committee, in good faith, hi-jacked the proposal and used it for their own purposes. I was saying to them that we needed to begin where the priests were at, what they were doing, what their problems were, what they saw to be the signs of the times that the Church in South-East Queensland needed to respond to. As a lone voice on the committee, I was not heard. I remember one influential person saying, "The priests would not be able to articulate where they were at. They would not be capable of doing that sort of work."

It was a vote of no confidence in the priests. I left the meeting with a heavy heart, knowing that we were putting off something that was vitally important.

The seminar went ahead, of course. It was a passive, jug-mug affair, lecturers doing their stuff for us, their almost totally passive recipients.

I say 'almost' because Bernie Wallace, who had recently been ordained a bishop, was to give the key address, "The Ministry of the Priest Today". I was looking forward to the address, as Bernie had been one of our best lecturers at the seminary and was someone whom I respected.

I found his lecture very disappointing. If he used the word 'mystery' once, he used it twenty times in his lecture. He clouded the whole issue in mystery. As the lecture went on I became more and more annoyed, because I knew that what he was saying was of no help to the people who had requested the seminar. His last two sentences were: "The areas of the poor and justice are the province of lay-people, not for priests. As far as these areas are concerned, we, the bishops, have to make prudential decisions." I was seething. What a cop-out, what a sell-out of Vatican II!

Questions followed. About five or six of the young priests spoke openly about how, after two or three years of ministry, they were lost. They tried to ask Bernie questions which would help to clarify their position and give them some direction. His response was to put them down in no uncertain terms. I got to my feet and demanded that they be given a hearing. In fact I requested that the agenda be scrapped and that we spend time in small groups, listening and addressing the issues that these young priests had raised. After discussion, some of it heated, people decided to suspend the agenda for the afternoon and spend time in small groups. It was a small, token achievement. Insufficient time was given to the new agenda, and we were unable to take the concerns of the priests any further. We, as a presbyterate, had lost a golden opportunity to do something substantial about working out our vision and mission. My intervention did not endear me to Bernie nor to some of my brother priests.

There was another opportunity in 1983 at a Priests' Assembly at Banyo Seminary. I read all the material that was sent out, and wondered if I should attend. Most of the position papers dealt with structures in the Archdiocese, and nothing more. After a lot of thought and prayer, I decided to become involved. I phoned eight priests and invited them to a meeting to discuss the forthcoming assembly. At the meeting I suggested we formulate responses to the position papers, since the papers did not mention poor or marginalised people, and did not consider justice. They agreed and asked that I prepare a paper and submit it to the next meeting. I prepared the following.

The Role of the Church in Brisbane – July 1983

Some of the young people I lived with at the Lodge are now dead. None of these reached their 20th birthday.

Joe was one of the Valley boys. I first met him when he was 15 years old. He was a shy, gentle lad—homeless, unable to get a job—living under bridges, in railway carriages and in deserted houses. He jumped off the Storey Bridge when he was 18 years old.

Tricia was placed in a home when she was 7 years old. The thing that always puzzled her was why she was placed in a children's home, but her brothers and sisters were not. I first met Tricia when she was 14 years old. She'd been locked up in a secure children's home because she kept running away to find her parents and her brothers and sisters. She lived at Kedron Lodge for several months when she was 16 years old. While she was there, she tracked down her parents, who were separated. Her mother (at 38) was having an affair with a 19-year-old boy, and both were on dope. Her father, on their first meeting in nine years, tried to seduce her, his eldest daughter. Tricia herself got into drugs (heroin) and prostitution, and died in March of last year of a heroin overdose.

Bill was 13 years old when I met him. His father was a chronic and violent alcoholic. Bill, though intelligent and gifted, never had a chance. His family was poor, they lived in a Housing Commission area a long way from anywhere, with few local resources and an almost non-existent public transport system. Bill wanted to leave home and try to make a new start, away from his violent father, but no family could be found to take him. He stayed at home, got further and further into trouble and died this year aged 15 years from sniffing glue, so the papers said.

Jenny died at 17 years of age of a heroin overdose. A very capable and intelligent girl, her mother had a stroke when Jenny was 9 years old and was rendered immobile and speechless. Her father was a chronic alcoholic.

Sam died aged 16 years......

Mary died aged 20 years.....

These stories are merely the tip of the iceberg. They are representative of a large and ever-growing number of people—not only young ones—who have no hope, nothing to live for, no future.

The Catholic Church in the Archdiocese of Brisbane is heavily involved in commitments to parishes and to Catholic Education. I guess, since the inception of this diocese, properties have been purchased, boundaries designated, priests assigned and the parish plant established with its church, presbytery, school and convent. Heroic efforts have been made and are still being made to establish new plants in new parishes, and to maintain older-established plants.

The Archdiocese has, mainly through its religious orders and lay organisations, endeavoured to cater for the poor, especially those with special needs: for example, children at Saint Vincent's Nudgee, girls at Mt Maria Mitchelton, homeless men and women through the hostels sponsored by the Society of Saint Vincent de Paul and the Legion of Mary.

But still we have the Joes and the Tricias and the Marys and Sams dying at a very young age. Still we have the despair of the solo parent and battered wife. Still we have families where the bread-winner is unemployed, living on the dole which maintains the family in poverty. Then there are the Aboriginal people, and some of the migrant women working in dehumanising conditions in factories, the prisoners . . .

What is our Church saying to the poor of Brisbane? Does our Church see the poor? Do the poor feel welcome in our parish communities and our educational establishments? Do our parishes and our schools cater for and stand side by side with the poor?

Or do the poor see us condemning them to a life of frustration and hopelessness by our seeming lack of concern, lack of action, our saying "yes, I think it's OK for you to live under the poverty line!"

Do we, as a Church, support the injustice of poverty by saying and doing very little? Are we a scandal to his 'little ones' (Matthew 10:42) —the poor? "For I was hungry, thirsty, sick and you gave ME ..." (Matthew

25:35-36) says Christ to us. "Blessed are those who hunger and thirst for righteousness," (Matthew 5:6) says Christ to us.

Our Scripture is prolific in references to the poor, to justice and the oppressed, and to the stance that our God commands us to take. Our tradition is also rich with examples of men and women who went into bat for justice and the poor. Even in our own day—Archbishop Romero, Mother Theresa, Brian McMahon [a priest from the Toowoomba diocese who had recently been expelled from Chile because of his stance on justice and the poor].

But what of us, what of our parishes, what of our schools, what of our Archdiocese?

How do we see the needs of the poor in the Archdiocese? What are our plans to give "preferential treatment to the poor"? What do we want our Church to be in seventeen years' time: the way it is now but a little more developed? Or do we want to see a church serving the poor, doing justice, living by faith in the Lord, who will and does provide?

Could we, the presbyterate of the Archdiocese of Brisbane, either formulate here, or make concrete plans to formulate the tasks which the church of Brisbane will address in the next seventeen years?

"The Church by its very vocation is called to be the faithful protector of human dignity everywhere—the mother of the oppressed and those on the fringes of society—the Church of the weak and the poor." So said John Paul II in May 1981. Can that be said of the Church, the parishes and the schools of Brisbane?

Proposal -

That groups of the poor be brought together

    a) to break down their isolation

    b) to enable them to support each other

    c) to help them address the causes of their poverty, that is, ultimately to empower them.

(These groups made up of -

- pensioners
- handicapped people
- unemployed
- migrant women
- solo parents
- Aborigines

- women
- migrant women in factories
- people in rented accommodation
- people being exploited by hire purchase companies and/or banks e.g., Walton's
- secondary students
- factory workers both male and female
- rural poor
- farmers exploited by fertiliser monopolies)

Representatives from these groups should be on the parish council, together with other representatives of, for example, liturgy, catechists, school, peace, etc.

I gave copies of the paper to the priests at our next meeting. The main comment was that the document was too direct, abrasive and blunt. I was asked to take it away and re-write it in the light of the comments of the group.

At our next meeting I submitted the following to them:

The kinds of things I would wish to be included on the agenda of the Priests Assembly would be as follows:

1. Justice: I believe that this concept is fundamental to the message of the Bible and the mission of Christ. I would like to see a day spent on this topic with sessions on

- The Bible on Justice
- Justice as an integral part of the Mission of the Church
- Injustice within the Church in Brisbane in terms of allocation of resources
- The Church of Brisbane and its stance or lack thereof on the issues facing the poor: for example, housing, transport, prisons, Walton's, pensions, unemployment

2. The mission of the Church in Brisbane to the poor

- Who are the poor?
- How are they poor?
- Why are they poor?
- Does our Church cater to the needs of the poor? How adequate/inadequate are these responses?
- What more can we as a Church do so that the poor see us as their advocates?

-    What proportion of our resources of time, personnel, money are used for middle-class Catholics—poor Catholics—poor unchurched non-Catholics?

3. Can the assembly formulate a vision for the Church in Brisbane for the eighties with long-term goals and short-term task oriented steps to achieve those goals?

An extract from "Law, Love and Language" by Herbert McCabe:

"Again, the sacrament of order is an exploration into the deep meaning of revolutionary leadership. The Christian minister is meant to be neither the pillar of an established quasi-feudal order, as conservative Christians are inclined to think, nor is he the democratic representative of a quasi-bourgeois society as the progressives seem to suggest; he is a revolutionary leader whose job is the subversion of the world through the preaching of the Gospel. He exercises authority amongst his people but not as maintaining an established structure; he is the leader of his people in a movement towards a new community. He is representative of his people but not necessarily in the sense of being their elected spokesman; he may represent them in the way a revolutionary leader does, a way that is not obvious to them and only becomes clear when the revolution is achieved. I think it significant that, according to Saint John, the first thing Jesus says about the missionaries he commissions before his death is that the world will hate them.

"Father, I have given them your word, and the world has hated them because they do not belong to the world, just as I do not belong to the world... As you have sent me into the world, so I have sent them into the world. And for their sakes I sanctify myself, so that they also may be sanctified in truth." (John 17:14, 18 &19)

The group said: 'Yes, it was an improvement on the previous one but, no, they did not think it was suitable for general distribution to the priests prior to the Assembly'. I suggested that it might be made available to the priests at the Assembly itself. No, they said, they did not think that was a good idea either. Finally, I suggested that we, as a group, should meet of an evening, or another suitable time, to monitor what was happening and to offer support to each other should it be needed. They thought not.

The Assembly went ahead as planned. I was heartened that a priest raised the issue of unemployment which caused some spirited debate: in the end a motion was put to the Assembly and passed. It was left to individual parishes and their pastors to respond and, to their credit, some of them did.

A final word?

1985 was designated as International Youth Year. In late 1984, the Catholic Leader asked me to write an article. The article went under the title, *Young people: will we listen, do we care?*[62] I reproduce a substantial part of that article here.

Will the 1985 International Youth Year be mere 'word magic', totally without substance, a 'gong booming or cymbals clashing', empty sound?

Do we really want our young people to participate in decision-making? Do we really believe that they have something worthwhile to contribute?

Do we really want to know about their problems, their hopes, their ideals?

They have a great deal to say that is well worth listening to—things to say that would surprise many of us if we took the time to listen to them.

"In what they say and do, young people show us what our society is like. Their varying life experiences point out the good and bad in society. Their dreams and hopes challenge and judge us."[63]

I believe this should be discussed from the viewpoint of what is happening to our young people in their families and in society though the eyes of these young people themselves—especially those who are most disadvantaged, those whom the family and societal systems seem to reject.

I believe it is they, most of all, who could tell us about the society and the world which we have bequeathed to them. It is they who could tell us what it is like trying to survive at 15 years old, with no family to back them up and no income guaranteed by the governments. They could tell us what it is like to be 16 or 17 years old, unemployed on $45 per week, on the dole and paying $50 per week for a dingy flat.

If we took the time to seek them out and consult with them, they would be able to give us some insights into our education system. They could explain to us why they felt the system had failed them: why, for instance, after nine years of schooling they are still illiterate or semi-literate; why they don't have the basic skills to survive in our society—things like cooking, or budgeting, or how to fill out a dole form, or even how to grow a few vegies; why they don't know how to organise themselves so that their voice would be heard.

Some of them could tell us what it is like to be on the wrong side of the law and how ignorant they are of their basic legal rights and of how the

62 *The Catholic Leader*, 2 December, 1984 p 15.
63 'It's a Rocky Road,' Australian Bishops' Social Justice Statement of 1984.

legal system operates. A few who have experienced the deficiencies of our child welfare system would be in an excellent position to give us their valuable insights from a consumer's point of view.

Would we want to consult these young people? Would we be able to listen to their cries or would be wanting to defend the system?

Would we want to work with them so they might have a real say in the policies and the plans of our State and our nation—policies and plans which affect these young people most?

People might think that when I speak of these most disadvantaged young people that I am thinking of an insignificant minority. I'm not. The most recent estimate of the number of young people living in poverty in Australia was 750,000. A horrifying statistic—but certainly credible.

Three issues stand out from consultations with young people:

- unemployment and income security;
- relationships;
- nuclear war.

The facts on unemployment are very disturbing. From 1970 to 1983 the number of unemployed teenagers grew from 21,000 to 165,000 and their unemployment rate grew from 3% to 23%. We need to ask: What is the demoralising effect of unemployment on the young people of this nation? Do our present policies contribute to their solution? Do we need policy options which will remedy the inequities in existing programs and provide more and better opportunities for young people, whether in conventional employment, in education, in training or in alternative modes of living and working? It must be kept in mind that youth employment rates may not recover to the pre-1973 levels.

Youth is a period when new relationships are explored and old ones reassessed. Young people enter wider relationships as they move beyond the immediate circle of school and home. These new relationships raise questions and concerns for them. Certainly, many disadvantaged young people find their family relationships to be destructive. Family life for them is a place where domination exists, not only on the basis of age, of children by parents, but also domination on the basis of sex, of women by men. They find it difficult to avoid repeating these patterns of relationships in their own lives.

Experiences of unstable family and personal relations make it more difficult for young people to form stable relationships of their own. Sexual relationships especially are affected. Young people want to give and receive love. They all reveal a need for loving relationships. The difficulties which stand in the way of such loving relationships reflect the growing self-centredness of our society as a whole. A significant number of young people don't live as a member of a family unit. In fact, the number is estimated at 442,000 of under 25-year-olds, of whom 127,000 are aged between 15 and 19 years.

For many young people, the possibility of nuclear war is a major concern. There are two parts to this: fear of nuclear war and concern over the use of resources. The fear of nuclear war is a present fear. The possibility of destruction is real and, of itself, personally destructive. This threat reduces the future. It makes planning and preparation seem useless. It also builds up a sense of powerlessness in people. The problem is so great, so remote and so threatening that individuals and even whole nations seem insignificant before it.

The other aspect of the nuclear question is the consequences of the huge expenditure on weapons, which channels resources away from areas of pressing need. Even in Australia the Defence budget was more than $5 billion for 1983-84. As one young person said: "The super-powers of the world should get rid of the bomb and spend all their money on developing Third World countries. No money spent on bombs." Another said: "Who wants to be blown up? Homes rather than nuclear arms. Although this may never come to be, it would be something everyone should strive for. Ban the bomb!"

Young people understand well the danger of nuclear war. They identify what concerns them:

- lack of progress in disarmament talks
- the development of new weapons systems and
- the continuation of uranium mining.

Yet they have difficulty in knowing what to do. We need to ask ourselves some questions:

Do we—and our society—keep young people powerless in order to facilitate our own power?

Do we keep young people in a state of identity crisis in order to stabilise our own identities?

Do we pretend that the needs of youth are naturally different from our own in order to avoid giving them the power to satisfy their own needs?

The United Nations has declared that next year will be International Youth Year. Australia is promoting this year under the themes of participation, development and peace.

Participation: having the right to make decisions about family, school, work, government and carrying them out.

Development: young people mixing with others, achieving their full potential through personal achievements.

Peace: confronting basic problems like inequity, homelessness, unemployment and racial discrimination. If society were tolerant and flexible people could be at peace with each other.

I have to ask: Are we really prepared to consult with youth? Are we prepared to take their views seriously?

The article was to be my swan-song, my farewell to working with young people. A week or so after the article was published, I was going on long service leave.

While I was on study leave overseas, I had formulated in my mind the kind of centre that I thought was needed in Brisbane. The work I had done at the Lodge, as well as the research undertaken by Justice for Juveniles, had taught me a great deal about the needs of disadvantaged young people. At the Lodge we were a necessary ambulance at the foot of the cliff. Our study and research, listening to the cries of young people and their reflections on what had happened to them, challenged us to climb to the top of the cliff to examine what was happening at the source—to see what we could do to prevent the tragedies we were witnessing. It seemed to us that young people were falling through huge gaps in the system, and that there was little or no preventive work happening. Much of the suffering experienced by young people and their families could be averted.

* * *

A new model to assist
young people

IN AUGUST 1980 I drew up a model for a multi-disciplinary youth legal centre which we decided to call the Youth Advocacy Centre (YAC). I was keen to have the word "advocacy" in the title as I had for many years been a fan of the Holy Spirit: "When I go I will send the Holy Spirit. With his help you will do greater things than I. He will be the Advocate, to assist, guide, and strengthen" (John 14:26 and 16:7).

Advocacy meant supporting young people in their legitimate aspirations, defending them in and out of court, promoting their needs and their concerns. It also meant empowering young people with advice and information, so they could exercise their rights and make informed decisions.

During my study leave, I came across several youth legal centres overseas. They were of two kinds: centres for legal advice alone, or centres with lawyers and social workers working together. From the research carried out by Justice for Juveniles, we knew young people in Brisbane needed much more than that; so we designed a new model.

The proposed Youth Advocacy Centre was to have six elements: legal advice and representation; social work assistance to young people and their families; assistance for communities to solve their own problems of youth at risk; an after-hours service to assist young people questioned by police; consultancy and educational services to lawyers, social workers, welfare agencies, teachers, youth at risk and their parents, and the community; and finally, research into the juvenile justice system, including monitoring all proposed Parliamentary legislation pertaining to children and young people to ensure it was the best legislation possible.[64]

The rationale for the Centre was based on the following statements:

The child shall enjoy special protection, and shall be given opportunities and facilities, by law and by other means, to enable him/her to develop physically, mentally, morally, spiritually and socially in a healthy and normal manner in conditions of freedom and dignity. In the enactment of laws for this purpose the best interests of the child shall be the para-

---

64 Most of the information in the early section of this chapter is taken from "Youth Advocacy Centre—a proposal", presented by the Justice for Juveniles Group, January 1981.

mount consideration[65] (Principle 2 of the United Nations Declaration of the Rights of the Child).

"Two attitudes about children underlie the Danish juvenile justice system. The first is that the child is innocent, good and born with a clean slate. Thus, if a child misbehaves, makes a mistake, the reaction is not one of blame, but rather of looking for causes in a child's life that can be remedied. The second is that a child is an individual with his/her own inalienable rights, which no one, not even his parents, can deny."[66]

"No single action holds more potential for achieving procedural justice for the child in the juvenile court than provision of counsel. The presence of an independent legal representative of the child, or of his/her parents, is the keystone of the whole structure of guarantees that a minimum system of procedural justice requires. The rights to confront one's accusers, to cross-examine witnesses, to present evidence and testimony of one's own, to be unaffected by prejudicial and unreliable evidence, to participate meaningfully in the dispositional decision, to make an appeal, have substantial meaning for the overwhelming majority of persons brought before the juvenile court only if they are provided with competent lawyers who can invoke those rights effectively. The most informal and well-intentioned of judicial proceedings are technical; few adults without legal training can influence or even understand them; certainly children cannot."[67]

We wanted to ensure that children being questioned by police or appearing before the courts had ready access to quality legal advice and representation; that children had access to information regarding their legal rights and responsibilities; that children remain with their families as long as possible, and if this is not possible or advisable, then with a substitute family; that children should remain in the community, preferably within their own local community; that local communities be alerted to the needs of at-risk youth and their families, and be stimulated to address these needs; and lastly, that only those children be incarcerated in secure institutions who had committed serious offences and who were a danger either to themselves and/or the community.

With assistance from many friends, including Anne McMillan, we developed a detailed proposal. We made a draft available to selected professionals and young people for criticism and comment. By January 1981 the proposal

---

65 Ibid., p 1.
66 Wager and Wager 'Child Advocacy in Denmark', 1975.
67 President's Commission on Law Enforcement and Administration of Justice—The Challenge of Crime in a Free Society: A Report of the President's Commission on Law Enforcement and Administration of Justice. 1968 USA.

was printed, complete with name, logo, aims, method of work, services, developmental proposal, board of management, budget and rationale. The rationale took up 16 pages of the proposal and was an integral part of it. We knew that most people, including funding bodies, would be somewhat ignorant in this area, so the rationale was written both to inform and to raise awareness.

On the logo we chose for the Centre, a younger person raises their arms for help. The larger person, or the adult, stands behind the younger person. We wanted our Centre to stand behind young people, to act with and for them.

The next step was to obtain funding. Staff in youth legal centres overseas had told me that it could take two years to get a centre up and running. Most of their centres had taken as long as that, some even longer. The ideal would have been to have the Centre privately funded. Since we did not know any millionaires who would be prepared to invest in such a venture, we applied for funding from some of the larger foundations, but without success. I approached a number of people and institutions for letters of endorsement; we did receive such a letter from the bishop.

We approached both Federal and State Governments for funding. We organised a meeting with the Queensland Director of Children's Services and his Minister. After our meeting with the Director in early November 1980, he noted in an internal memo that "it might be a worthwhile pilot project for which funds might be sought from the Office of Child Care" (Federal). Apart from this typical passing the buck, he was helpful in requesting that his staff do a pilot for two months to ascertain:

(a)   the number of white children who appear before the
      Children's Court without benefit of counsel: this would
      apply to all the metropolitan Children's Courts, not just the
      one at Wilson Youth Hospital;

(b)   the number of status offenders who are placed in institutions;

(c)   the number of Aboriginal children who appear before courts.

He noted that "as far as (c) is concerned, I have pointed out to Father Dethlefs that we have no way of telling this as statistics are not kept."[68]

Extremely enlightening, and damning, statistics about legal representation in the metropolitan Children's Courts were forwarded to us several months later. Besides the Brisbane Children's Court, still at Wilson Youth Hospital, where 56% of young people were now represented, the overall figure for legal representation in the suburban courts was only 35.63%. Of young people appearing in the Redcliffe Court 97% were unrepresented; 93% in the Sandgate

68   Director of Department of Children's Services to A/Principal Child Care Officer (Residential Care) 11 November, 1980.

Court, 92% in the Holland Park Court, and 87% each in the Inala and Petrie Children's Courts.[69]

Interestingly, in the Cleveland and Brisbane courts, the figures for those legally unrepresented were only 50 percent and 44 percent respectively. The Cleveland court figure was low because a lawyer, who had done voluntary work at the Lodge, single-handedly spent whatever time he had representing children in the court closest to where his office was situated. The positive Brisbane figures were largely due to the publicity associated with the Justice for Juveniles group and the response of the Law Society in setting up a Duty Solicitor scheme.

We arranged a meeting with the Minister for Children's Services for 5th March 1981. In a briefing document to the Minister, the Director states,

> I should first give you some information on the Group. Justice for Juveniles is a group which at one stage, was particularly critical of the Wilson Youth Hospital. Father Dethlefs was the Chaplain at the Hospital and might be described as rather radical and perhaps a little unstable and emotional in his approach ... Mrs McMillan is a very pleasant person and I feel brings a great deal of stability to the Justice for Juveniles organisation.[70]

As for the proposal itself, the Director was in favour of the Government Departments concerned cleaning up their own acts:

> The recurrent funding is a lot of money for something which might be cured intra-system, that is, if the police behaved themselves better and if the courts were conducted better. The latter, at least, is envisaged in the new Family Welfare Legislation.[71] Perhaps the major point is the real wisdom of children being "hooked in" to the formalities of an adversary system, including the pre-formalities.[72]

Did the Director wish to keep the young people of Queensland, especially the children under his guardianship, ignorant of their rights? Such ignorance would leave them powerless in an adversarial system which often dealt with them harshly, inhumanly and unjustly.

69 Figures kindly supplied by the Department of Children's Services for the year 1979-1980.
70 Brief for the Honourable the Minister re: Deputation from the Justice for Juveniles Group to be received at 3pm on 5 March 1981, p 1.
71 Since the legislation was enacted in November 1993, twelve years later, the Department was apparently in no hurry to bring about much needed reforms. The Lucas Inquiry recommendations into police practices had been shelved, so there was little or no chance of the police "behaving themselves." The reform of the Queensland Police had to wait until the late eighties for the recommendations of the Fitzgerald Inquiry.
72 Ibid., p 3.

In a section titled "Opinion", the Director made the following remarks:

There is no doubt that children and young people are confused by police and court procedures. There is also little doubt that police do not adhere to appropriate practices in questioning juveniles. There is evidence cited in the submission and there have been an ample number of cases rejected to demonstrate this point.

As far as courts are concerned, one only has to attend the Children's Court to be impressed by how little children understand of the proceedings and therefore the eventual contempt which must be generated to the so-called "process of justice" …

The question must be asked—what will come from a child knowing in detail his rights? For example, the right to refuse to answer questions. Surely it is better for there to be some informal arrangement between departments than to set up an elaborate mechanism which will complicate rather than simplify the juvenile justice system."[73]

What is the point in anybody having rights if they do not know them? And what is the point in anybody knowing their rights if they are unable to exercise them?

The Director voiced his strong criticism of our proposal:

I see this proposal as a reaction to the very obvious wrongs in our existing system, but one which, if it comes into effect, will cause more wrongs than presently exist."[74]

Obviously we could not have expected any assistance from this quarter. In fact, in his concluding paragraph he said as much:

My recommendation is that the deputation be heard and that an indication be given that the submission will be studied in detail, *[which of course had already occurred]* but no commitment or support be provided."[75]

The Minister was unable to see us on 5 March. However we did have an interview with the Director who subsequently wrote of this meeting to the Minister. He began by stating that "the views that I expressed in that brief about the proposal are unchanged."[76] In other respects his views were even more strongly expressed, particularly about the police and the courts:

73 Ibid., p 3 and 4.
74 Ibid., p 4.
75 Ibid., p 4.
76 Brief for the Honourable the Minister undated and unsigned, p 1.

My personal view is -

(a) That the Police do abuse their powers in the questioning of children, but it would be better if there was some modification of this abuse within the system rather than children being instructed in their legal rights...

(b) The Children's Court as it presently exists and I should make it clear that this implies no criticism of the Magistrate, is a charade. Proceedings are very often over before a child knows that they have begun, but I can't see how every case being defended can improve this system.

Mrs. McMillan in her comments has said that she would behave reasonably, but Mrs. McMillan is a very moderate and reasonable lady, other Youth Advocates may not behave in this way.[77]

The Department knew that children were being abused by police when they were being questioned. I would have thought they had the duty, in justice, to do something substantial about this abuse of power rather than wistfully hope for "some modification of this abuse within the system." It is dumbfounding that a Department charged with discharging its function that "the best interests of the child shall be paramount" would prefer that children not be instructed in their legal rights. The point made above in (b) by the Director that "I can't see how every case being defended can improve this system" is astounding. Defence in legal proceedings is a fundamental right in our system of law.

The Director's final recommendation was bland:

May I suggest that you indicate your interest in the proposal and say that you will refer it to the Attorney-General for his comments as far as the legal profession is concerned.[78]

We ploughed on, still hopeful of funding. We took every opportunity to give talks to groups and clubs.

In every public address I gave, I was asked why children needed legal representation. If there was a policeman in the audience, he would confront me with his view that we were encouraging young people to be dishonest. My response was that if he disagreed with the few legal rights young people had, then there were ways and means to work towards changing them. However, while they existed, young people ought to know their rights and be able to exercise them. I would add that when policemen are questioned in relation to alleged offences, they almost always exercised their rights—especially the right to silence.

77 Ibid., p 2.
78 Ibid., p 3.

We believed that young people needed legal representation because of their immaturity, because current legislation provided for the legal representation of children, and because the process of the Children's Courts was adversarial—requiring legal representation to balance the prosecution. Children, and especially disadvantaged children, needed somebody with knowledge of the law to be readily available to help protect their rights. Many children and young people felt that the court had the power of life and death over them. They felt that the court could "put them away" and that frightened them. They were going into a totally unknown situation with a whole lot of adults, not knowing who those adults were, nor what was going on. As I have already noted, the situation regarding the lack of legal representation of children in some of the suburban Children's Courts in and around Brisbane was a scandal.

Opening the Centre

Finally, in April 1981 the Queensland Legal Aid Commission decided to fund the Youth Advocacy Centre by providing the services of a solicitor on secondment, by funding a clerk typist and receptionist, and by funding rental money and providing some furniture. Mr David Hook, a senior member of the Legal Aid staff, was our seconded solicitor initially, replaced by Anne McMillan after two months.

The Centre opened its doors in the Hibernian Building in Queen Street, Brisbane, on the 9th June 1981. Gwenn Murray was our administrative assistant. I did the coordinating work as well as some counselling. We were fortunate to have the voluntary services of a social worker for two days each week.

Soon after the Legal Aid Office had indicated that they would fund us so that we could begin operations, I met with the Archbishop to give him an update and to point out what still needed to be done. I had intended to ask his permission to work at the Youth Advocacy Centre, at least on a part-time basis. When I had finished my briefing, he said:

"It looks as though you will have your work cut out for you in that Centre."

"I was about to request your permission to work there," I said.

"You certainly have it."

I was overjoyed. Certainly an extra pair of hands would prove helpful during the early stages. I assured the Archbishop I would be seeking funding for any position I occupied, so that I could leave the Centre and move on to other duties.

Some months later, the Honourable, Mr Terry White MLA, Minister for Children's Services, officially opened the Centre. Also present were Archbishop Rush; Mr Viv Gillingwater, the Children's Court Magistrate; Mrs Elaine Darling, Federal MP and Member for Lilly, who had tabled our proposal in Federal Parliament earlier that year; Sir John Rowell, chairperson of the Legal Aid Commission; the Public Defender, Mr R. Plummer, Director of Children's

Services; Mr Merv Fagg, Queensland Director of Social Security, whom I had first met when I was working in the parish of Yeronga; Sister Kath Bourke, Congregational Leader of the Sisters of Mercy; Professor Edna Chamberlain, Head of the Social Work Department of the University of Queensland; and Mr Barber and Ms Quentin Bryce of the Law Faculty of the University of Queensland.

In my welcoming speech, I told those present that the Youth Advocacy Centre had evolved from the many needs of young people at risk and from the experience and research conducted over many years by the Justice for Juveniles Group. "Basically," I said, "as we see it, too many young people are needlessly penetrating too far into the juvenile justice system and into secure care. We feel that more needs to be done in preventative areas."

When our doors opened, young people began to trickle in. Rather than sit around and wait for the word to spread, we produced brochures about our services and small cards which young people could carry in the pockets of their jeans. With the assistance of some young people who had been in Wilson, we produced an eye-catching poster and put it up in many prominent places around Brisbane where young people gathered, as well as in the offices of youth services.

To assist the maximum number of young people in need of help, David Hook began acting as duty solicitor at the Children's Courts at Holland Park and Beenleigh. By August 1981, he, and later on, Anne McMillan, had arranged a system of duty solicitors to be available at Wynnum and Cleveland.[79]

79 *Courier-Mail*, 4 August 1981.

The Youth Advocacy Centre under way

O NCE WE were up and running at the Centre, we worked to find funding for a full-time social worker. The legal problems of young people were often symptoms of their underlying problems (family dysfunction, health, education, accommodation). Therefore if the Centre was to respond to these young people's needs in any sort of appropriate manner, it was essential we have a full-time social worker.

On 15th December 1981 the Centre received advice from the Minister for Welfare Services that approval had been given for the employment of a social worker. Our first full-time social worker was Jenny Felton. Jenny commenced work with us at the end of February 1982.

David Hook and then Anne McMillan began negotiations with the Department of Children's Services to allow the Centre to access children and young people being held on remand in Wilson Youth Hospital and Westbrook Training Centre near Toowoomba. These negotiations were successful, and Anne commenced visiting these centres regularly early in 1982.

During the negotiations, I remember travelling with David to Westbrook. To say that we were warmly welcomed is an understatement. We were shown through the institution, introduced to staff as well as inmates and allowed to speak to whomever we wished. All our questions were answered with refreshing frankness. In fact, David was asked if he would, there and then, look at a boy's file and if he thought it appropriate meet with the boy. The superintendent and his assistant were concerned about the lad because he was slightly intellectually disabled, and because he had been continually remanded into Westbrook on a monthly basis (mainly due, they said, to the efforts of a senior policeman who had taken a strong dislike to the boy). The lad had been attending a sheltered workshop in Toowoomba, where the people in charge were willing to have him back as he caused few, if any, problems. However, because of the trouble with the police, his foster family were unwilling to have him live with them any longer.

David began work on the legal side, while I moved to have him placed in suitable accommodation. As a result of the interventions of the Centre, the lad returned to his community within the next month. As a result of this visit, arrangements were made for the YAC solicitor to visit young people on remand in Westbrook every month.

Twelve months later the Department of Children's Services reviewed YAC's service to Westbrook and Wilson; they stated that it had provided "a high quality of service."[80] Furthermore Mr Trevor Carlyon, the Acting Superintendent, Westbrook Training Centre, reported that Mrs McMillan "has provided an excellent service to the boys on remand as well as supplying information on solicitor/client relationships, rights during questioning and court procedures."[81] Mr John Bull from Wilson Youth Hospital said that there were no problems with the practice of the Duty Lawyer providing a service to children who were on remand in Wilson.[82]

The children and young people who were incarcerated in institutions were alienated from society and possessed few rights. I knew from my chaplaincy at Wilson Youth Hospital, how positively they responded to another human being who treated them with respect. I also knew how mystified they were by the legal system—how much it confused many of them. I also knew many were wrongfully held on remand, and that remand was often used, especially for girls, as an accommodation facility (the justification being that the young woman needed a psychiatric assessment).

The child care officers from the Department had no alternative accommodation available, or did not know how to access it. As a result, their young charges would be popped into Wilson for up to six weeks for an unnecessary assessment. But with Anne McMillan attending these institutions regularly, I knew that the young people were meeting a warm-hearted human being, a committed and competent lawyer, and a person passionately committed to justice—with the courage to match that dedication.

The first twelve months[83]

The first twelve months were heady days for the Youth Advocacy Centre; setting up a new agency and attending to all the organisational responsibilities. We brought together a Management Committee, drafted a constitution and obtained tax-deductible status. We drafted and printed a suitable card for young people, briefly explaining our services, and explaining in detail the rights of a young person when they were apprehended by the police. I remember one young person coming in and requesting two cards. When I asked him, "why two cards?" he responded: "One for me to keep and the other for the cops to rip up."

80 Miss B. J. Flynn, Residential Care and Court Services, to Acting Assistant Director, Specialist Services re: Duty Lawyer Service to Wilson Youth Hospital and Westbrook Training Centre, dated 4 January 1983, p 2.
81 Ibid., p 1.
82 Ibid.
83 In this section I have drawn from the Chairman's Report, First Annual General Meeting of the Youth Advocacy Centre, 8 September 1982.

We also designed an attractive brochure and eye-catching poster to advertise our Centre and its services. We made submissions to the Director, Department of Children's Services, regarding the development of educational facilities and positive educational opportunities for children in Wilson Youth Hospital and Westbrook Training Centre, and we prepared a detailed submission on the Parliamentary White Paper on the Proposed Family Welfare Legislation.

During this same period we ran several innovative projects. As well as distributing 14,000 cards outlining our services and young people's legal rights, we disseminated 10,000 brochures explaining the procedures, personnel and dispositions of the Children's Court. We set up legal education programs for youth workers, and the Youth Advocacy Solicitor attended as Duty Solicitor at Brisbane suburban Children's Courts.

The brochure on the Children's Court was produced by the Centre, with the assistance of an artist, Peter Fogliani. Most children did not understand who the people were in court and what their functions were, or the determinations of the court. The Commission of Inquiry into The Nature and Extent of the Problems confronting Youth in Queensland under Judge A.G. Demack (1977) recommended that printed information about the procedures of the Children's Court, the right of trial by jury, and the procedures that follow after the court appearance, be prepared by Officers of the Department of Education and the Department of Children's Services, in consultation with the Children's Court Magistrate, for distribution to the parents and children who attend the Children's Court. As little had been done (and as we perceived it to be important) we went ahead with printing and distributing thousands of these brochures to all the Children's Courts and police stations throughout Queensland.

A number of people generously provided many services on a voluntary basis. They collated our resources, did our book-keeping, did the artwork for our posters and brochures, provided our printing free of charge and assisted us with general office work. In that first year of operation, 19 households offered to accommodate young people needing emergency, short or long-term accommodation.

One of the important initiatives we undertook soon after we opened was to set up a Young People's Advisory Group. From as early as 1981, a young person who had been in Wilson was on the Steering Committee and then on the Management Committee. She made important contributions to the fledging Youth Advocacy Centre. We decided to set up an advisory group of young people who had been in contact with the juvenile justice system. Most of our meetings were held in one of their flats, and we supplied the group with information.

Almost from the first meeting, the young people set their own agenda and the group took on a life of its own. At the very first meeting, because some of the participants did not know each other, we had a getting-to-know-you session. At once the members realised that they had all been in Wilson. One of the youngest members had recently been released from Wilson and spoke of the sexual harassment she had experienced there. The others listened to her and believed her—and she, in turn, felt she was understood. The others related similar damaging experiences. They were concerned about the plight of young people still in Wilson, subject to the same predators. "What can we do to stop this?" they asked.

I was keen to put time and effort into this advisory group, as I knew from experience that those who had experienced the juvenile justice system would have a lot to contribute. Some of these young people did offer to do voluntary work at the Centre, but sometimes there were difficulties associated with this. For example, some of them were in great need, bouncing along from crisis to crisis, and when they came in to do some work their own problems had to be addressed. Also, it was not always easy to combine paid workers and volunteers.

Conflict with the authorities

The first major drama at YAC occurred towards the end of 1982 when the Director of Legal Aid announced he was recalling Anne McMillan to his office and replacing her with another member of his staff. The announcement really threw the cat amongst the pigeons. Anne did not wish to return to the Legal Aid Office. She had completed her legal training specifically to work in the children's jurisdiction. In meetings with the Director he informed us that it was his policy to rotate his lawyers so that they could gain experience in different aspects of the law—and as Anne and I had worked together as a team he wanted to see if the Youth Advocacy Centre could survive without Anne. We tried to negotiate with him, but he was adamant.

As a result, the Management Committee decided to employ Anne. This meant that we had to fund the position—no easy task. Anne unselfishly indicated that she did not need to be salaried to the extent she had been as an employee of the Legal Aid Office.

The second drama followed hot on the heels of the first. In September 1981 I was interviewed by a journalist from People magazine about the Youth Advocacy Centre and, later on in the interview, about Wilson Youth Hospital. The journalist also interviewed the Minister for Children's Services, and was able to have a conducted tour of Wilson. As could be expected, the published article was a damning indictment of Wilson as well as of the juvenile justice system in Queensland. The article was published under the provocative title: "They call this a hospital—Like Hell! It's really a prison...for children."

The repercussions were considerable. The Minister had some uncomplimentary words to say about me in Parliament[84]. He was kind enough to send

---

84   See *Hansard* 14 October, 1981, p 2584.

me a copy of his remarks with a note saying that we would work better together if I did not publicly criticise his Department.

I was given a stern reprimand at our first Advisory Committee Meeting by its Chairperson, Sir John Rowell. Sir John stated forcefully that, in his opinion, the recent publicity had been detrimental to the Youth Advocacy Centre, that he himself had been personally castigated by the Ministers for Justice and Welfare, and that any further such media coverage would irrevocably alienate both himself and possibly the other members of the Advisory Committee. He suggested that the Youth Advocacy Centre work for change within the system and exercise extreme care with media contacts. Anne McMillan's comment after the meeting (which she had also attended) was that Sir John had "admonished and discharged" me!

We knew that if we wanted to do a good job at the Youth Advocacy Centre, standing up for young people and their few rights meant that we would come into conflict with the authorities. It was a tension we knew we would have to live with.

The after hours service

After we had established the social work position at Youth Advocacy, I was keen to set up an after-hours service regarding the questioning of young people by police. I had heard too many stories from young people about what happened to them in police stations, and I had witnessed a few situations myself. Mostly this questioning took place in a police station, without the young person having their rights explained to them and without the presence of a parent, guardian or independent adult. As a result, the young person was often severely disadvantaged in law, namely by making and signing a confession. In *R v. C*, Judge McNamara stated:

> It is quite clear from the authorities .... and from other matters that the interrogation of young people must be dealt with quite differently from the interrogation of adults who are not under any disability.[85]

In a number of cases, judges had pointed out that whether or not any allegations of impropriety had been made against the police officers concerned, the circumstances of the interview itself between a police officer and a child in the absence of a parent or other person present on that child's behalf, could cause "the child to be overborne by the situation." The courts had therefore been concerned to ensure there was a balance between the parties during the interview. As Judge McNamara said in the case of *R v. C:*

> It seems to me that in a situation such as this, the position between the parties—that is the interrogator and the person being interrogated—should be as equally balanced as can be reasonably possible in the circumstances...[86]

As a result, following the Report of the Committee of Inquiry into the Enforcement of Criminal Law in Queensland (the Lucas Inquiry of 1977), the Queensland Police Commissioner issued a general instruction in these terms:

> ### Questioning of children, Aborigines, Torres Strait Islanders by Police:
>
> When a child or Aborigine or Torres Strait Islander is being questioned by a member of the police force about his implication in an offence for which he may be apprehended or detained in custody, the member of

85   Unreported District Court at Brisbane, 31 July 1979.
86   Ibid..

the force interrogating the child or other person will question any one of them in the presence of, in the case of a child, the parents or guardians of that child or in the absence of the parents or guardian, an adult person nominated by him or them or if not nominated, an independent adult person, preferably of the same sex as the child.

In law, an independent person being present meant an independent and responsible person. The fact that the person was an adult did not of itself qualify him or her to fulfil the role adequately. Further, the directive was intended not only for the protection of young suspects but also, just as importantly, for the protection of the police officer. If the Commissioner's directive was followed, then no word of criticism could properly be levelled at the form of the investigation.

Finally, under our system of law, a suspect's right to silence is still paramount and dominant. Unless and until some authority, be it legislative or judicial, says that the right to silence is no longer a dominant and paramount principle of our criminal justice system, then courts must respect that right and give effect to it. An adult can be presumed to understand his or her right; a child cannot necessarily be presumed to understand his or her right. It is therefore for others to explain it to him or her, and to support that child in the choice that they make to exercise the right to silence.

Initially we had tried to set up a fully-funded after hours service of three or four trained field officers who would be available for police questioning of young people in the Brisbane, Redcliffe, Wynnum-Manly and Ipswich areas. However, the exercise would have been costly, and nobody was prepared to back it with hard dollars. I decided to investigate the possibility of setting it up with rostered volunteer lawyers. I knew it would be vital to use the services of lawyers, because if police respected anyone, it was lawyers.

I talked this over with a lawyer friend of mine, Terry O'Gorman. He agreed it would be best to use lawyers: however he did not think it would be possible to find enough volunteer lawyers. Fourteen, he told me, would be a necessary minimum number for a roster. I told him I could get seven, and challenged him to find seven. We agreed to meet in two weeks' time. We had, as it turned out, little trouble in finding 14 lawyers—so we decided to try for 30. Many lawyers from the Public Defender's Office and the Legal Aid Commission expressed interest. We conducted two lunchtime training sessions and another after work, to familiarise them with what we wanted the project to achieve, their part in it, and the manual we had produced for them.

On 17th January 1983, the after hours service began operation. 43 volunteer lawyers were on its first roster. It is a tribute to the legal profession that so many of its members made themselves available.

Some saw this new project as radical. However, young people were vulnerable in police interviews. I knew of many who had suffered in these situations.

The Lucas Inquiry had recommended such a service; even the Police Commissioner had issued a special directive about the vulnerability of young people. We were not doing anything radical. We were meeting a publicly-acknowledged need. The young people we dealt with knew the law could work against them. They also needed to realise they had a few rights which they should be able to exercise—and that the law could work for them. Many of these young people had no parent or guardian to be with them in these situations.

Preventing homelessness

I was constantly on the look-out for suitable accommodation for young people. I considered stable and secure accommodation to be a basic right of all people, especially vulnerable young people. The following stories indicate the type of requests YAC was receiving. The names are fictitious, but the stories and the needs are not:

"My name is Barry. I am 13 years old. I attend a High School on the south side of Brisbane. I need accommodation with a family who will provide the care and nurturing I have missed out on. I know that the Department of Children's Services will provide some assistance to you by way of allowance and support.

"I am 16 years old and my name is Mary-Anne. I attend High School also. Due to circumstances beyond my control, I cannot live at home any longer. I need to live with a family until I complete Year 12. I have a part-time job and I would be willing to make a contribution towards board and lodging."

"I am coming to Brisbane to undertake a six month course and I would like to be with a family. I am 16 years old and I've never been away from home before."

"I'm only 13 years old and my name is Joe. I need to stay with a family for three weeks only, while an assessment is done on me and my family by a social worker. They told me that I'd have to go to a 'home' if a family couldn't be found to take me. I don't want to live in a 'home', not even for three weeks."

I had never been homeless. I knew something about homelessness from listening to, living and working with homeless young people; it was always better to get young homeless people to speak for themselves as much as possible. The following poem was unsolicited. 'Diane' wrote it when she was staying temporarily with us at the presbytery at West End. She readily consented to my using it:

A LETTER TO GOD

Dear God, I want to go home
To some parents who care
About why I'm alone,
By asking for this, do you think I'm unfair?

You, dear God, had a mother and a father,
Even though you still suffered a lot of pain,
And I'm sure for you it was harder
but for you there were things to gain.

God, you worked miracles on the sick and the lame,
Can't you work one, and give me parents and a home?
Why do you let us kids go through this pain?
God, the ways in which you work are strange.

You just sit up there and watch all of this,
When I know damn well you could prevent it
Stop kids hurt and pain and bitterness,
Because I'm telling you being alone is the pits.

God, my mind feels like it's exploded,
My brain by far is well overloaded.
Can't you feel the fears I'm feeling today?
Don't you understand what I'm trying to say?

This whole damn world is full of frustration,
I'm at the point of self-destruction,
God, here I go telling you again,
Knowing you'll put me on the mend.[87]

Even before I had been freed from doing the administrative work at the Youth Advocacy Centre, I began doing community development work aimed at sensitising local communities to the needs of homeless youth in their areas. A further aim was to assist local communities to work with these young people and their families to prevent homelessness. The work was exciting, creative and innovative.

In 1975 I met 'Morris' and 'Johnno' in Wilson Youth Hospital. They came from the Wynnum-Manly area on Moreton Bay to the east of Brisbane. Morris was eleven years old and his brother nine. Both were illiterate. Both had been placed in Wilson for not attending school. Their parents were separated. Whenever the boys ran away from Wilson (and they often did), they would return to Wynnum and would be found by the police somewhere near the water. They told me that they liked water and boats and fishing, and sometimes their dad would take them fishing.

I met Johnno again in 1981 in Woodford Prison. He was still illiterate and homeless, and he was locked up for 18 months for driving without a licence. He had been involved in an accident—not his fault, he told me—and the driver in the other car had been killed.

---

87 'Diane', 16 years. 7/10/1982.

These two boys needed and wanted to be in a family; they wanted to live in their local community among familiar people and surrounds. Why was the local community not responsible for Morris and Johnno, and others like them?

The impetus for doing some community work in the Wynnum area came initially from the Wynnum Catholic Youth Group. They were concerned about youth homelessness, and wanted me to speak to them on the work I had done and was presently involved in. I told the contact person that, while I would be prepared to do as they requested, I also wanted to speak to them about the homeless young people in their area. I suggested it should also be a public meeting, advertised locally. They agreed.

At the Sunday night meeting in October 1982, there were 70 people present. I had some knowledge of the area. I knew that Wynnum people identified as a community; that they did not regard themselves as part of Brisbane; that they had pride in their local area (which had been boosted by their team winning the premiership of the Brisbane Rugby League just prior to the meeting); that one of the local service clubs had produced a resource book about the local agencies in the area; and that there had been several local meetings in the previous twelve months on the topic of youth homelessness. I had also found out that approximately two young people per month were being accommodated somewhere in Brisbane, or locked up in Wilson Youth Hospital, because there was nowhere suitable for them to stay in the Wynnum-Manly area.

I presented the meeting with the facts, and then suggested there could be several responses to the situation in their community. One was a boarding program which could cater for the two young people per month who were being sent away from the local community. During the following week, I spoke at the local religious Ministers' Fraternal meeting. They passed a motion that they would bring the matter to the attention of their congregations, and try to recruit two families each.

After more meetings and publicity, the local Catholic Youth group and myself arranged an information evening. The group called itself initially 'The Wynnum Community Ecumenical Boarding Group'. At this meeting a Departmental social worker spoke of the need, I explained the proposed model, two foster parents spoke of fostering, and two teenagers who had been fostered on a number of occasions talked of their experiences. I was particularly keen to have the involvement of foster-parents, as well as young people who had been fostered. Young people have a lot to contribute, but often their reflections are not sought. Twenty-one local people, including representatives from ten interested households, attended this meeting in February 1983.

We based the model on local community people volunteering to board local adolescents for a maximum of three months, while intensive work was carried out with the young people and their families with a view to the young people returning home. The households were trained, assessed, supported by local professionals, and formed into a group with its own structure. The house-holds were paid a fee of $74 per week; the children were aged from 12 to 17; there were written contracts for all interested parties about the objectives of the placements; the young people were expected to stay for varying lengths of time, depending on the individual agreements (but no longer than three months); the households were expected to attend training sessions and sup-port group meetings; and the group had built-in "baby-sitters" for emergencies arising from within the group.

After this night, six to eight households committed themselves to eight hours' training, held over one weekend. Soon after the training, the group made a commitment to the program for twelve months.

A few months after the group began boarding young people, I remember receiving a phone call at Youth Advocacy late one Monday morning, to be accosted by the coordinator of the group demanding where I had been over the weekend and why I had not answered my phone. (I had been supplying Masses that weekend on Stradbroke Island). On inquiring what had happened, she told me this story. On Sunday afternoon two young girls were riding horses on a back road in Wynnum West. One was in the boarding program, the other was a daughter of the boarding family. A police car came along, and the police thought one of the riders was a person they wanted to question. They put on their siren, the horses bolted, and one of the girls ended up under the police car. Fortunately she was only bruised and scratched, not seriously injured.

The boarding parent phoned the coordinator and, after seeing to the girls, marched up to the police station with another boarding parent and demanded to see the police person in charge. After explaining who they were, they insisted that the police involved be called to account for their actions. The next morning they again fronted at the police station and demanded to see the Inspector-in-Charge.

Local citizens were demanding accountability and standards of behaviour from their local public servants. "We, the local community, are trying to raise our young people to be responsible. We demand that your officers conduct themselves in a responsible manner also."

I was proud of them—I was not needed at all. They had handled the situa-tion perfectly. I committed myself to work closely with them for the first twelve months, passing onto them the skills I had gained.

The first coordinator of the group, which decided to call itself Bayside Adolescent Boarding Incorporated (BABI), was an experienced foster-par-ent, Marie Stokes. Under her leadership, guidance and dynamism, the group flourished.

At the end of its first year the group conducted a major review of its pro-cedures, including the needs it had discovered and the ways in which the local community could meet these needs. The group liked living in the local area, loved the people and enjoyed the tasks they had undertaken together. They owned the program and had the power to shape its future direction.

In 1988 BABI presented oral and written evidence to the Human Rights and Equal Opportunity Commission Inquiry into the situation of Homeless Children and Young People. The Commission, of which I had been appointed a member, spent a morning at the offices of BABI where they spoke with young people who had been boarded, the coordinator, boarding parents, and parents of children who had been in a boarding household. The Commission was so impressed by this program that it commissioned a research report to be carried out on community preventive programs for homeless young people.

Despite the lack of government funding, similar programs were established in other suburbs of Brisbane. One, at Carina in Brisbane, was set up for young people held in Wilson on remand for status offences or for minor criminal offences. Instead of having to stay in Wilson, young people could live in a household in the community while awaiting their appearance in court.

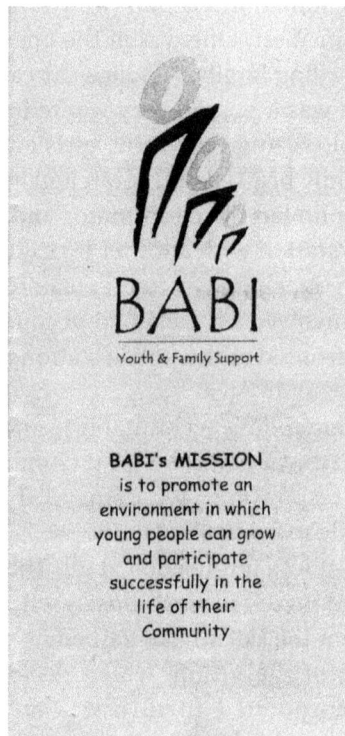

BABI
Youth & Family Support

BABI's MISSION
is to promote an
environment in which
young people can grow
and participate
successfully in the
life of their
Community

Renewing the face of the Church[88]

T HE VISION and mission of Jesus is something I have been intent on discovering since shortly after my ordination. Having discerned something of this vision and mission, I have wanted to develop my understanding of it and participate in its dynamism. The vision and mission of the Church needs to follow hand in hand with the vision and mission of Jesus. From an early stage in my priesthood—in fact, right back to when I was in my first parish—I struggled to understand even the need for vision and mission. Why the need for vision? The Church or the parish priest told us what our vision should be or, to be more truthful, took it for granted that they and I knew what we were supposed to be on about.

As for mission, that was pretty simple: visit all the members of the parish, make sure they were baptised, confirmed and attended Mass and the sacraments regularly and, of course, contributed to the weekly collections and sent their children to the Catholic schools. However, I never found this understanding of mission satisfying or satisfactory. Surely mission meant more than that, but what it did mean, I didn't know.

Then Vatican II came along with its documents on the Church in the Modern World, on the Laity and on the Church. To understand Vatican II more fully and deeply, I attended classes at Banyo Seminary. Living with disadvantaged young people, and working on the oppressive issues that burdened them, grounded and deepened my understanding of the vision and mission of Jesus and consequently of the Church.

Soon I came to the conclusion that the Church would only be renewed by mission, and not merely by maintenance. It seemed to me that the Brisbane Church was intent on renewing itself by maintenance only, and that this approach was a road leading nowhere.

I attended gatherings for priests, including deanery meetings. When given the opportunity, I would tell those present something of what I was discovering on the edge of Church and society. I tried to prompt some action on these discoveries by making recommendations, but sometimes I was not even able to obtain the support of a seconder to the motion.

88 The material for this chapter largely comes from notes and reports made available to the Council of Priests

Things changed in the early to mid-nineties when Michael Fallon was appointed as Coordinator of the office of Continuing Education of Priests. Michael was a fellow-priest from the Archdiocese of Brisbane, whom I knew a little. I knew he believed and practised many of the things I held dear.

Soon after being appointed, Michael convened an overnight meeting of invited priests at Manly, a bayside suburb on the eastern side of Brisbane. I was one of the invitees. Tentatively I attended, curious as to what I would be experiencing.

Michael was not slow to ask us hard questions, which I warmed to, and was challenged by, at the same time. The aim of the session was to reflect on the dimensions of the priesthood where we as individuals were active, to share this with one another, and at the end of the meetings to indicate to Michael if we were prepared to be a reference and support group for him in his role as coordinator of Continuing Education for Priests. In for a dime, in for a dollar: I put my hand up, indicating I was prepared to be a member of Michael's support group.

We were certainly concerned about what was happening, and more importantly what was not happening, in the Church in the Archdiocese of Brisbane. Did we know where we were going? Did we know what we were on about? My answer to both questions was an emphatic 'No!'

Brisbane Priests: Creating the Future in Hope

We worked towards organising a time for in-service training and reflection for priests. The group consisted of Michael as our convenor, Joe McGeehan (a classmate of mine), John Fitzherbert and myself. Our title for the in-service was *Brisbane Priests: Creating the Future in Hope*. Father Gerald Arbuckle, a Marist Father, was engaged to assist in facilitating the sessions and support the attendees' learning. Gerald had written a number of books and articles on renewing the Church, including one I had read entitled *Refounding the Church: Dissent for Leadership*.[89]

Garry Everett, deputy executive director of Queensland Catholic Education, was engaged as overall chairperson for the three days. The in-service was held at Banyo Seminary in May 1995. I was hoping that as many as 50 priests might attend, but thought realistically we may only attract 20. Small is beautiful, anyway, I mused. I was amazed when 85 priests attended on the first and third days, with 103 attending on the second day.

The overall theme for the first day was *Surfacing and Identifying Issues*. The questions asked on this first day were challenging. For example, under the banner of "My experiences of Church in the Archdiocese" they were as follows:

---

89   Maryknoll, NY: Orbis Books. 1993.

I.   *What do I regard as being DEAD in the Archdiocesan Church?*

II.   *What is DYING in the Archdiocesan Church?*

III.   *What is STRUGGLING TO LIFE in the Archdiocesan Church?*

IV.   *What is ALIVE and WELL in the Archdiocesan Church?*

These questions caused some uneasiness from some, especially identifying what they regarded as dead, but also being asked to express their feelings. Some were upset about writing up the conclusions of the group on butcher paper and displaying these results publicly around the room. But the answers that emerged were wide-ranging, honest and challenging.

Just a few of the issues identified as *dead in the Archdiocesan Church* were: Vatican II—its hopes and vision; a common vision; professionalism among clergy; and devotions and sacramental practices.

Some of the answers to *what is dying in the Archdiocesan Church* included: faith practice in the marriageable group; clergy—numbers, culture and morale; simple acceptance of Church teaching; pastoral intimacy in large impersonal parishes, current model of priesthood, and Eucharistic involvement of young people.

The question *what is struggling to life in the Archdiocesan Church* produced some interesting insights, for example, facing sexual abuse; ability to handle controversial issues like divorce, homosexuality, married clergy, women's affairs; justice for ex-clergy; consciousness of Aboriginal people and their culture; collaborative ministry and hunger for scriptural-based spirituality and small Christian communities.

To the fourth question, *What is alive and well in the Archdiocesan Church*, some of the responses were: individual people living out their faith and living out their role as Church; sacramental programs; Catholic education; liturgical worship; cooperation among clergy and caring groups.

The second session was under the banner of *What are my experiences of being Pastor in the Church of the Archdiocese?*

The priests were invited to reflect on the following and/or other aspects of being pastor:

I.   *The clarity of mission to today's world in the Archdiocese*

II.   *Your sense of community, intimacy, and support with people in the Church of the Archdiocese*

III.   *Changes in emphases in your ministry as priest*

IV.   *Those aspects of your being pastor, which give you life*

Reflecting on the clarity of our mission, the priests disclosed that there appeared to be no clear, precise understanding of mission. This was borne out by the following statements:

- No community sense of mission
- No sense of vocation of the Church
- Several different ecclesiologies in existence
- No clear strategies to bring about the reign of God
- We have a mission statement (1992), but there is uncertainty about how to carry this out
- No clear prophetic voice in the Church today
- A question: are we Kingdom-centred or Church-centred? We are not clear about our mission to the world, we are merely clear on our mission to our own people
- We have a clarity of vision in a general sense (to promote the reign of God), but there is a blurring of how we do it
- There is no clear mission regarding the homeless, young people, victims of sexual abuse, usury, unemployment, peace, racism, sexism, Aboriginal apostolate, mal-development, the broken and those outside the Church
- Our focus is insular to the detriment of a wider community outlook, especially regarding matters of social justice
- Our mission at the moment caters for Mass-goers (20%); how do we respond to the other 80%?
- In the Archdiocese there is an emphasis on collaboration in ministry, but there are problems when all are not in harmony on vision, viewpoints and beliefs e.g., ecumenism, community spirituality, social (or Gospel) justice, community development
- The structures of an over-centralised Church block the energy flow of the Gospel so that the Church is preoccupied with maintenance rather than engagement in mission
- We need a common vision for mission among priests but not uniformity.

I loved the challenge of the questions and was keen to jot down a few notes and to interact with my colleagues in discussion. Most participants put energy into participating, but some were skeptical, others quite unhappy with what they were being asked to do.

The theme for Day 2 was *Leadership for Mission*. It began with an inspiring liturgy, followed by reflections on the previous day's discussions by Gerald Arbuckle.

After morning tea break we worked in our small nominated groups considering the question:

What are the implications of mission today?

a)   *For me personally?*

b)   *For the Archdiocese?*

The process in small groups was firstly to share reactions to input from Father Arbuckle's session and then develop a list of preferred options about *mission* which you believe the Bishops should consider, and record on paper. Finally, time was set aside for personal reflection: in the light of a) and b) above, what are the implications for me personally?

After lunch Father Gerry spoke to us about leadership. Later on, we moved into our small groups to discuss the topic *Implications of Leadership for Mission*. The process for this discussion was to prepare some preferred options regarding Leadership for Mission based on the group's views of the implications from Gerry's input for Leadership:

a)   At the parish level

b)   At the Archdiocesan level.

Individuals and groups expressed the following convictions:

- That within the context of the local Church (Archdiocese) there is a need to clarify our mission. Several groups recommended calling on the resources of those skilled in areas such as inculturation, Australian anthropology and community development to assist in this work.

- There is a pressing need for us to get together to clarify what relationship there should be between the *real* world and what Christ is calling us to. We, the Church, need to find our prophetic voice: to announce those good things in our society which promote the reign of God, and to denounce those things which are obstacles to the reign of God. We need to be game enough to look at and respond to the *real* issues: are we Kingdom-centred or Church-centred?

- Under the title of *Implications of leadership for mission*: that the presbyterate of the Archdiocese of Brisbane get together to tap into its own expertise in order to identify the challenges (signs of the times), pastoral strategies and structures. The presbyterate should exercise corporate leadership.

- That the bishops gather the presbyterate together for conversion from 'the maverick' to collaboration, from the spirituality of individualism to the spirituality of collaboration.

- That the presbyterate search together for a message of hope for our mission to the poor. This needs to be done not only personally but corporately, realising that out of our unity of purpose we can act in our different ways.

- We want the Bishops to critique the institutions of the Church, especially those to which it gives pride of place, i.e. Catholic schools.

The theme for the third and final day was *Mission in Action*. However, Gerry, aided by Garry our chairperson/facilitator, had a huge challenge and surprise for us. At the first session of that final day they asked us to consider and vote on the following hypothesis:

In this group neither the vision nor the mission is clear for the Archdiocese. Therefore, without clarity of vision, there is no operative force energising this group for mission (i.e. strategising) and action.

Just articulating such an hypothesis was like throwing a cat amongst pigeons. Arguments were passionately put forward as to why this hypothesis should not be discussed. However, sanity prevailed and we moved into new groups to discuss and vote.

While there was not complete unanimity, there was overwhelming agreement with the above hypothesis. In fact nine out of the ten groups agreed with it.

In the last session of the in-service, the participants considered how vision and mission could be clarified. We broke into new groups and spent time discussing the following:

a) Discuss those factors and their interactions, which cause the lack of clarity about vision and mission and then implementation for this group of priests.

b) Brainstorm suggestions as to how this lack of clarity can be overcome, and the implementation of mission and vision be improved.

c) Develop, to share in a whole group forum, an overview of a process whereby during this year, the priests can make considerable progress towards clarifying the vision and mission and implementing them effectively.

Among the proposals put forward were:

- A three-tiered assembly of presbyterate, lay people and religious with a time line. This proposal surfaced in more than one group.
- Regular meetings of all the priests.
- Ecumenical-style dialogue to discuss the differing ecclesiologies in the presbyterate.

After this final heady and energising session, the organising group including Gerry and Garry met with the Archbishop in a private session. Each of us put forward our reflections on the three-day gathering. I told the group that the priests had been formally invited to look at the chaos in their work and in the Church, and they had responded honestly. They, I felt, were almost compelled to own this chaos, which mostly they did. They had been given some frameworks to make sense of this. I concluded by saying that the leadership and authority of the Archbishop was needed to make certain what had happened over the past three days was not side-tracked, captured or destroyed.

The Archbishop told the group he was disappointed more of the deans were not present. He felt the in-service finished on a good note. However, further action would have be endorsed by the Council of Priests; all but one member of its executive had not attended.

Sometime later, Michael Fallon presented a full report on the in-service to the Council of Priests. All members of its executive, except the one who had attended, spoke strongly against the in-service, its conclusions and recommendations. They were supported by one of the auxiliary bishops who was present at the in-service. They said the process was flawed. The Archbishop said nothing. No further follow-up action was taken.

Again I felt as I did many years previously, that if a body like the Council of Priests can ignore recommendations from a majority of its members, then it has successfully passed a motion of no confidence in itself.

Another moment of grace had been ignored. Another golden opportunity for renewal of the Church in the Archdiocese of Brisbane had been rejected.

Special studies

Later that same year, 1995, Michael was asked by the Council of Priests to submit to them suggestions on special studies for priests in the Archdiocese of Brisbane. He was not asked to consider the needs of the seminary nor the need of special ministries in the Archdiocese as other forums were responsible for such matters. Michael convened a group of twelve interested priests including myself. The group met for one full day only.

Our starting point or context was the gathering of priests the previous May, *Brisbane Priests: Creating the Future in Hope*, and the hypothesis regarding the lack of commitment to a common vision and mission which made strategising almost impossible, agreed upon by the majority of priests. The group began its work by also considering the following expressed convictions from the May in-service: the need to clarify our mission using the resources of those skilled in the areas of inculturation, Australian anthropology and community development; the need to find our prophetic voice; a need to identify the challenges (signs of the times), pastoral strategies and structures and exercise corporate ministry; the need for conversion from the maverick to collaboration, and from the spirituality of individualism to the spirituality of collaboration; the need to search together for a message of hope for our mission to the poor; and finally the need for bishops to critique the institutions of the Church, especially those to which it gives pride of place.

We also considered the Archbishop's vision of "spirituality, ecumenism and social justice" and the changing role of the pastor, following on from changes in the Church and society.

We concluded that the selection of special studies should take into account the following pastoral perspectives:

- We should name and spell out the principles we work out of, the competencies we ought to acquire and the specific training necessary for presbyteral leadership in the Church today;

- We need to be trained as community animators to bring people to life again;

- We need assistance to work towards the formation of small Christian communities;

- We need to acquire special skills in the management of human resources, preaching, leadership in prayer, personal and small group reflection and insights and expertise in the way we should use our power;

- We need a robust diocesan spirituality;

- We see the need for the asceticism of action and intentional reflection, and for a way of learning how to do this; we need help to be contemplatives in action – to contemplatively read the signs of the times and decide together on a Christian response;

- We need procedures and structures in the diocese which offer pastoral care to the pastors;

- We note two major and diverse systems in the Archdiocese, namely, the institution of Catholic Schools and the institution of the Parishes, noting that in our experience these systems were often in conflict and often indifferent to each other.

The group identified another special area of concern, namely that of sexual abuse. Sexual abuse issues were being regularly reported in the media. We asked ourselves the question: should we be gathering to examine some of the questions which arose?

The discussion identified the following needs:

- The need to integrate sexuality and celibacy and how we might deepen our understanding of ourselves as celibate sexual men;

- The need to make opportunities to tell the stories of how we are living celibate love;
- The need to take responsibility for our own lives;
- The need to promote our well-being and decide on adopting a healthier lifestyle;
- The need to formulate for ourselves as a group our own professional code of behaviour.

We noted that *The Church in the Modern World*, a document from Vatican II, presented us with the image of the Church in service to people who were poor, oppressed, dispossessed and marginalised. Again we posed the question: what needs to happen for our Church here in Brisbane to faithfully show the face of that kind of Church to society in South-Eastern Queensland? How can we learn such disciplines as structural analysis, scrutinising the signs of the times, how to co-operate with international organisations such as the United Nations, how to understand culture in the world, in the Church and even in the priesthood itself? And finally, are we allowing these issues to be addressed in the secular media only and thereby surrendering our prophetic role?

In our conclusion we noted that we were not proposing a definite list of specialised studies, but had put forward to the Council of Priests the lines of a solution towards our reclaiming presbyteral leadership at the service of the Archdiocesan Church in its mission to society. Sadly, I think this report also ended up in a big black hole.

Other comprehensive reports Michael and this group submitted to the Council of Priests and met with a similar fate were *A Resignation Package: Further Provision for those leaving the Priesthood and the Diaconate of the Archdiocese of Brisbane*, and a Clergy Car scheme especially targeting priests in country parishes. This latter scheme was promoted and adopted for all priests in the Archdiocese some years later.

St Francis Parish, West End

TOWARDS THE END OF 1983, I resigned from my position at the Youth Advocacy Centre. The Centre had been successful in obtaining funding for the two positions of Coordinator and Community Development Worker which I had held. There was a possibility of my doing some part-time voluntary work there on my return, but that would have to be discussed and decided with the Youth Advocacy Centre.

I had applied to become parish priest of West End, but the bishop decided that the parish priest should have overall pastoral responsibility for Dutton Park, West End and South Brisbane. Tongue in cheek, I told my friends that I did not possess the high standards of maturity and responsibility demanded by the Church to handle such an exalted position as parish priest, nor did I obviously possess the requisite pastoral skills.

I became Priest-in-Residence at Saint Francis Parish, West End, in October 1983. West End is an inner-city area, with people of more than 70 different nationalities living in the area. There were many flats and boarding houses, including a number of hostels for people discharged from psychiatric hospitals.

In my first three months at Saint Francis, about 30 people left the congregation. "We come to Church to hear that God loves us and to be comforted. When you are preaching you disturb us." "We are only interested in peace in our hearts, not world peace." After Mass, on one occasion, a woman in her mid-thirties confronted me: "You spoke politics from the pulpit this morning. If you continue doing this, I will not come back here." I told her I had related the Bible readings to the situation in our own community and to the poor in our nation. I added, "If you continue to come to this Church, I can assure you that you will hear more of the same." I did not see her at Church for the next six months, but she later attended regularly.

Looking back over my homilies from this time, I can see that what I was saying, while based on the readings of the Sunday, certainly contained a strong social or Gospel justice flavour. I believe if we are not alert to the social dimension of the Bible and of the Gospels in particular, then we fail to understand 90 per cent of its message.

The presbytery at West End is an old Queenslander, with verandas on three sides. Built in the early 1920s, it has three bedrooms, two offices and a large lounge-dining room. I moved into the bedroom (which had been the housekeeper's quarters) at the back of the building, away from the noise of the road. I was amazed at how comfortable the lifestyle of a priest could be—house rent-free, food, electricity, gas, telephone, newspapers, and even stationery and stamps all paid for. The downside was to be living 'above the shop', available almost 24/7. However I had been living in the 'shop' with the doors open, during my time at the Lodge.

The job also came with an amazing amount of power. There seemed to be little, if any, accountability. If I wanted to—and I did not—I could have made all sorts of decisions and done very little work and nobody, but nobody, would have called me to account. In contrast to the Lodge days, I was not required to submit an annual report. Basically all I was required to do was submit regular financial returns. The bishop did visit the parish, spoke at the Masses one weekend and met the people afterwards. He did not want to talk about how the parish was going, nor did he want to see any parish registers. His visit was not a pastoral one; it was more like showing the flag.

Neighbourhood communities

Noel McMaster, a Redemptorist priest, joined me at Saint Francis in 1984. Noel worked as a part-time industrial chaplain. Before Noel decided to move into West End, we had met on several occasions to discuss our vision, theology and methodology. Noel was keen to do some community-building, in the style of the Basic Christian Communities, in an inner-city, disadvantaged area.

In the West End parish, the Care and Concern group were run off their feet answering calls from people in need in the different areas of the parish. They were a very small group, most of them in full-time employment, and they were exhausted. They were running all over the parish ministering to people whose neighbours, Noel and I felt, should have been looking out for them. After discussing the matter with us, we suggested that they disband, which they did. In their place, Noel proposed that if someone was in need in a certain part of the parish then he would visit the households nearby, no matter what their religious affiliation, to see if they would be prepared to help.

He certainly had some successes. 'Jacob' was elderly and lived alone. He had no immediate family and he was arthritic. Meals on Wheels called on Jacob each day, Community Home Help kept his place in order. The problem was weekend meals, and some company for Jacob from time to time.

As a result of Noel's efforts, a roster was set up for people to bring a hot meal to Jacob on weekends. The sisters in the Convent and ourselves at the presbytery were backstops, should anyone on the roster be unable to meet their commitment. The system seemed to work well. Jacob was bothersome at times, prone to panic at eight o'clock on a Sunday morning about whether he would receive his midday Sunday meal. One Sunday, Jacob received three hot meals—one from the person who took him Holy Communion, one from somebody on the roster whom he had harassed and, of course, one from the person designated to bring him his meal on that day.

People soon got to know Jacob and persuaded him to exercise some patience and trust. One neighbour would drop in every morning at six o'clock, to take Jacob for a short walk up to the corner and back. Then he would get Jacob's paper and whatever he needed from the corner store. Another would make sure his bills were paid and that he had enough money on hand for incidentals.

Noel and I lived and worked well together. We shared a similar vision of the mission of Christ and the Church. We knew that the Church should be opting for the poor and for justice, and that small Christian communities were the way to go. Noel was and still is a great devotee of Juan Luis Segundo, one of the great liberation theologians from South America. He would often give me selected pages from one of Segundo's books to read, and I would enjoy and profit from the resulting discussions.

One wet afternoon, soon after he had started as an industrial chaplain, Noel came home and told me he had spent the morning visiting the cemeteries and speaking with the grave-diggers. He had arrived at Bulimba cemetery at morning tea-time in the pouring rain. The six grave-diggers welcomed him and invited him to have a cuppa. After remarks about the weather, four of them resumed their card game. Noel sat down opposite a man who was reading a book, and next to another who was staring into space. Conversation soon petered out and the three sat in silence, drinking their tea. One of the card players said to the others, "Did you hear about Bill?"

"No. What about him?"

"He was down the pub, day before yesterday, drank 23 beers in a row, keeled over and died."

The silence was broken by a card player, murmuring, "Musta 'ad a dirty glass."

Expo '88

Soon after I arrived in the parish I was invited to community meetings about the staging of World Expo '88 in the South Brisbane area, adjacent to West End. Many local people had concerns about Expo. They had done their homework and knew the effects this extravaganza would have on local housing, and especially on housing for the poor. From their research in other places in the world where Expo had been held, they knew that these giant fairs always ran at a loss. Most were not against Expo as such, but all were against Expo being held in our area. Five years before the planned event, they were doing all that they could to influence the government to use another site, rather than Southbank, as the venue.

As well as attending meetings, I spoke about the group at the Church, and displayed the literature which they had produced. I noticed that the literature was always taken, and some of the parishioners attended the meetings.

Expo '88 was, of course, another battle that was lost. Expo went ahead and was a great success, in terms of the numbers who attended—twice as many as had been estimated. It was also a great cross-cultural experience for many who attended, especially for Australians who had not had the opportunity to travel abroad. However, Expo did run at a loss, some $160 million, which meant that it was heavily subsidised by taxpayers. Moreover, as predicted, it affected the poor of the area, especially those in boarding houses, cheap flats or other rented accommodation. Housing was pulled down with no provision made for the tenants. Rents skyrocketed. People who had been paying rents of under $100 in 1984 were being asked to pay over $300 in 1987 or, if they were unable to pay, to vacate the premises.

Afterwards, the fight was on to prevent the Expo site from becoming an extension of the Brisbane central business district. Fortunately this was largely successful, as the site was given over to public places which all could access, especially those who still lived in the West End area.

Rumour also had it that the Brisbane City Council had decided to put a bridge across the river from Toowong into West End to facilitate access from the western suburbs to the city. There were several public meetings, and I was asked to chair one at which the Lord Mayor of Brisbane, and others would be speaking. Our concerns were that a major bridge into West End would overload the narrow streets of our suburb, further carve up our community, and destroy its character. We were also upset that the Council had made little or no attempt to consult the local people, despite stated policies on local community consultation. We had hoped that 50 or so people would attend, and optimistically had placed a hundred chairs in the hall, so we were more than happy when in excess of 200 people attended. As the night wore on, the Lord Mayor, under sustained questioning from the locals, revealed the plans the Brisbane City Council had in hand. She said publicly that she would consult local people and listen to their concerns but, sitting next to her, I could see and hear that she was far from comfortable putting rhetoric into practice. The bridge was not built, and the meetings played a small part in stopping it.

A Canterbury Bulldog

Early one morning, soon after I arrived in the parish, the presbytery doorbell rang. A gaunt old man stood there dressed in a Canterbury Bulldogs football jersey and blue jeans, and carrying a walking stick. I had seen him at Sunday morning Mass. He said he wanted to sit in the kitchen and talk over a few things he had on his mind. We dealt with them, and he stood up to leave. I said, "Don't go yet. I'd like to know more about who Mr Bonsey is."

"Thank you for addressing me as Mr Bonsey, but I'd be happy for you to call me Nigel."

He went on to tell me about his life, pausing to ask if I minded him smoking his rollies. When I stood to fetch an ashtray, he waved me back to my seat, producing an old tobacco tin for an ashtray. "It is bad enough that I smoke. Others shouldn't have to clean up after me."

Nigel had been born in England and had come to Australia as a young man. During the Depression, he had nearly died on the streets of Brisbane from hunger, but had been picked up literally half-dead by Father Mills, a Catholic Priest. Nigel decided to become a Catholic, although he never lost his affection for Anglicanism. He had been a journalist, had worked for the Housing Commission, had a great love for cricket, especially the West Indies and the 'great' Viv Richards, was a passionate member of the Labor Party, and a follower of the Canterbury Bulldogs. He often walked around West End in a Bulldogs football jersey, not bad for someone in his late seventies. By his own admission, he was an eccentric.

At that first of many meetings, I discovered he was well read in theology, the Fathers (and Mothers) of the Church, both East and West; had read and understood most of what the liberation theologians had written; and was a passionate student of Fr Pedro Aruppe, and later of Fr Peter Hans Kolvenbach, successive world leaders of the Jesuits.

I asked Nigel if he would like to take responsibility for the Reflection in our weekly parish newsletter. He jumped at the opportunity. From then on, he would regularly appear at the presbytery with three or four weeks of Reflections in advance, and come in for a cuppa and a chat. He often turned up at the presbytery at seven in the morning and, as this was my prayer time, I asked him if he could make it at 7:30, to which he readily agreed.

Many a morning, Nigel, Noel and I enjoyed deep theological discussions over breakfast. Nigel's weekly reflections in the Parish Newsletter were a mix of the ancient Fathers, liberation theologians, the readings of the day, and an apt quote from cricket, in particular Viv Richards, or from Mal Meninga, a local Rugby League football hero. He was able to connect the Gospel with life and with social justice, and his reflections often complemented what I and Noel were saying in our homilies and trying to do in the parish. Once he asked me if it was OK if he did not participate in the Prayers of the Faithful at Mass, because it seemed to him that we were giving God his instructions for the week, and he was not prepared to do that.

Although he would never admit it himself, Nigel in his own way cared for the *anawim*, the poor of Yahweh. In his street, living in flats, there were people who had few friends, were handicapped and generally doing it tough. Nigel befriended these people, often dropping in with the excuse that he wanted them to have a copy of his newsletter Reflection. In fact, he personally delivered more than a dozen to various people. If he had quoted from Aruppe or Kolvenbach, he would send them a copy too, having first (quite unnecessarily) sought my permission to do so.

He died at the age of 87. I visited him from time to time during his last illness. Eighty-seven had special significance for him, he told me, as this was the number of runs which many first class cricketers floundered on (being an unlucky 13 runs short of a century). Several months before he died, he gave me instructions for his funeral. He wanted "no panegyrics, no eulogies and, above all, no bullshit." He wanted 'Amazing Grace' to be played, and an Anglican Priest, Malcolm Bell (whom I had worked with in the prison) to concelebrate. At the funeral Mass we used one of his favourite readings, Romans 3:23-24, "For there is no distinction, since all have sinned and fall short of the glory of God; they are now justified by his grace as a gift, through the redemption that is in Christ Jesus."

Nigel often quoted the text, saying "We are all sinners. All of us fall short of the glory of God. Thanks be to God for Christ Jesus." Others times he would just say: "Romans 3:23, you know what I mean."

Celebrating church festivals

I wanted to work co-operatively with the people of Saint Francis parish, sharing decision-making and responsibilities. However a certain group of people, in my opinion, were power-hungry, wanting to dominate and influence every person they could to their way of thinking. They seemed to me self-righteous and closed-minded.

At the beginning of Advent, this group told me they always displayed an Advent wreath in the Church with candles. I asked them what the significance of a wreath with candles was. They did not know. I said there was no point in using a symbol which had no significance. Instead we decided to use a gum tree, which we stripped of its leaves. We tied onto its branches yellow leaves which had an item of food written on the back. People were to take one home, return with the item of food, and replace the yellow leaf with a green one. Gradually, throughout Advent, the tree changed colour from yellow to green. After I began working in the prisons, we decorated the tree with yellow and red leaves. The red leaves had the name and address of a prisoner, male or female, on it. If a person took a red leaf, it meant that they were prepared to send a Christmas card to the prisoner. Sometimes there was further correspondence, and some parishioners even made a few visits to prisons.

Later I invited the Vietnamese and Filipino communities to share our Christmas Mass. Although the Vietnamese community always had a weekend Mass in Saint Francis, they did not have a priest available on Christmas Day. I said that I was certain they would be welcomed at Saint Francis. The Filipinos told me that they had no chaplain and no church. I told them they too would be most welcome.

We had several preparatory meetings for the Christmas Vigil Mass. It was slow work, communicating with people whose first language was not English, but we managed. The Vietnamese people offered to decorate the Church (and thirty young men turned up at the Church one Saturday morning to do just that), while the Filipino people hung up their beautiful Christmas lanterns.

We produced a special booklet for the English speakers, so they could follow anything not sung or spoken in English. After a short introduction, two carols each were sung in Vietnamese, Tagalog and English, with all the people holding lighted candles. As the first carol was being sung, Mary and Joseph walked slowly down the centre aisle and sat on the sanctuary. Mary was a white woman, and Joseph was very black. I didn't have the courage to look at the colour of the baby when it was placed in Mary's arms a little later.

During the second carol in each language, people from that country brought a special gift and placed it at the foot of our gum tree. The responsorial psalm was prayed in each language, with each major language group reciting one verse each. The prayers of the faithful, as well as the hymns at Communion, were also in the three languages.

Basing my homily on the words from Luke 2, "There was no room for them in the inn"[90], I asked the question: why was the inn crowded? I explained that it was because the Romans were conducting a census of the whole world, in an effort to discover those who were to be taxed, and to find out who was eligible for service in the armies of the empire. The tidings of great joy were not announced in the inn, because it was too crowded and too noisy. "The Great Joy is announced after all in silence, loneliness and darkness to shepherds living in the fields or living in the countryside." The shepherds remained outside the agitation and were untouched by the vast movement of peoples. I finished the homily with the story of one of the most damaged of the young people who had been at the Lodge, who was supporting her two young children by working in an aged care home as a domestic worker. She had invited a number of the old people from the home to spend Christmas Day with her and enjoy Christmas dinner with herself and her children, sharing the little that she and her children had. I concluded by saying that there is room in the inn, and the spirit of Christmas leads us to make room for those who would normally be excluded.

The Vietnamese, the Filipinos, and most of the people were thrilled with the liturgy. I even used a special Aboriginal Eucharistic Prayer. However some parishioners hated it, and told me so at every Parish Council Meeting for the next 12 months. "That was not Christmas. That was not Mass. I will have to go again in the morning. Why did the Vietnamese and the Filipinos pray in their own languages?" And to top it all off: "I even saw one woman breast-feeding her baby during Mass." Nevertheless the Vietnamese and the Filipinos were grateful they had been able to enter into such a Liturgy; some even had tears in their eyes when they thanked me and asked me to thank the people of the parish.

---

90   The ideas came from Thomas Merton's *Raids on the Unspeakable* (Burns & Oates, 1977) p 44ff.

We did a similar thing at Easter. I rewrote the whole of the Easter Liturgy into comprehensible language, mixing in liberal doses of the 'signs of the times'. We had people joining in from the Vietnamese, Filipino, Sri Lankan, Fijian, Lebanese, Italian and Anglo-Australian communities. The local Catholic Worker community also gave some special input. On Palm Sunday we blessed the palms in the parish hall at the rear of the Church, and processed to the Church, stopping on four occasions. At each of these stations, a mime was acted out, while a relevant section of the Passion story was read.

The first one was for political prisoners in Vietnam and in the Philippines (where Father Brian Gore and others had been imprisoned). We read the section about the arrest of Jesus.

The second, at the entrance to the convent, was set up to look like a Commonwealth Employment Office with a young woman going for an interview with a sign on her back which read: "I am not a dole bludger." We read the section about Jesus being wrongly accused.

The Vietnamese organised the third station. One of them had painted a huge picture of a boat in rough seas, superimposed upon a map of their home country. A few boat people stood in front of the painting while another section of the Passion was read.

The final station was in the Church. Again, a large picture had been painted to depict the sanctity of life both in the embryo and in relationship to war. A final narrative about the crucifixion of Jesus was read.

Some parishioners were again disturbed and unhappy. Others were challenged by the marrying of the Gospel and the events of the day—the signs of the times.

The following Christmas was even better. I discovered that the Vietnamese sang a number of carols to the same tunes as ourselves. So we sang one verse of "Silent Night" in English, and then they came in with their musical instruments and sang a verse in their language. That year, we had a man playing the didgeridoo in the choir loft after Communion, with the church in almost total darkness. That year, Mary and Joseph were black people—from Sri Lanka.

I had various contacts with members of the Vietnamese community. In 1984 I spent some time with two sisters who were studying at university and their two younger brothers who were attending the local high school. After the second Christmas Mass, one of the sisters approached me and, bowing with hands joined, said very solemnly, "Happy Christmas, Father."

I bowed and returned the greeting with equal gravity.

She said, "I have bought Father a little Christmas present."

"You should not have done this." I knew they were struggling financially.

"I have bought Father a box of chocolates," she continued.

I repeated that there was no need for her to do this, that her greetings and best wishes were more than sufficient.

She said: "I must tell Father that I am very sorry. I ate them all."

"These Sunday night Masses"

The Catholic chaplain to Aboriginal people, Leo Wright, used to celebrate the Sunday evening Mass. Leo gave the Mass a strong social justice flavour and many people from across Brisbane attended. Twelve months prior to my arrival Leo had taken on a parish, and the numbers attending the evening Mass at Saint Francis had dropped dramatically to an average of 20 people.

I could have cancelled the Mass, but I decided instead to reintroduce the social or Gospel justice dimension to see what would result. From the very beginning, I attempted dialogue homilies, not from the pulpit but by walking up and down the centre aisle of the church. For three months, nobody, but nobody, responded. The first person who responded was an elderly lady, Nancy Weir, a famous Australian pianist who was partly deaf. Altogether, 13 people made comments that evening. Soon more people began coming—mainly people working for justice, peace and with poor people. They began to request more participation and more responsibility for organising the Mass. As the seating in the Church was not conducive to discussion, Noel and I removed some seats and placed others on an angle.

Some of the parishioners from the other two Masses nearly rioted. They called a Parish General Meeting to discuss 'this Sunday Night Business'. I told the Sunday night people that I was not prepared to speak alone for the Mass and what happened there. If they were convinced of its value, then they had to come to the meeting and speak up. The meeting was quite brisk, almost fiery. The Sunday night people spoke eloquently and, to our surprise, some people listened. The turning point came when one of the 'oldies' (who was young at heart and open-minded) said, "It all sounds good to me. Why can't we have these things happening at the other Masses?"

Eventually we moved the Sunday night liturgy to the Parish Hall, and the seating in the Church returned back to almost normal. The laity now totally prepared the liturgy. I never knew what was going to happen until I arrived. The liturgies were very creative, on the whole, and the message often stayed with me and with many who attended for the whole of the following week. After the liturgy, we enjoyed supper together. The people who attended the Mass from the psychiatric hostels and some of the boarding houses particularly enjoyed these suppers. Once a month we held a meeting to review the previous weeks' liturgies, and to give people the opportunity to indicate which of the forthcoming liturgies they wanted to put together.

Noel and I agreed that if I was not available for the Sunday evening Mass, he would not stand in for me, and that the group should go ahead themselves without a priest. It was a difficult question for many, but one which we discussed and worked through over several months. When I went on holidays later that year, the liturgies continued without a priest, although some felt the need to attend Mass in a 'regular' church.

Guests in the Presbytery

On frequent occasions I welcomed to the presbytery some of the young people I had worked with, or was currently working with, when they turned up on the front doorstep. Sometimes they needed accommodation, and the convent had a small bungalow which could provide the space. The nuns were wonderfully welcoming of these young people and their children. At other times, Noel and I accommodated them in the presbytery, sometimes only for a night or two, sometimes for much longer periods. Our house was a large one, and it was important to share it with others in need.

Some of the young people phoned in the middle of the night, or turned up on our doorstep in the early hours of the morning. Some were in serious strife and trouble, were mainly unsupported, and in need of whatever assistance we were able to provide. Others used our place to recover from a crisis situation.

One night, just after midnight, a 17-year-old young woman turned up. She told us that she had been picked up by the police and offered money in exchange for information about her brother. Although she was unable to assist them (and thought it was a case of mistaken identity) she was taken to the Woolloongabba Police Station where she was interrogated and bashed. I offered to take her to the hospital so she could be checked out, but all she wanted was to lay her head down and sleep. Later on she woke me up, saying she was very sick and sore, and wondering if she had a depressed fracture of the cheek. I again suggested that I take her to the hospital, and this time she decided to go.

At the hospital I told the doctor to take meticulous notes, as they could be used as evidence against the police. While we were waiting, I suggested to her that she should tell me exactly what happened. As she did, I took down notes. The doctor examined her, took down notes, and asked that she return to the hospital in the morning. I took her back to the presbytery.

I typed up her statement in draft form the next morning and, when she felt up to it, I asked her to read and correct it. Then I outlined her options. She could just let the matter rest, or she could contact her local State Member of Parliament, take out charges against the police, make a complaint to the Police Complaints Tribunal or talk with a solicitor. She decided on the latter, so I made an appointment for her with Stephen Keim, a friend of mine. He suggested that she make a complaint to the Police Complaints Tribunal, and went with her to the interview.

The police conducted an investigation, during which I was interviewed twice. Finally, a police inspector arrived unexpectedly on my doorstep. He told me the investigation had been concluded. The young woman was unreliable, the doctor had not submitted any notes, the police concerned were exonerated and the matter was closed. We had known this would probably be the result, but it was important to take the matter further as, in a democracy, citizens have a right to complain. If young people embarked upon this course of action, our obligation was to assist them to the best of our ability, using whatever means we had at our disposal.

Welcoming the excluded

While we, as a parish council, were slowly trying to work out how and why we should respond to the signs of the times in our local community, local needs were ceaselessly presenting themselves. One Saturday I received a phone call from a woman who had just opened up two hostels for people discharged from psychiatric hospitals. While she herself was a practising Anglican, she was inquiring about the times of weekend Masses, as some of her residents were Catholic and she wanted to drive them to Mass.

Eight of her residents arrived at Mass the following day. One or two stood up at the wrong times, and some made noises from time to time. After Mass, one of the parishioners told me that I had to get rid of these people as they were a distraction to all the people in the Church. I told her that these people were more welcome in the Church in the eyes of God than we were, and that our job was to befriend them and do what we could to integrate them into our community.

We struggled with this issue for a while, but gradually the parish began to look out for the people from the hostels. As the parish fête was approaching, and knowing that many were gifted in craft work, I approached some people from the hostels to see if they would be prepared to do some work for the fête. I then approached the fête committee to obtain some of the materials they needed. Materials were grudgingly given: "This material is expensive, they had better not waste it." Most people from the hostel completed some excellent work, which was sold at the fête, and the proceeds went to assist the work of the Saint Vincent de Paul Society in the parish.

The Philippines: the struggle after Marcos

Driving in my car one day, listening to the radio, I happened to hear a community announcement. Jose Maria Sison from the Philippines was to speak on 'The Philippines after Marcos' at the Saint Francis Church Hall at West End on 18th September, 1986. Although I often received information this way, it did not concern me, as I trusted the judgment of the people making the bookings for the hall.

In the Sunday Mail newspaper that weekend, there was a short article on the speaker, with a photograph, under the title: *'Red' Filipino revolutionary in Brisbane*. The article had this to say:

> The man who founded the Philippines Communist Party in 1968 will visit
> Brisbane later this week. Jose Maria Sison became a commander of the
> New People's Army, the military wing of the party.

The Premier, Sir Joh Bjelke-Petersen, yesterday offered a less-than-warm welcome. Mr Sison's philosophies were exactly opposite to those of the State Government, Sir Joh said.

Mr Sison will lecture at a West End hall on Thursday night.

Sir Joh said: "He believes in exactly the opposite of our free way of life and private enterprise. I'll bet you anything you like there will be heaps and heaps of Labor people there to listen to him and clap and cheer."

Police will be on standby because they expect Mr Sison's presence may anger many in Brisbane's anti-communist Vietnamese community.

Mr Sison, 47, from a wealthy family, is credited as the founder of modern communism in The Philippines.

He was arrested by the Marcos regime in 1977 and spent more than eight years in jail, much of it in solitary confinement. President Corazon Aquino released him last March despite the objections of military officers in her government.[91]

On the Sunday before the function, I received a phone call from the bishop. He began by saying that some of our friends who are dedicated to keeping us honest had protested to the Archbishop about Saint Francis Parish being the venue for Jose Maria Sison, a founder of the Communist Party in the Philippines. He also said the Catholic Commission for Justice and Peace had been caught up in co-sponsoring the speaker, and that they had been taken for a ride. He told me the Church could not provide a forum to those who had been violent in the Philippines. He told me there were a few days left for the organisers to arrange another booking. After arguing with him, I told him that I was prepared to talk the matter over with some of the people who were sponsoring the speaker.

As a number of the members of the Philippines Support Group attended the Sunday evening Mass at West End, I asked them to discuss the matter with me. As a result of that meeting, I wrote the following letter:

This evening I had discussions with some of the organisers of this event. These people were able to inform me that:

- The vast majority of the members of the Philippines Support group are Catholics;

- The speaker is advocating reforms, particularly land reforms, which would halt the spiral of violence;

- The speaker is a person who has spent nine years in prison—at no stage was he convicted of an offence. Many of these years he spent in solitary confinement. Like Father Brian Gore, who also spent several

91 *Sunday Mail*, 14 September 1986.

years in prison, he could possibly have something worthwhile to say;

- The speaker is presently a lecturer at the University of The Philippines and his analysis could be worth hearing;
- People, namely Australians, need to inform themselves on what is happening, especially from people who have suffered;
- The Church in the Modern World encourages dialogue and cooperation within the Church, with other Christians, with all who acknowledge God, with men and women of good will and even with atheists while rejecting their atheism.

The discussion further highlighted two matters of justice:

- that people have the right to inform themselves and that Catholics especially need to inform themselves about situations of injustice or oppression;
- that the hall has been booked and the venue publicised. It is felt that at this late stage it would be almost impossible to obtain another venue and terribly inconvenient for those attending.

The policy of our Parish Council is to encourage responsibility and decision-making among our laity. Certainly since I have been here the Parish Council has given the responsibility for the booking of the hall to the laity. While at times both the Parish Council and myself may question the use of the hall by particular groups, I would see my duty as one of discussing my concerns with the lay people entrusted with the hiring out of the hall.

Several of the organising committee for this function are available to discuss this matter further with you at your convenience.

This letter prompted another phone call from the bishop. He was not convinced by the arguments in the letter. I presented further arguments. I quoted again Vatican II, urging us to "work with all women and men of good will".

"How do you know he is a man of good will?" the bishop asked.

"How do you know he isn't?" I replied. "He has an uncle who is an Archbishop. He spent years in solitary confinement. He has never been convicted of an offence."

He was unimpressed. I told the bishop that we were adults and that we should be able to discern the truth of the matter and the integrity of the speaker. At the end of the conversation, I further inflamed him by suggesting that maybe he would like to control the future bookings of the parish hall.

The organising group decided to change the venue to a hall at Red Hill. They did this because they did not want to put further strain on my relationship with the bishop, and, more importantly, because I had applied for the prison chaplaincy job, and this could hinder my chances of appointment.

I heard Jose Maria Sison speak, and found the presentation interesting and informative. Sison's basic message was that little had changed since Marcos had been ousted, and that the land reform platform which had swept Aquino into power had not been implemented. At the meeting, there were at least a dozen right-wingers, possibly from the National Civic Council. They often interrupted the speaker and tried to control question time. In fact, the first question was directed to me. The questioner took over five minutes to ask his question and because I saw that he just wanted to have a debate between himself and myself, when he finished I declined to answer, saying that I had come to hear the speaker answer questions.

As a result, I received a couple of anonymous letters in the mail, pointing out the evils of communism. I also received a mention in one of the NCC newsletters, stating that I was the only Catholic Priest in Australia prepared to host Sison. (I do not suppose that too many Catholic priests in Australia were approached). As in the past, while I was trying to follow the directions of Vatican II, once again the local Church either had a different interpretation, or was not prepared to live explicit Church teachings.

A watershed retreat with 'Kermit'

I N MID-1984, against my better judgment, I decided to do a retreat at Banyo Seminary. I had not had anything to do with the seminary since June 1979, when I was helping out Dan Grundy with pastoral formation. What attracted me to the retreat were two things: first, it was on *The Meaning of Jesus* and was to be given by Father Kevin O'Shea, a Redemptorist (whom I nicknamed Kermit from the TV show The Muppets, because in looks and some mannerisms Kevin reminded me of Kermit); and second, the middle day of the retreat was to be conducted by Juan Luis Segundo, a South American liberation theologian.

We were asked to meet at Banyo at 8pm on the Sunday evening, but, because I had the evening Mass at West End, I was unable to leave for the seminary until 8:30pm. As I was driving, I kept saying to myself, "You are a fool for going down to Banyo. You'll only open yourself to more criticism and invective." It took willpower to make myself keep driving.

When I arrived, I found an empty room, put my gear down, and went looking for the other retreatants. I encountered a priest whom I had not seen for years.

"What are you doing here?" he asked.

"I'm here for the retreat."

"That surprises me," he said.

"Why should it?"

"I'm pleased you've still got a little faith left in you to come here for a retreat."

I walked off, saying to myself, "I told you so, you stupid idiot. I told you not to come to this place."

The next priest I met asked, "Where are you these days?"

"I'm at West End."

"How long have you been there?"

"Nearly 12 months."

"You haven't sold the presbytery to the Blacks as a sacred site yet?"

"What a good idea. I'll give that one some thought."

What a start! I decided to stay in my room as much as possible and keep out of further trouble. I attended lectures and meals, and spent the rest of the time in my room, which suited me down to the ground.

'Kermit' based much of his input on *Jesus before Christianity*[92] by Albert Nolan, a Dominican liberation theologian from South Africa. In the first session on Jesus and John the Baptist, he told us that John had a universal message with regard to justice, prayer, asceticism and fasting, but no particular message regarding the poor, was not into healing, and never forgave anybody their sins. Whereas Jesus went to Galilee to the poor, where he healed and forgave, and worried about present problems like the lame, the blind and the oppressed. The poor for Jesus were those who were tugging at his heart. Jesus went out to the needy, the scum of the earth, as a living symbol of God's love. In doing so, Jesus threatened the whole system, because his commitment was to the poor, not to spirituality.

In the second session, which he called *From Purifier to Healer: A Change in Personality*, Kermit told us that tenderness is the name of the living God, who is infinitely in touch with pain, woundedness and crying out. We must learn to feel, if we want to be a real Jesus person, and to feel the pain of the other as an issue of justice, not merely one of sympathy or charity. "I stay in there, with people who are oppressed", he said, "to reveal to people something of the feeling capacity of my God."

He called the third session *Fidelity as Courage*. Jesus was a strong courageous man in his commitment to the poor. He wanted to avoid trouble and to keep on loving the poor. He stood his ground, always faithful to the poor, and continued to throw himself faithfully into the impossible. His fidelity showed itself in his courage. However, he got the cross because he loved the poor.

On the Monday night, we were encouraged to attend a public lecture given by Segundo on *Theology as an Art not a Science*. Segundo told us that Vatican II had changed the scope of our Christian faith: the place of salvation is the whole world, not the Church. The function of the faith, he said, is to direct the mind to solutions which are truly human.[93] This is a practical art, not a science. Fidelity of conscience leads the modern Christian to join with others to search for truth—truth which will humanise human beings.[94] The reason for becoming a priest or a theologian is to give more humane solutions to human problems. Blessed are the poor when they cease to be poor. The Our Father is a prayer of a revolutionary: *Thy will be done on earth as it is in heaven.* I was thrilled with what I was hearing, and looked forward to spending time with him in two days, when he came to the seminary to take the third day of the retreat.

The second day with Kermit was as stimulating as the first one. In the first topic of the day, 'The Grandeur of the Man Jesus: Beyond Courage', Kermit

92 *Jesus Before Christianity: The Gospel of Liberation.* Albert Nolan. Darton, Longman and Todd. 1977.
93 Vatican 11: *"The Church in the Modern World (Gaudium et Spes)"* para 11.
94 Ibid.. para 16.

told us that the emphasis of Jesus on the poor changed to sinners: that is, the ones outside the Covenant. Jesus told these people that they belonged to God, because the expansiveness of God can encompass the sinners, the tax-collectors and the prostitutes. He offered free forgiveness to people who were not technically forgivable. Through his contact with the poor, sinners and the oppressed, Jesus was wounded, opened and transformed, which is the mystery of the transfiguration through suffering. An opened-up man through woundedness is a truly open man. His break-down was an invitation to break through.

Kermit called the second session 'The Gethsemane Experience(s) of Jesus'. Here he dealt with the death of the Messiah. *How can I face annihilation as the Messiah of the poor, or as a shepherd king? What have I done wrong?* In the garden, Jesus touched the whole nature of evil in profound solitude. Jesus was astonished by the invasion of terror into his own being: the whole world was ending, and its ending was dirty. Luke tells us in his Gospel that we cannot mature in the priestliness of the New Testament covenant without some sort of suffering.

The final session of the day was called 'Consecration of Commitment'. We heard how it was normal for the Jews to take vows, which they mostly did at family meals. Table fellowship, meal sharing and vow-taking went together: a person would drink from the cup and take their vow to the Lord. Jesus at the Last Supper made his act of commitment, despite what was going to happen very soon. "This is my blood poured out for you, the poor and the oppressed," was Jesus' commitment. The Eucharist, the poor and the socially oppressed must go together with vow-taking and consecration. At Mass we do not just consecrate bread and wine, we consecrate and dedicate ourselves to the poor and to sinners.

The third day of the retreat was open to all priests, to hear Juan Luis Segundo speak. In the first of two sessions he dealt with 'The Divinity of Christ in the Past and Today': happy are the Third World countries because theirs is the kingdom of God; happy are the Aboriginals, the unmarried mothers and the unemployed, for theirs is the kingdom of heaven. Jesus was for the poor, the hungry and the outcasts. He was not interested in the well-off. In this, Jesus was partisan. The real scandal of Jesus was that he got involved with people who were moral failures.

In his second session, Segundo told us that the Council of Chalcedon was worried about Jesus becoming an object of idolatry. Jesus fought and died for historical values. The faith of Jesus needs to be emphasised, rather than faith in Jesus. Theology can be a tool of oppression used by the ruling classes. The Church is needed because there is suffering in the world. If, for example, nothing can be done about cancer, this is because resources and energy are going into armaments.

Kermit called the third segment of the retreat 'The Paschal Mystery'. In the first section, he considered the Dying of Jesus. Kermit contended that Jesus was arraigned because of his position with regard to the poor. The cry Jesus emitted on the cross was the cry of a man in his last agony, when he can do very little else. It is a cry of dereliction, forsakenness and abandonment. In John's symbolic Gospel, Jesus is described on the cross: "having bowed his head he passed across his breath, his life." That is, Jesus leaves his spirit to them for the cause of the poor, imparting his spirit of love for the poor to all and, somehow, to all the *anawim* in the cosmos.

The next session was titled 'The Marvel of Continuing Life'. God raised up the poor man Jesus, as the crucified wounded one. Easter is the symbol that the poor shall live. The poor live. Jesus lives. The poor live in him. The fidelity of the Father and of Jesus will never cease and it empowers the little ones. We need to leave the Paschal Candle in the Church and go out and show poor people that they have brothers and sisters by working for the resurrection of the poor in our areas. The resurrection does not remove the crucifixion of Jesus. Rather, it eternalises the wounds of the cross. Jesus is raised as crucified, as poor, as wounded and as all-embracing of sinners.

The final lecture on the last full day was 'Risen Life'. What is risen life? Even in heaven we might not have our acts perfectly together. We may still have our wounds. Our gaps and openness will still be there. We'll still look like us: people who have spent ourselves.

At the final session on the last day, Kermit discussed "Who is Jesus? Who is God?" The dynamic in the life of Jesus was the Spirit. It is the Spirit-beyond-words which makes us move from stage to stage in our lives. The Spirit drives us on, is inside us making it all work. Who then is Jesus? God's own son in the Spirit. What sort of son is Jesus? God's own grown-up son who has gone around the whole track, even through Gethsemane. He was always discovering further ways of being the Son of God.

Who is God? The Spirit-opened Father. The Spirit binds the Father and the Son so that they can pour themselves out on the poor of the earth. God is an historically-involved Father, not a closed, sedentary Father. The Trinity is therefore one of the most political doctrines in the Church.

What does the Spirit do? He takes the stigmas of poor people and turns them into the stigmata of God's only son. The Spirit is the spirit of mercy to the poor: "Come to me all you who labour and are overburdened; be ye merciful as your heavenly Father is merciful." If the Trinity means anything, it takes us out to the bleeding ones, to the outcasts, and it is there that we give glory to God.

Needless to say, I was excited by all that I heard and prayed about during the week. On the last day, one of my friends said: "This retreat must have been right up your alley."

"Certainly," I replied. "I can't believe that this stuff is being given out publicly, to priests and in the seminary setting as well. This week meant a lot to me. How did you find it yourself?"

"Each lecture I attended was like a great kick in the guts."

Before I left, I had a cuppa with one of the retreatants who had been ordained two years previously. "What did you make of the retreat?" I asked.

"I've heard it all before. We did all that stuff in the seminary," he said in a bored tone. I refrained from asking him how he had been able to live "that stuff" as a priest since ordination.

Baptism of fire at Boggo Road

Prison chaplaincy: a change in direction

IN 1986, the Catholic Prison Ministry team, approached me about taking on prison chaplaincy. They assured me it was only a part-time job, one and a half to two days per week, and could easily be combined with the work at Saint Francis.

Peter Kennedy had been prison chaplain for six years and wanted to retire from the job. He had asked me on a number of occasions if I would consider taking it on. After discussions with Peter and the other members of the team, Tim Riddell, a social worker with Catholic Prison Ministry, and Sister Bernice Heffernan, a Holy Spirit nun who worked in many prisons including the Women's Prison, I applied for the job in September 1986.

I noted in my letter of application that I had experience as a part-time chaplain at a juvenile detention centre, and that from time to time, I had visited individual prisoners in adult prisons. I am sure the Church authorities were not inundated with applications. Nevertheless, it took them longer than usual to select and recommend my appointment to the Queensland Government. It then took another month for the State to give approval. I knew there would be difficulties for both sets of authorities, because of my 'track record' and my commitment to Gospel justice.

I received notification that I was to be appointed to the position of Catholic chaplain to prisons in South-East Queensland. But almost before I could begin work, the Prison Department changed the way chaplains were to work in prisons. From being a part-time job two days a week, it became a full-time job. I decided that it wouldn't be too difficult to combine the work at West End and the prisons because Noel was there to assist. My work in the prisons meant more work for him in the parish, but he said he didn't mind.

The past catches up

Having approved my appointment in October 1986, the bishop arranged a meeting with the Minister for Prisons, Mr Geoff Muntz, for him to run his eye over me, and for me to receive his formal approval. My impression, from those who were present at this interview and from what was said, was that this was not to be merely a rubber-stamp approval, but that the Minister's minders were keen for him to hear certain messages about me, and for me to hear particular messages regarding my future conduct as a chaplain, should the Minister so ordain.

The bishop, Tim and myself turned up at the Minister's office at the appointed time, which happened to be a few days before the 1986 State Election. Accompanying the Minister were the Under-Secretary of the Department and the Assistant Director of Prisons. These latter gentlemen were both practising Catholics and quite conservative.

Fortunately for me, but to the annoyance of his minders, the Minister kept being called out of the room to the phone or to other consultations. I say 'fortunately' because both the Under-Secretary and the Assistant Director wanted to raise in front of the Minister, matters relating to my previous record. When this proved impossible, they were forced to raise the questions in front of the bishop and Tim only.

They mentioned my troubled relationship with the Department of Children's Services in Wilson and my involvement in the Justice for Juveniles Group. I assured them that all that was in the past, but they did not seem totally convinced. Obviously they were wary of me, my views and my past actions, especially my having had certain matters publicised in the media. Asking me questions in front of the bishop and in the Minister's office was a vain attempt to call me to heel. The attitude was: if we allow you to enter our prisons, then you must conform to our unwritten rules—we do not want you working for justice and taking up prisoners' rights. It struck me as sad that these powerful public servants had not grasped the essence of the Catholicism they professed: that is, the dignity of the human person, the human rights which flowed from that dignity, and of course, Gospel justice. About a month later, approval was granted.

When I began working in prisons, I took with me my Cardijnian methodology, my social analysis, my human rights perspective, my understanding of twelve-step programs to overcome drug and alcohol addictions, my option for the poor, and my vision of Gospel justice. These were my tried and tested tools of trade. I knew they could be put to good use in any situation, especially with disadvantaged people. I had been around and was, to a certain extent, 'streetwise'. All of this would stand me in good stead in my work in the criminal justice system. When friends asked me why I took on prison chaplaincy, I would reply tongue in cheek: "I have a conscience. I failed with a lot of young people over the years. I've taken on this work to try to assist those whom I've failed."

"Shut up! You're a hostage."

I hate prisons. They are dehumanising institutions. At least 70 per cent of prisoners should not be there. Most prisoners are incarcerated for non-payment of fines, because of poverty, for non-violent offences or drug/alcohol related crimes. The offences are dealt with, but the underlying causes of the offences (for example, addiction) are given scant attention by the courts, and even less by the prison system.

I went into prisons with some understanding of what happens to everyone 'inside'. A few years earlier, I had read a report on some American research on the effects of prisons on prison officers. The report concluded that those who administered a dehumanising system were, in turn, dehumanised themselves.

The prisons were in ferment when I began work, especially the main reception and maximum security prison, Boggo Road, situated close to the centre of Brisbane. Riots, escapes, bashings, rapes and drug abuse were almost everyday occurrences. I was nervous about working in adult prisons. I knew I related well with young people who were incarcerated, but wondered how well I would be able to relate with adults.

My introduction to Boggo Road was at a Saturday morning Mass, to which Sister Bernice kindly decided to accompany me. The Mass was held on the stage of the concert hall. Despite my nervousness, the Mass seemed to go well, the men participated, and the prison officers who watched what was going on seemed suitably unimpressed.

After Mass, I was talking with Josh, an elderly prisoner, when I felt a blunt object pushed into my back. A deep voice above me said, "Shut up! You're a hostage."

Without thinking, I turned and faced two huge men, whose names I found out later to be 'Matt' and 'Dennis'.

"That's great," I said.

"What do you mean 'great'?"

"Well, if I'm a hostage, that means I get to spend more time with you guys, and that's what I'm on about."

"You're (expletive) useless, aren't you?"

"You're right," I said. "That's why the bishop gave me this job."

The big men backed off, and Josh and I were left to continue our conversation. That was my first test, and I can only believe it was the Holy Spirit who helped me through it.

Ecumenical chaplaincy

Shortly after I started, the Prisons Department made the position full-time. The Department had guidelines for chaplains and a State Chaplaincy Board. In practice, the chaplains were on roster, doing one full week at a time as a 'duty-chaplain'. In theory, the chaplain had access to all parts of the prison, was available to prisoners and staff alike, was equipped with a beeper and could be called into the prison any time, day or night. There was an office with a telephone, and a prisoner looked after the chaplain's library, fetched prisoners for religious visits and made a brew from time to time during the day.

The Assistant Director had responsibility for chaplains. He went through the guidelines with us, conducted us on tours of the prison, and introduced us to the Superintendent and senior administrative staff.

The new Departmental arrangements involved working ecumenically with the other chaplains. On the whole, this worked rather well. At Boggo Road, most of the chaplains had a Gospel vision which included working for justice and respecting the dignity of all, which made it possible for us to work together on various issues: for example, trying to get the underground cells closed down, which we were successful in achieving—but more about that later.

At the time I knew that the community, by and large, did not care about the prisons or the prisoners. The prison walls kept the inmates confined and isolated, and kept the community physically excluded, and ignorant of what was happening inside. Prisons, according to Arlene Morgan, a Professor of Psychology at the University of Queensland and a member of the Management Committee of Catholic Prison Ministry, had an impossible task: firstly, to promote change and growth in an atmosphere of incredible repression; and secondly, to teach new values and new skills in an atmosphere of hostility and vengeance.[95] At the time, the characteristics of prisoners were as follows:

- 35% of Queensland prisoners were in prison for the non-payment of fines
- 86% were sentenced for less than one year
- 90% had no education beyond primary school
- 30–40% were functionally illiterate
- 80–90% were unemployed at the time of arrest and/or had unsuccessful employment histories
- 40% were Indigenous.

Professor Morgan concluded:

> The 86% minor offenders should not be in prison. There should be 'correctional' facilities in the community with an educational focus, not a punitive one. Otherwise, a large proportion of these offenders will work their way up to the 14% who become committed to a criminal lifestyle. We give them few options[96].

I enjoyed working with Tim and Sister Bernice. We shared a common vision and methodology, and supported each other well. We met and prayed together

---

95 *Guidelines for a Program of Community Education on Prisons. A Preliminary Draft*, A. Morgan (May 1985) p 1.

96 Ibid..

frequently, and became good friends. Among other things, Tim was involved in community development work—recruiting, assessing, training, empowering and supporting people in local communities to assist prisoners and their families. Tim set up groups to assist the families and friends of prisoners, to help reduce the effects of imprisonment on the prisoner and family before and after release, and to promote public awareness of the prison system.

The work Tim was doing in the community was of vital importance. I could work conscientiously in the prison, but I needed people in the community to assist the families and loved ones of prisoners. For example, I would meet a prisoner who had just come into the prison system. He would be very concerned about his wife and children. I would assure him that I would have a person visiting his family within 24 hours. I would let him know the outcomes, sometimes that very day, which helped him settle down and not do anything stupid to himself or to anyone else. Some needs, like a food parcel, were easily met. Others were more difficult—for example, taking families to prisons for visits, and assisting people obtain pensions and benefits. Bernice was doing counselling with very difficult clients in both the women's and men's prisons. All of us were involved in justice issues, whether with individual prisoners or with reform of prisons generally, to make the criminal justice system more just, humane and rehabilitative.

"I'm the duty chaplain"

In my first week as duty chaplain, I had my first full day in prison. There had been a riot in the prison on the Friday, and on the Saturday and Sunday the prison had been in a lock-down situation with all prisoners locked in their cells and extra staff rostered on. I was to begin at 8am on the Monday. I quietly hoped I would not be allowed in. I was unsure of myself: would I be equal to this task? My prayer throughout that day was: "My grace is sufficient for you, for power is made perfect in weakness." (2 Corinthians 12:9) I knew my limitations and felt I could be getting myself into something beyond my capabilities.

I arrived at the prison at 7.45am, met the chaplain who had been on duty the previous week, and received the beeper and the badge we wore for the week. He gave me a run-down on what had happened during the previous week. He had been excluded from the prison for the previous three days and did not think I would be allowed to enter. I myself thought (and hoped) that would be the case.

I fronted up to the officer at the boom gate.

"You can't go in," he informed me.

"But I'm the duty chaplain," I said pointing to my very obvious badge.

"We've had a riot. The prisoners are in their cells. Nobody's allowed in."

"But I'm the duty chaplain," I persisted, "and under this new system we, the duty chaplains, are supposed to be allowed in at all times."

After some discussion, he permitted me to proceed to the door opening on to the area between the huge double gates which allowed vehicle access into the prison. I banged on the steel door. After a lengthy period, a metal spy-hole opened up and an unfriendly voice challenged, "Wha' da ya want?" I repeated my spiel, argued and was lectured, but was finally allowed to enter the area between the gates.

The next person I had to front was the officer-in-charge of the gate. He controlled all movement in and out of the prison.

"Who are you and who let you in here? Don't you know we've had a riot in here? Don't you read the papers? Are you stupid or something? This prison is closed to civilians."

I stood my (shaky) ground, repeated my speech, kept my cool, resisting the temptation to walk out and have the day off. After long delays and further lectures, he finally decided to allow me to enter 'his' prison. While I was waiting, a very young officer was also admitted into the section and stood near me.

"What section are you assigned to today?" I asked.

"I don't know," he replied courteously. "I'm half-way through my induction program at the staff training college."

"What have you been mainly learning there?"

"Up till now, mainly how to crack skulls efficiently and effectively."

After putting my briefcase in my office, I started out on chaplain's rounds, which meant visiting all parts of the prison to see if anybody wanted to speak with the duty chaplain.

My first port of call was the prison hospital. I pressed the buzzer adjacent to the barred door. Eventually a young 'agro' prison officer dressed in white (white because he worked in the prison hospital, not because he had any nursing qualifications) confronted me from the other side of the bars. After explaining who I was (I wore the "duty chaplain" badge on my shirt), he told me that I could not come into his hospital. Again I stood there like a big dummy, mumbling again who I was and what I was on about. I could not tell him that I had the right as chaplain to visit 'his' hospital as that would have meant a too uneven confrontation. I was being treated as a prisoner, with neither rights nor dignity.

Finally he must have realised I was not going to go away, so he said belligerently, "Well, I can't allow you to wander willy-nilly around my hospital. Do you have anyone in particular you wanted to see?" Fortunately the previous duty chaplain had given me the names of two prisoners who he thought were in the hospital. Their families had phoned him over the weekend, inquiring and worrying about the safety of their loved ones. From my notebook I produced two names. He told me to wait while he checked to see if they were indeed patients in his hospital.

Ten minutes later he returned and unlocked the gate to let me in. As we walked down the corridor to the locked door of a ward, I received another lecture: "You are to talk to these two, and nobody else, do you understand? I'll be standing right next to you. If you or they mention anything about the riot or what has been happening in this prison these last few days, you'll be out of here faster than you came in. Do you understand?"

He unlocked the steel door of the small ward, which normally contained six beds but was now crowded with 12 men. I called out one of the names I had in my notebook. A young man stepped forward, little more than a teenager, with his head swathed in bandages. I told him his family was worried about him, and I asked him how he was. He told me he was in for three weeks for non-payment of fines and had been placed in Two Jail (the older section of the prison and the scene of the recent riot) on the Monday prior to the riot. I asked him how his head was. He told me he had 18 stitches in it and that he had injured himself by walking into a door. (In fact, as I later found out, he had sustained his injuries by being bashed on the head by an officer's baton when he had had to run the gauntlet of baton-wielding officers—he had wanted to leave the area and take no part in the riot).

While he was talking, I kept wondering about the prison officer who was standing somewhere close by. I spoke quietly, hoping that the prisoner would do likewise. I was waiting for a tap on the shoulder and the order to leave 'his' hospital. The second young man I saw also had his head covered in bandages. He told me he too had walked into the same

Wally was never allowed into this punishment room

door. He had 10 stitches in his head. He had been placed in Two Jail the day before the riot and was serving two weeks for non-payment of fines.

Other men talked to me. They wanted me to get messages out to their loved ones to assure them they were OK. I wondered how my officer friend was handling the extra people talking to me as I jotted down names and phone numbers. I did not want to overstay my welcome, but I also wanted to speak with all who wanted to speak with me. Finally, I received a tap on the shoulder from my friend, the prison officer, who without further ado, escorted me out of 'his' hospital.

I felt as if I had done a morning's work, and it was not yet 10 am. My next port of call was Two Jail, the scene of the recent riots. Two Jail is separated from the main prison by what prisoners called 'the track', a stretch of cement with iron barred gates at either end surmounted by rusty barbed wire (later to be replaced by razor wire). On one side was a red brick wall approximately 10 metres high, while on the other was a low building which housed some offices. A guard sat on a chair halfway between the gates, and controlled access to and from Two Jail.

He saw me waiting at the gate and continued to sit. I waited patiently. After 10 or 15 minutes, he slowly got up and approached me. "Who let you into this prison? You shouldn't be in here. We've got enough trouble looking after our own backs without having to look out for a civilian. What do you want?"

I repeated my now well-rehearsed speech and respectfully requested I be allowed to visit the prisoners in Two Jail. Initially he was flabbergasted but, having recovered, gave full vent to his fury and called me every name he could think of. I had not received such abuse for years, but my years of training at the Lodge and Wilson served me well.

"This is a dangerous place. There is a riot on [there wasn't, it was over]. You can't come in." With that, he turned on his heels and walked away. After he had walked a few paces, he turned to see if I had gone. I still stood there. "Go on! Go away!" he shouted. "You can't come in here!"

"Excuse me," I countered.

He stopped, obviously puzzled. "What?"

"Excuse me," I repeated. "When do you think I would be able to visit this part of the prison? I would be grateful if you would let me know." I cannot write his response, but it was neither a compliment to my parents nor encourage-ment to keep my vow of celibacy.

Having failed to enter Two Jail, I continued on my rounds. I climbed three flights of steps to visit the prisoners on C Wing. I pressed the bell at the top of the stairs and went through the waiting game again. Finally, I was ushered into the Senior's cubby-hole of an office and met the talking Pole, 'Vince'. Vince's uniform was always neat and spotless. He was such a compulsive talker that he could probably speak underwater without drowning. He invited me into his office, and talked on and on about his woes and the situation in the prison. He granted me permission to visit the yards fronting the catwalk on C Wing, to speak with the prisoners through the thick bars.

At the first yard, I was accosted by a prisoner who wanted to know what I was doing about his mates in Two Jail. He then went on to describe to me what he had heard during the riots, with graphic descriptions of the bashings and the screams of the prisoners. The yard he was in was adjacent to and over-looked Two Jail.

I moved on to the next yard. Here a 'lifer' (a prisoner who has been sen-tenced to life imprisonment) confronted me with what had happened during the riot. He again was worried about his fellow-prisoners: whether they had received medical attention, or were being fed. I told him I had met some in the hospital.

"You have to get into Two Jail," he urged. I told him I had tried and that I would try again. This seemed to placate him a little. I had a brainwave. I chal-lenged him to do what he could. He said he was powerless, locked in his yard. I replied that I was doing what I could and he had to do whatever he could.

"What can I do? I'm locked in here."

I told him I didn't know, but again asked him what avenues he had. It was then he told me he was a lifer, and that there was a lifers' group in the prison. I urged him to talk with them. He asked how could he, locked in his yard. I told him he would have a better idea than I and that, if he expected me to do some-thing, then he also had to do what he could. Somehow or other he was able to communicate with other lifers over the next two days, and they put pressure on the administration to allow an independent person into Two Jail.

I continued to move along the C Wing catwalk. Further down, a prisoner approached the bars. "Do you know who I am?"

"I wouldn't have a clue."

"Have you heard of Whisky Au Go Go?" (This was a night club in Fortitude Valley which had been deliberately burnt down, killing 15 people). "I'm Jim Finch," he said belligerently. "Who are you?"

"I'm Wally Dethlefs. I'm the duty chaplain this week."

"What are you doing about the blokes in Two Jail? They've been belted up. They're not being fed. No one's givin' 'em any medical treatment. You get in there and do somethin' for those blokes."

I was thankful that I had already tried: it seemed to mean a lot to Finch and the other prisoners who had crowded around him. I asked him what he was doing and when he said there was nothing he could do, I said I could not accept that he could do nothing at all. At that point he bunched his fists, and I realised that I was in range. I considered moving out of range, but decided against it, realising he would notice and it would lessen his respect for me. I wondered if I would be fast enough to duck if he did decide to throw a punch. After a short argument, he told me about a prisoners' discussion group, different from the lifers' group. I told him that he needed to get them to do something, and moved on.

I completed my rounds by lunch time, and then retreated to the privacy of my office to catch my breath, write up my notes, and lick my wounds from all the abuse I had received that morning.

After a while, I made my way to the officers' mess, where chaplains were allowed to receive a free meal. The mess was controlled by an officer, but prisoners worked there, cooking the meals and waiting on the tables. I endured the usual quiz from the officer-in-charge of the mess. There was one spare seat at a long table. Politely asking if the seat was occupied, and receiving no replies, I sat down, saying hello to those on either side of me and opposite. I hardly rated a grunt, and they continued with their conversations. A prisoner served my meal in silence, and I ate it, feeling the obvious resentment of those around

"I hate prisons": revisiting Boggo Road jail

me. I was invading their space, and at a difficult time. I was the new boy on the block, a civilian, a priest, and I was receiving the 'treatment'. I finished my wordless but nourishing meal, and returned to my office.

In the afternoon I continued my rounds, receiving similar abuse as I had done in the morning. I left the prison at 4pm. I visited the family of a young prisoner at Salisbury, a nearby suburb, on the way home, as they did not have a phone and they were anxious to hear news of their son.

When I got back to the presbytery I collapsed on my bed, thoroughly exhausted. I had never in my whole life received so much abuse from so many people in the one day. The job was too tough for me. I had bitten off more than I could chew. It was too hard. Then, the doorbell rang, and in walked Tim. He said I looked pale and grey, ashen-faced. He asked how the day had gone and was amazed that I had been able even to get into the prison. He listened as I related the story of the day, and consoled me by saying it could not get worse: I had done well. I really appreciated him dropping in and his encouraging words.

The next day I lined up for more of the same. I knew it would be difficult but, since I had survived the worst that could be dished out to a non-prisoner, I would be able to continue. In fact, the abuse on the second day was not as bad or as intense as on the previous day—or maybe I was already becoming used to it. The prison was still in lockdown, with neither workshops nor laundry in operation, and the barest minimum of prisoner movement. However, I did notice a few more prisoners were working at their jobs, mainly running messages for officers. I continued to try to enter Two Jail, but was continually rebuffed.

On my third day, Wednesday, I was called to outside administration for an interview with a senior officer. He wanted to know if I would be willing to go into Two Jail that afternoon to observe prisoners coming out of their blocks and entering their mess for the evening meal. He knew I was in a position to reassure the prisoners in the main jail that things were returning to normal in Two Jail. I was not allowed to speak with any of them. I agreed to do this.

Later that day I was escorted into Two Jail by 'Jake', a senior prison officer for whom I came to have great respect, and watched as the prisoners shuffled from their blocks to the mess. Many had bandages around their heads, some had their arms in slings, a few limped. Before I left that day, I was able to tell a couple of key prisoners in the main jail that their fellows in Two Jail were being released from their blocks for meals and that many had received medical attention. Gradually, as the week progressed, more and more prisoners were released from their cells and the prison slowly resumed its normal routine. At my sixth lunch in the officers' mess, an officer spoke civilly to me.

Many prisoners serving life sentences knew that the prison would be their home for a very long time. A number of these men did excellent work with other prisoners, especially the younger ones. Some were also heavily involved in the wider justice issues affecting all prisoners. I realised that these men were key people. I resolved to be their back-up and sounding board, and to support them in the faith dimension of their lives. Thereafter, when I began my week as duty chaplain, I would write out the names of these men, and make certain that I saw all of them before I finished on the following Sunday.

At the beginning of every week, one or two used to land in my office, and immediately brought me up to date with what had happened since I was last in the prison. They would often indicate some men whom I should see and those who had been bashed and locked away in isolation. I would ask them about themselves, their work, their families. I used whatever skills I possessed to assist them in helping others. When I met a prisoner who was depressed, I would listen to him and, with his permission of course, notify one or another prisoner to chat with him and help him through his crisis.

The Rambos and Two Jail

For the next year or so, most of the troubles in Boggo Road were in Two Jail. The longer I spent there, the deeper my understanding became of why this was happening. One reason was the senior officers who controlled that section, and the other was the type of prison officer who was attracted to work there.

Because the culture in Two Jail was particularly violent, it attracted the more violent officers—the "Rambos". Also, it was built prior to 1900 and was a ghastly place. Tins were used as toilets in the cells, huge cockroaches abounded, the yards (or pig-pens as I called them) offered little space and less shelter from the elements. Two Jail was a cesspit of degradation and dehumanisation. It did not surprise me that most of the troubles in Boggo Road began in Two Jail.

When I had been working in the prison for about six months, the chaplains were relocated on the "track", that is, the section between the main prison and Two Jail. This meant that our office was technically in Two Jail, so we came under the jurisdiction of the officer-in-charge of that Division. On arrival in the prison each morning, we had to find our way into the office of 'Charles', who held court there from behind his huge desk. There were at least four or five officers in the room as well, and Charles would give his views out in a loud voice. His views were punitive, violent and dehumanising of prisoners. He bemoaned the lot of prison officers. Next to his desk was a wall with the name of the block at the top, the number of the cell, the surname of the prisoner who occupied it and the offence he had committed. We always had to approach 'Charles' for permission to see one of 'his' prisoners, and he often kept me waiting next to his desk as he gave out his latest bit of wisdom. Invariably when I asked to see a particular prisoner, he would glance at his board and reply, "What do you want to see that (expletive) rapist for? He's no good. You'll never do any good with him."

He was the man I had to approach every morning, when I was the duty chaplain, to obtain the keys to the chaplain's office and the telephone we were allowed to use. The telephone was a bone of contention. In his opinion, we had no need for a phone, and could very well be allowing prisoners' use of it. Every morning, Charles went on and on about how prisoners were not like they used to be. "Years ago prisoners did what they were told to do." "Prisoners used to be compliant." I was sick of his endless grandstanding, so one day I interrupted asking. "What do you put this change down to?"

"What?" he stammered.

The attention of the officers in the room focused on me, because nobody interrupted Charles when he was giving forth.

"What did you say?"

"You were saying that in your experience prisoners have changed. I am sure you are a man who reflects on your experience, so I'd expect you'd be able to tell me, a newcomer to prisons, what has brought about these changes in prisoners." Still flabbergasted at my interruption, he asked me to repeat my question.

He said he did not know. "That surprises me," I replied. "Do you think drugs have made the difference?" He had not thought of that, he said. Not wishing to push my luck any further, I requested my keys and telephone and beat a hasty retreat. I continued to cut in on his conversations at every opportunity, sometimes gently, often mischievously sending him up, other times trying to provoke him to reflect upon what he was saying.

A few months later, Charles was nearly killed by a prisoner. 'Nick' was a huge, strong young man who had been on anabolic steroids and was prone to violence. If Nick was quietly asked to do something, he normally was compliant. However, if he was ordered, or worse, provoked, he mostly reacted violently. Nick was being kept in the cages, which were punishment cells at the end of C Wing, and something fired him up. Charles bought into it, even though the cages were not under his jurisdiction. He went up there and confronted Nick, who picked him up by the throat and nearly throttled him. Charles blacked out. The guard in the tower above the cages would have killed Nick if he could have gotten a clear shot at him. Charles had to have a few days off to recover and, when he returned to work, I happened to be duty chaplain. A more subdued Charles related his near-death experience to me. I showed him compassion and encouraged him to talk it out and reflect on the incident. Over the next few days, I continued to ask him how he was feeling.

On my last day that week, he told me he was retiring the following year. Tongue in cheek, I said, "You're kidding me. A man as young as you can't be retiring."

He was clearly pleased with the compliment: "Yes, I'm out of here in April of next year, and I'll be pleased to see the last of it."

"You and your experience will be a great loss to this establishment and the prison system," I ventured.

Charles agreed. "This show doesn't value its key and experienced personnel."

Charles was moved to the classification board. The board, which sat in an office in Two Jail and was chaired by 'Tim', allocated prisoners from the reception prison to other prisons on the basis of beds available and the security status of prisoners. A prisoner appeared before Tim and Charles, and told his story: they reviewed his case and classified him as maximum, medium or minimum security. Tim was a compassionate man who, despite the pressures on him, listened to prisoners. For the first time in his career as a prison officer, Charles was forced to listen while prisoners told something of their story.

Soon after Charles began working in classification, Tim summoned me to his office. He had tried unsuccessfully to interview a prisoner from Central America. Would I talk with this prisoner, find out what his problem was, see if he had any legal needs, and report back? "Your knowledge of Latin might help you in understanding his lingo," said Tim.

I saw the prisoner, gradually pieced the story together, and reported back to Tim and Charles. I recommended that the prisoner be sent to Wacol Prison, which I also visited regularly, so that his family who lived in nearby Inala would be able to visit him without too much trouble. Tim, to my surprise, said, "If that's your recommendation, then we'll go along with it, won't we Charles?"

Charles reluctantly agreed, as Tim instructed him to log the decision. "He'll be on the bus tomorrow for Wacol prison."

I was in Wacol two days later for Mass and could not find the man from Central America. The next morning I was in Boggo Road and walked into the classification office. Tim was on the phone and Charles, in an officious way, asked me to state my business. I told him I did not think the prisoner from Latin America had made it to Wacol. After discussing the matter, Charles opened the log register, found the man's name and said, "Yes, he went to Wacol the day before yesterday." I continued to question whether the transfer had actually taken place, praying that Tim would finish his phone conversation, as Charles was becoming more and more agitated.

Tim finally put the phone down, caught on straight away, picked up the phone and called Wacol. After he had put the phone down, he said, "Well, isn't that interesting? We send a prisoner to Wacol, do all the paperwork and presume that others have done what they are supposed to do. That man is still in this prison. They didn't put him on the bus when they were supposed to. We wouldn't have known about it unless you had come in and told us. Charles, we need this man and those like him. Thanks, Wally. If you come across anything like this again, you let us know immediately."

About six months later, I was caught between the main gates, trying to gain entry into the prison. There had been another fracas the previous day, and I had to 'fight' my way into the prison. Between the gates were also a number of officers from the Security Squad (SS), the prison police, dressed in black riot gear and armed to the teeth.

I had been waiting there for 20 minutes when Charles walked past, on the inside of the prison. He saw the SS people, stopped and yelled at them, "Why don't you men get out of your fancy dress clothes and come in here and do some honest work, instead of loafing around between gates doing nothing?" When he had finished mouthing off at the SS, he noticed me. "Wally, what are you doing in there?"

"I'm waiting to get in."

"Officer of the gate! Unlock this gate and allow this man in to do his job. If you goons in black did some honest work like this chaplain, this prison would operate more efficiently."

As I passed through the gate into the prison, Charles invited me to his office for a cup of tea. When we arrived there, he said to me, "I retire at the end of this week."

I was genuinely surprised. "I didn't think it was so soon."

He talked on for a few moments, then said reflectively, "If only I knew 27 years ago, when I started this job, what I've learnt in these last six months."

Prison: community and carpet snakes

BOGGO ROAD, a place of dehumanisation and violence, was often in a state of ferment, particularly in my first two years, when riots and bashings were the order of the day. Racism was endemic. Attempted suicides, even among non-Aboriginal prisoners, numbered as many as 13 each week.

During my second full week as chaplain, I was approached by one of the elected Aboriginal elders. 'Terry' asked if he could have a yarn with me. He sat down, and we chatted together over a brew. Two days later he was back again, wondering if I had time to talk with him. This time, he told me, he wanted to have a serious chat.

He spoke to me at great length about the situation of his people in prison— the racism, the lack of jobs and, in particular, the many Aboriginal men who were culturally estranged. He and a number of his people had been reflecting on this situation for some time, and had formulated a plan. The plan encompassed three aims for their people in prison. Their first was to gather into the one yard all prisoners of Aboriginal and Torres Strait Islander descent. "The thinking here," Terry said, "is that too many of our people are subject to racist attacks by some prisoners as well as by some prison officers. If we are together in the one place, we can and will look after each other. We can stop our blokes attempting suicide. We can keep a better eye on them than the authorities." Their second aim was to establish Aboriginal cultural studies. "Many of the brothers who come in here," Terry told me, "either have little or no knowledge of their spiritual heritage, or they think it is worth nothing. We aim to turn that around. We want our people to be conscious of their Aboriginal heritage. We want them to stand tall and proud in the knowledge of it." The third aim was to establish Aboriginal arts and crafts. "Our blokes either don't get jobs or get the lowest paid jobs in the prison. We'll sell the crafts we make, so our blokes will obtain some income and be able to contribute to the support of our families."

"What do you want of me?" I asked.

"I've checked you out," Terry replied. "You're OK. I want you and your Church to help us."

Terry and his friends achieved all three aims by the time I finished as prison chaplain. I worked in Boggo Road maximum security prison in Brisbane from 1986 to the end of 1989. During that period, there were no Aboriginal deaths in custody and, as far as I was aware, no attempted suicides by young Aboriginal men.

But I remember the upheaval when most of the Aboriginal men were transferred into the one section. A hue and cry was raised by non-Aboriginal prisoners and many prison officers. Non-Aboriginal prisoners were jealous of the achievements of the Aboriginals. The Aboriginals told their white brothers that they too could achieve things if they organised themselves.

There was quite a deal of suffering involved in achieving these aims. On one occasion, because of the stand he was taking, Terry was placed in the punishment cells, or cages, as the prisoners called them. I visited him there on several occasions. He said to me, "I've told them they can keep me in here for as long as they like, for six months if they wish. But, when they release me back into the general run of the prison, I'll be continuing on right from where I left off."

Terry was unusually depressed on one of the occasions I visited him in the cages. Amazingly, the officer-in-charge of the cages allowed me to sit in his cell with him so we could talk privately. They placed no restriction on my time with him. After a month or so, Terry was released from the cages and, true to his word, continued on with the struggle.

On one of the rare occasions when an officer referred a prisoner to the chaplain, a young man came to my office. He told me it was his first time in prison, and he mentioned the minor offence for which he had been 'slotted'. He told me he had a girlfriend on the outside whom he loved dearly, and that he was sad, depressed and worried that he might do himself in.

I asked him where he was from. He told me he had been living in Toowoomba, that he had been born in Mt Isa and that he was of Aboriginal descent. I asked him to stand up and, sure enough, he stood tall and strong like a Kalkadoon man. I asked him if he would give me permission to talk to other Aborigines about his situation and put them in touch with him. He said he was tribal, and would not be able to talk with others. I told him there were other tribal people in the prison, and he consented to meet them.

I sought out Terry and told him of the plight of this young man. Terry said, "I don't know how he was able to slip through our net, but I'll get one of the brothers to spend some time with him." I contacted the man from Mt Isa later in the week. Contact had been made and he was happier. I caught up with Terry, too, and he instructed me to let him know immediately about any of his people who were in a similar situation.

Terry worked in the education centre as an assistant to the full-time teacher, John Nunn. John was a dedicated, committed and capable teacher, and also a social activist. I always made it my business to have a brew with John each week I was on. His job was a very difficult one. Many prison officers resented prisoners receiving any education at all, even in basic literacy and numeracy. Some would prevent prisoners from attending classes they had sought and obtained permission to attend. It was a regular occurrence for officers from the Special Squad to interrupt the classes, charge in and strip search prisoners, sometimes in front of female part-time teachers.

Terry and many others, including myself, worked hard at formulating a curriculum for Aboriginal cultural studies. One day I came across a good article and offered it to Terry. I did not know if he was literate. The next time I saw him, I asked him about the article, and he gave me a precise summary. Later on, I gave him another article, this time a little more difficult. He seemed to have no trouble devouring that one either. Then I loaned him Paulo Freire's "Pedagogy of the Oppressed," a book, as I mentioned earlier, I had found difficult to comprehend on first reading. The next time I saw him he said, "That Freire book is magic. It speaks to my heart. Oh, and by the way, you're not going to get it back."

A few months later, Terry was relating a recent non-violent Aboriginal action. "And that," he said, "was a classic Paulo Freire action."

Sometime later, on a Monday morning soon after I arrived in my office, Terry knocked on the door. "Do you have a few minutes?"

"Always for you."

"Did you hear what happened to 'Rachel'?" Rachel was a part-time art teacher in the prison, and she and Terry had fallen deeply in love.

"I've heard something, but I'd like to hear the story from your point of view."

"You know Rachel and me have got somethin' goin' between us?"

I nodded.

"Well, we don't see much of each other, so we've got this little arrangement where she appears on the Dutton Park railway station at about 7pm each night. My cell is high up on the back wall. It overlooks the Women's Prison and I can see the platform of the railway station. When Rachel appears, I stand on my bed and yell, and she yells back. If the wind is blowin' the right way, we can actually hear a bit of what is said.

"A few nights ago, we were carrying on our courting as usual, when I noticed this bloke stalking her with a knife. I yelled and yelled and yelled to warn her, and she just probably thought I was more ardent in my love for her. The last I saw of her was this bloke dragging her into the darkness with his knife at her throat. I nearly went berserk. I was totally powerless. The guards paid no attention, and I spent one of the most miserable nights I have ever spent in my life. The word spread around the prison, about what had happened to Rachel.

"She begged and pleaded with him, told him the names of many Aboriginal men that she knew and was able to escape from him with a few bruises, a couple of cuts, caused by grabbing the knife, and lots of shock. She rang the police and the police picked him up.

"Three days later, last Wednesday, in fact, he arrived here, in this prison. The whole place was waiting for me to deal with him. I can take care of myself, and they know that I am quite capable of dishing it out.

"As soon as I could, I went up to this young bloke, embraced him and said, 'I know what you've done and why you've done it. I don't excuse it, but I'm not goin' to give you a floggin'. I've already told the rest of the blokes in here that if anybody lays a hand on you they'll answer to me. We've got a lot of good things goin' in this prison for our Aboriginal brothers, so I hope you'll take the opportunity and tap into some of these positive things."

Terry looked at me and continued, "You know, I had to break the circle of violence. Violence causes more violence and gets us nowhere. I had to break that circle.

"By the way, do you go up to David Longland Prison? That young bloke I was telling you about has just been transferred up there. I want you to tell him from me that I had nothin' to do with his transfer. In fact, I wanted him to stay here and get into some of the good cultural stuff we've got goin' here. Will you tell him that for me?"

The next day I dropped in to see Rachel, who lived nearby at West End. She told me her story. At the end she added, "I've written him [her attacker] a letter, telling him that I'm OK and that I forgive him. I've also mentioned that I want to help him in any way he thinks I can. When you see him, will you make sure he has my letter and, if he hasn't received it, would you mind telling him these things for me?"

A few days later, I looked up the young man in David Longland Prison. He had received Rachel's letter. I gave him Terry's message also. He told me that when he arrived in Boggo Road he was expecting a belting from Terry or one of Terry's mates. He was surprised that it hadn't happened. He told me it had given him a lot to think about.

For this and for many other reasons I often said to Terry, "You have more spirituality in your little finger than I, as a professional Christian, have in my whole being."

The chaplain's office situated on the 'track' was the hottest place in summer, and the coldest in winter as the wind whistled through. A guard was stationed in the middle of the track, half-way between the two gates. I would arrive at the gate, the guard would see me and I would have to wait, sometimes as long as 20 minutes. If another guard came along, he would jump up immediately and let both of us through.

One day I was waiting patiently at the gate for the guard to come and let me through. A prisoner joined me. We chatted while we waited. The guard eventually came and let us through. As we were walking down the track, this Aboriginal man astounded me by exclaiming, "I love this part of the jail the best."

That blew me out. I looked around again at the stark walls, the razor wire, the armed guard in the tower above watching us.

"How come?"

He pointed to a small stunted tree, growing out of a crack in the third row from the top of the high red brick wall.

"You see that tree?" he said. "Every time I walk through here, I look up there and greet my brother. He says to me, 'If I can survive and grow up here on this arid wall, you can do the same and better down there'. That tree gives me hope."

The Racing Guide Bible

Josh, whom I mentioned earlier, was a lifer and a lovable old man. He was a chronic asthmatic, suffering from emphysema. He always had a nebuliser and oxygen at hand. He never missed Mass. When I first began working in the prisons, Josh worked in the maintenance gang outside the walls of Boggo Road. His responsibility was the rose gardens. He came back into the prison after lunch, and was allowed to rest on his special tilted bed. He played a key role as a father figure to many young prisoners. On one occasion he told me that he had a never-ending stream of prisoners dropping into his cell for a chat during the afternoon, when he was supposed to be resting. Nobody will ever know the amount of good work done by Josh and other prisoners like him. I always made it my business to have a long chat with Josh each week I worked in the prison.

One day I arranged to meet him at 2pm in J Wing mess, which was adjacent to his yard and his cell. I walked past the guards at the door of the mess, telling them that I was meeting Josh inside. Josh was sitting at a table. I greeted him and sat down. It was then that I noticed that he was having great difficulty in breathing. I waited for him to catch his breath, but his condition did not improve. I asked him if I should seek assistance and he vigorously shook his head. I then asked him if he wanted me to leave. Again he shook his head and placed his hand on my arm, pressing me to stay.

Ten minutes later he had regained his breath. He told me what had upset him was that he had walked into the mess one or two minutes ahead of me, to see two prisoners shooting up heroin. He could not believe their brazenness in taking drugs in a public part of the jail and with two guards on duty at the door. A week or two previously, he told me, he saw something sticking up from an overflow drain in the toilet. He bent over and pulled it up. It turned out to be a sock containing syringes.

Josh was a great punter. He had no relatives and used his weekly phone call to place his bets through his TAB phone account. After Saturday morning Mass, I often asked him what horse he had his money on that afternoon. He would say, "I just happen to have my bible in my back pocket," and pull out the racing guide. I would write down the horses he was betting on, and I noticed that nine out of 10 Saturdays he backed winners.

As he never had any visitors and was interested in receiving a visit, we arranged for one of our volunteers to visit him. She did so on a regular basis for six years, and they fell in love. Josh would pick a few of his best roses and present them to her in the visiting area. On one occasion, he told me, he was making his way to the visiting area when a guard challenged him about what he was carrying—which was obvious. The guard took the roses from him and dismembered them one by one. This done, he then ordered Josh to pick up the petals, wrap them in newspaper and give them to his girlfriend.

Josh's medical condition slowly deteriorated. He spent long periods of time in the prison hospital and was confined to a wheelchair. Prisoners organised among themselves to take him for a "walk" in his wheelchair around the oval, and made certain that he was brought over to Mass. Josh was deeply grateful for all that was done for him and, as Josh was classified as minimum security, we tried to have him released on parole as he had served 10 years of a life sentence (and was therefore eligible to apply for parole). We applied to have him work each day at Catholic Prison Ministry, helping around the office. Instead, he was transferred to the prison farm at Numinbah near the border of New South Wales. The move was nearly the death of him: Numinbah was wet and cold, and his cell did not have any heating. As he was constantly ill, he had to be transferred back to Boggo where, he was told, the hospital was equipped to deal with his needs. We tried every avenue we possibly could to have him released over the next two years. His girlfriend's flat was inspected, she was interviewed, and she and her flat were approved by the authorities.

A number of applications for parole, on the grounds of his medical condition and good behaviour, were rejected by the Queensland Community Corrections Board, as "lifers" are not generally considered for release until they have served a minimum of 13 years. A few days before he died, Josh was advised in a letter from the Board that "No exceptional circumstances exist in your case which would warrant the Board's variance from those guidelines."

Josh was hopeful and cheerful to the end. I would take him Communion in the hospital, and he would break into a smile of gratitude, tidy up his bed and compose himself to receive his Lord.

The failure of the system to release Josh so that he could die decently and in dignity was another manifestation of its heartlessness and its inability to assess the security risk and respond in a humane way to an invalided old man. Despite all this, Josh died with his dignity intact in the prison hospital. I am sure he rests in peace.

"The do-gooder"

One of the places I visited regularly on my rounds as duty chaplain was the reception and discharge area. This, as in most sections of the prison, was staffed by prisoners working side by side with officers and under their supervision. I would wander over there to receive the print-outs on the recent admissions which, amongst other details, noted religious affiliation. Another task was to see if any of the workers wanted to speak with the duty chaplain. If there was no action, I would chat for a while and keep on going.

On one of these visits, 'Jack' asked me if I had time for a brew. He asked permission of the officer to speak with me, and we moved to a space where we were able to speak semi-privately.

"What sort of a do-gooder are you?"

"I'll never be as good a one as you," I said. "What's on your mind?"

"This morning we discharged a couple of young blokes who come from down South. They have no money and nowhere to stay. They're not bad young fellas, but they'll be back in here quick smart 'cause they've got no contacts. What I want to know is can you or your Church help? It's too late for these young blokes, but there will be others."

I told him to give me a couple of hours, and I'd get back to him that day. I contacted Tim and the manager of the Saint Vincent de Paul Men's Hostel at South Brisbane. Tim assured me that a bed or beds could be made available at a little hostel he supervised at Oxley, and the manager of Vinnies made a commitment to reserve two or three rooms for people coming out of prison. Armed with these names, addresses and phone numbers, I returned to the reception area and handed them over to Jack. He dutifully pinned them on to the notice board next to the counter. "They'll be handy when any of us need them." Then he added, "You're not bad for a do-gooder, are you?"

Next time I was in that part of the prison, Jack again invited me to join him for a brew. "How long have you been working in here now?" he asked.

"Over six months."

"Have you come across any prisoners who have told you they are guilty of the crimes they were arrested for?"

"I could have. What's on your mind?"

"I just want to tell you that all of those blokes out there are guilty, but I'm not. I, in fact, have done more than most to create employment, to help the building industry along at a depressed time and what thanks do I get? They shove me in here for eight years. There's no justice in our system."

"Go on. Don't stop there," I urged, wondering what was coming next.

He went on to tell me that he had 'dropped' a building for an insurance job. He was an explosives expert and was engaged to destroy a building so the owner could obtain the insurance.

While we were sitting there, a few new prisoners arrived, including a young lad who could have been barely 17. Jack excused himself and hopped up. He called the young man over, extended his hand to him and said, "My name's Jack. I work in this section and I'm here each day. If anybody hassles you and you don't want to be hassled, let me know and I'll make sure nothing happens. This bloke here is the chaplain. He's OK. You can talk to him too."

Jack had been a mercenary, and knew how to handle himself. He was not prepared to look the other way if prisoners were standing over other prisoners, physically or sexually. Some time later, he was transferred to Wacol, where he continued to do what he could for other prisoners. I did my best to offer whatever support I could.

One time, we were following a matter through together and I needed to see him. I went to the place where he normally worked and was told that he had been transferred to the farm adjacent to the prison. I received permission to visit him out there, and drove out in my car.

I pulled up next to the little wooden office building to report my presence to the officer-in-charge. I could hear cursing, swearing and stomping coming from the office. I waited in the car, hoping it would settle down. When it didn't, and I hadn't the patience to wait any longer, I hopped out of the car, climbed the three steps and knocked on the open door. In the room were eight burly prison officers hopping around, swearing and cursing trying to get out of the road of a huge carpet snake and trying, at the same time, to get it out of the office.

"What do you want?" one demanded.

"I want to see Jack."

"See whoever you like. Can't you see we're busy?"

"You do seem to have your hands full," said I, as I retreated down the stairs. At that moment, Jack came around the corner of the building and greeted me.

"Why did you put that snake in there?" I challenged.

"Who told you I did that?"

"Listen mate, I didn't come down in the last shower. What the hell did you do that for?"

"Well, this morning they told me to work in the hay shed. I told them I'm an asthmatic. They insisted I go. I'd only been working over there a short time when I came across this huge carpet snake. I've been waiting all morning for all of the screws to be in the office together. A couple of minutes before you arrived—I didn't know you were coming out to see me—they were all in there, so as I walked past the door I threw it in. If they send me back to the hay shed after lunch, they'll get another one. I've found its mate."

Jack often came to Mass in the prison, but would get openly annoyed when I spoke about non-violence, which I often did. At one stage he stopped coming to Mass, but we continued to be good friends and to work together. Six months later, he came back to Mass. The Gospel reading was from Matthew 16:13-26:

> Now when Jesus came into the district of Caesarea Philippi, he asked his disciples, "Who do people say that the Son of Man is?" And they said, "Some say John the Baptist, but others Elijah, and still others Jeremiah or one of the prophets." He said to them, "But who do you say that I am?"

Simon Peter answered, "You are the Messiah, the Son of the living God." And Jesus answered him, "Blessed are you, Simon son of Jonah! For flesh and blood has not revealed this to you, but my Father in heaven." Then Jesus told his disciples, "If any want to become my followers, let them deny themselves and take up their cross and follow me. For those who want to save their life will lose it, and those who lose their life for my sake will find it. For what will it profit them if they gain the whole world but forfeit their life? Or what will they give in return for their life?"

Having read this Gospel, I asked the prisoners to say in one word, if they wished, who Jesus was to them. There were various replies as we went round the semi-circle. Jack was the last and his word was "courage." I asked him how he saw the courage of Jesus.

"Did you see the footage on TV on Tiananmen Square in China?" I nodded. "Did you see that young student walk out in front of the line of tanks, hold his hand up and stop them, then hop up on the leading tank and talk to the commander? To do that took raw courage. That to me is the courage of Christ.

"He didn't know he was goin' to be a hero. He didn't know that he was goin' to be on TV throughout the world. He did it because he believed in democracy for his people. He took up the cross of democracy and was prepared to lose his life for freedom of speech in China."

On another occasion after Mass, Jack called me to one side and asked, "Are you happy with the number of blokes who attend Church?"

"I'm happy enough. It takes courage to attend Mass in prison. All the prisoners know where you are going, as do the prison officers. The blokes get chiacked for coming here."

"I've got an idea how you'll get a lot more blokes. Substitute Glenfiddich whisky for that cheap claret you use and they'll roll in."

Our Eucharists in prison were somewhat informal. Most times, there was an opportunity to talk together informally for 20 minutes or more, while keys and an officer were found. We generally used only one reading from the Lectionary, mostly the Gospel for the following Sunday. We then discussed this reading together. In these discussions one would often hear the results of the men's own seclusion, isolation and contemplation. I enjoyed the Eucharists immensely. They tended to attract largely, but by no means exclusively, prisoners who were involved in social justice. The men responded positively to the social justice dimension in the readings from the Bible.

While in Wacol prison, Jack, with a fellow-prisoner 'Ted', built up a flourishing business in the delicate art of pressing flowers. They spent a few hours each day collecting wild flowers in the fields of the prison farm. Even some of the prison officers got involved, bringing in pieces of fern or flowers. They chose combinations and then pressed them, placing them on the front of greeting cards. They wrote a loving message or a moving poem composed by a fellow-inmate. Both of them had attended calligraphy and floral art classes organised by the education officer at the prison.

Their cards caught the eyes of other inmates who wanted to send them to their loved ones on the outside. Friends and relatives loved the cards and submitted more orders. Mother's Day was the turning point in their endeavours. The demand spurred them both to thinking about expansion. They knew that there were a lot of talented people in prison, doing mundane work, suffering from boredom and receiving little or no encouragement for their legitimate creative talents. Jack and Ted made application to the Corrective Services Commission to set up a commercial card-making business, employing another 10 prisoners. The Commission was interested, and the enterprise went ahead and was successful.

Rob

'Rob', a new prisoner, began coming to Mass at Wacol. Rob was a married man with two or three teenage children. His wife was a practising Catholic and his children attended Catholic schools. Rob had been to Mass with his family on special occasions and had intended to become a Catholic, but had never gotten around to doing anything about it. Now that he was in prison, he wondered if it were possible for him to take instructions and become a Catholic. I gave him a book to work through, told him I would meet up with him at least once a month, and encouraged him to talk things over with one or two of the men who came to Mass. We met regularly and discussed what he had been reading and any problems he wished to discuss.

One day I said to him, "Do you pray?"

"Every day."

"If you don't mind me asking, what form does your prayer take?"

"I take the first cell call each night, so I'm locked in my cell at 6.30pm. The first thing I do is write a letter to my wife. Then I spend a half an hour to an hour on my hobby. I make things out of match sticks. After that, I pick up my Bible and read a bit and just sit with it. I'm about half-way through the Gospel of Matthew at the moment. I just take a paragraph or two and read it slowly a couple of times and try to think about it."

We discussed this for a little while and then he continued, "After that I pray to God for my wife and my children and anybody else I want to pray for. After that I just sit there and talk to God about my day, who I've met and some of the problems they are having and maybe some of the problems I'm having with them."

I thought he was finished when, after a pause, he continued. "After that, it's beginning to get late, about 9.30 or so, and the prison is starting to settle down for the night. I switch off my light and sit there in total darkness. I try to rid my mind of all thoughts and just sit in the presence of my God, trying to be quiet and listen to what God might want to say to me."

I was very impressed. Rob's prayer-life encompassed meditation on the Word of God, talking to God about his day and the people in his life, prayer of petition, and finally contemplation. I had nothing to offer except encouragement. A few weeks later we received him into the Church in a special Mass celebrated in the prison chapel. Rob was another prisoner who had time for his fellow-prisoners. Because he was who he was—self-possessed, thoughtful and considerate—many sought his listening ear and wise counsel.

Changed hearts, changing systems

MATT AND DENNIS, the two 'hostage takers' who had welcomed me to prison chaplaincy after my first Mass in Boggo Road, were drug-addicts who had supported their habit by stealing cars and robbing banks. Both were big men in their late 20s, and both were members of the heavyweight weight-lifting team in the prison. During my first year in Boggo, whenever they saw me they would yell out some smart remark. If I could think of a quick retort, I responded; if not, I just ignored them. They were violent men and prone to violence in prison. They were known never to back off a fight with anyone foolish enough to take them on.

One day 12 months after I began work in the prison, Matt caught up with me. "I want to talk with you."

"What's on your mind?"

"I want you to help me, if you know what I mean."

"I wouldn't be able to do that."

"That's your job, isn't it?"

"Maybe it is, but I can only help people who want to help themselves."

"Well, that's what I mean. I've been in boys' homes and prisons since I was 12, and now I'm 27, and I want out, if you know what I mean. Can you help me?"

"Maybe. But only if you want to help yourself."

"Well, I'm talking to you, aren't I? What do you think my problems are?"

I was wary of answering a question like that. Was I being set up? Matt and his mates were much bigger and stronger than me. I took my life in my hands and listed a number of problems as I saw them: drugs, violence, and so on. I finished up by saying that I felt he lacked self-discipline, and would not be able to get his act together until he worked on self-control. He said he would think about what I had said, and we left it at that.

Six weeks later, he approached me again. "I've been thinking about what you said to me, and I'd like to have a go at it."

"What, in particular, did you have in mind?"

"That self-control stuff. I reckon that's what I need to work on, if you know what I mean."

We arranged a meeting in the chaplain's office and began an eight-week program of self-discipline. Ray Lyons, my parish priest at Bardon, had taught me this program when I was with him. True to his word, Matt was keen and did not falter on any of the steps. About halfway through the program, I was talking with Matt in the office when the door was flung open and in walked Dennis.

"What are you two talking about?" he demanded.

"None of your business. What we talk about in here is between us. If Matt wants to tell you about it, that's up to him. Don't come barging in here without knocking while I'm talking with somebody."

As Dennis retreated to the door, he threw back at us, "Whatever you're doin' is making a difference to him. He's changin'."

Soon after Matt completed the program, he was transferred to Woodford Prison, which I visited only once a fortnight.

A month or so later, Dennis walked into my office. "I want you to do for me what you did for Matt," he demanded. He too took to the self-discipline program like a duck to water, not faltering on any of the steps.

Unbeknown to me, a few prisoners, including Dennis, decided to occupy the roof of one of the blocks in Two Jail. They were protesting about prison conditions. They occupied the roof for a number of days, resisting the temptation to tear up roof tiles and throw them on prison officers below. Sister Bernice was called upon to negotiate with them and, after receiving some assurances, they ceased their protest. I was very proud of them, particularly since they had acted in a non-violent way. Soon after this, Dennis too was transferred to Woodford.

Sometime later, Matt and Dennis became Christians. Dennis asked me to baptise him by immersion in the lake at Woodford, to which I readily agreed. I pointed out to him that this made his baptism a public action and that some prisoners would not be slow to test him out.

He used one reading at his baptism, and gave his reflections on it after it was read. The short reading came from Galatians 5:22-23 and reads:

"the fruit of the Spirit is love, joy, peace, patience, kindness, generosity, faithfulness, gentleness, and self-control."

Both Matt and Dennis continued to be powers for good in the prisons they lived in, right up until their release. On one occasion Matt told me that prison officers were asking him if he would be prepared to have young people live in his block, and if he would keep an eye on them. Matt was more than a little proud of this new status and the opportunity to make a positive contribution to the lives of some young people. On a number of occasions I asked Dennis to look out for particular prisoners who were lonely, depressed and suicidal. Dennis was always willing.

Once Matt approached me, saying, "This business of being a Christian isn't easy, if you know what I mean?"

"What part isn't easy for you?"

"I've had a reputation for never backing away from a fight, if you know what I mean? Well, lots of blokes in here know that now I'm a Christian, and I'm no longer into that sort of stuff. A few of them try to provoke me into a fight, if you know what I mean. My brother's in here too, and he noticed this sort of thing. He said to me, 'I see these guys hassling you and I know you are not into fighting any more. But if you give me the nod I'll take care of them for you.' It'd be easy for me to give him the nod, wouldn't it? But that wouldn't be doin' the right thing, would it? If you know what I mean?" I could only agree with this now gentle giant.

Normally at Woodford, Tim, Bernice (if she was available), and I saw inmates on a one-to-one basis. In the afternoons we would meet as a group to celebrate Eucharist. One morning, soon after the episode described above, all the inmates arrived at once and we were able to meet as a group. We expected at any minute that a prison officer would burst in and break up our group, but we talked for nearly two hours. Matt and Dennis were part of that group, and they talked about their childhoods, the violence, the hate and the anger. One said, and the other agreed, that all they had known for most of their lives was hate, anger and violence. These things were part and parcel of their home lives, their time in children's institutions, youth detention centres, and of course in prisons.

They then spoke of Tim, Bernice and myself—how we preached and practised a different way, and how they thought we were fools, naïve, out of touch, and possibly phonies. They said they had watched us over a long period of time, and finally decided that maybe there was another way, apart from hate, violence and ripping people off. They spoke of the struggles to change themselves, and the peace they had achieved within themselves, which one of them described as "having a weight lifted from your shoulders" and "winning through to a sort of freedom, even in prison."

"Could you act like a priest?"

I often referred prisoners to the Prisoners' Legal Service. Prisoners are human beings and entitled to all legitimate means to uphold their rights. One of the lawyers associated with the Youth Advocacy Centre had taught me that all people in custody are entitled to anything which makes sense. For example, if a person in custody is sick they are entitled to see a doctor. He also told me people are entitled to know their rights and, if necessary, assisted to exercise those rights.

I was always coming across prisoners who had been bashed by officers or fellow-prisoners. I would be told of them by some of the prisoners with a social conscience. Even though these prisoners were being held in isolation, I would persist in trying to see them, until I was eventually allowed. I would walk into their cell in the hospital, with nothing but a mattress on the floor and a toilet in the corner, announce who I was, and ask if the prisoner wanted to talk with me. No one ever refused. I would chat with them for a while. Mostly they would want to tell me about the bashing. I would ask if they wanted to see a lawyer. A typical response would be: "How the hell can I see a lawyer when I'm locked away in here?"

I would reply, "I can arrange that for you if you want me to. If you decide different when the lawyer comes, that's up to you."

They always looked surprised.

The weeks I was on duty in Boggo Road, a prisoner would be bashed up one day, and a day or so later a lawyer would be in to see him. I knew that was risky, but I felt it was necessary to take those sort of risks. I did not condone the violence, and I did not want to be associated with any of it. I was intent on doing all that I could to stop the violence, and legal assistance was one of the means I had at my disposal. I knew that some of the authorities would take a dim view of what I was doing.

One day as I was doing my work in the prison, I happened upon 'Jake', a senior prison officer. I greeted him, saying that I had been phoning his office and I needed to see him. He told me he had been doing the same.

"You know, Wally, I admire the work you are doing in this prison and I am 100 per cent behind you. I am not of your faith and I do not want to sound critical of you or your work, but the SS [the special squad, the internal prison police] are monitoring your every movement at the moment. From the time you walk into this prison to the time you leave, they are plotting where you go, whom you speak with and how long you talk with them."

I said I appreciated what he was saying.

"Again, I am not critical of your work, but do you think you could act like a priest for about two weeks? If you do, the SS will lose interest and drop off. Do you think you could do that?"

I was grateful for the tip-off, and assured Jake that I would try my best to act like a priest. Jake was kind enough to tip me off on several occasions. We were able to work together on a number of issues. Jake was a man I could trust and recommend to prisoners.

On another occasion, I was visiting prisoners who worked above the hospital in the dentist rooms and around the doctor's waiting area. I was sitting in a room stacked with records, talking with a prisoner, when another prisoner dropped some forms in for filing. The forms were admission forms for new prisoners. I looked at a few of them and noted that they contained the classification 'boys'. ('Boy' is classified as being over sixteen and under nineteen years of age. 'Children' are deemed to be under sixteen years of age). At that time there was a provision in the Children's Services Act (1965) for the Director-General to request the Comptroller-General of Prisons to accept children into prison if it was felt that they were unable to be controlled elsewhere. I knew that any person over the age of 17 would be sent to an adult prison, but wondered how many young people under the age of 17 were moving through the adult prison system.

I raised my concern at the next management committee meeting of Catholic Prison Ministry, who agreed that the matter should be followed through. Arlene Morgan suggested I contact Jake, a student of Arlene's. He might, she said, be able to obtain the information.

As soon as I could, I approached Jake. He was immediately interested. "How many months of statistics would you require?"

I told him I thought three months would be adequate, but he suggested that six months would give a better indication. He was to work in that area on the following weekend, and having basically nothing to do, would be able to complete the research.

The results of his work were quite startling, so much so that when I showed them to the Management Committee they were incredulous, saying Jake must have made a mistake. They asked me to ask Jake to check his results, which he did, and came up with the same figures.

Break-down over the past six months: [of under-17s in the prison system]	
April, 1987	34
May	46
June	52
July	41
August	27
Sept. (to 11th)	15

In the above-mentioned period two children were admitted:

22/4/1987　(1)DOB 12/4/1971 (first admitted to this establishment on 30/10/1986 and still here)

1/5/1987　(2)DOB 10/5/1970 (first admitted to this establishment on 12/5/1985 that is, two days after his fifteenth birthday)

The average age of 'boys' totalled above is 17 years 4 months, at the time of being confined to this establishment.

We were shocked that so many young people were being sentenced by the courts to prison—this university of crime. The trickle of 'children' into the adult system was alarming, a concern later picked up by the Kennedy Review.

Harold

I had not been working long in the prisons when I was approached by Harold. Harold had recently lost an appeal to have his life sentence reduced. He approached me, told me about his offence, expressed remorse and his frustration in not being able to make up for the life he had taken. Pleadingly, he asked, "What could I ever do to make up for the life I have taken? There is nothing I can do, is there?"

"You could be a 'life-giver,'" I suggested. "You have taken a life. You are unable to restore that life. But while you are in this system, you could do all in your power to give life to those you are rubbing shoulders with."

He asked me to explain. "You know better than I do the numbers of needy blokes in prison. Some need someone to listen to them, a shoulder to cry on, some need to be confronted with the truth, some need to be challenged about their violent behaviour. If you decide that you want to go down this track, I'll support you to the best of my ability. You think about this and get back to me if you wish to pursue the idea."

The very next day he was knocking on my door, telling me he was interested and asking me how he could get started. True to his word, he began to be a life-giver to fellow-prisoners and to prison officers. I made certain I saw him every week I was in, to give him time to talk about himself, and especially to support him in his role as life-giver.

On one public holiday after Harold had been transferred to Wacol, I was very tired and tossing up whether I should go to Wacol or just take advantage of the public holiday and rest. About 10 a.m. I set sail for Wacol. I had no sooner walked in the door when Harold ran me down saying, "Am I pleased to see you. I didn't expect you in, today being a public holiday." He told me about a young prisoner he worked with in the stores whose wife had been pack-raped in her home the previous evening. The prisoner was beside himself with worry. Harold was concerned he would do something stupid, which wouldn't help his wife or himself and which would probably extend his time in the prison system. Harold wanted me to meet the prisoner, who poured out tearfully the terrible story as he had been told it in a telephone call from his wife. I assured him I would have someone out to see her in the next 24 hours and that I would give him progress reports.

I activated our community contacts until I found a woman who was capable of handling this complex situation and who, in fact, was able to visit the wife that afternoon. During the visit she heard the story, assisted with the young children, suggested rape counselling and promised she would be in regular contact. Before I left the prison that afternoon I was able to tell the prisoner what had happened. The prisoner found this reassuring and comforting. I also told Harold what had been done and we talked about how he would handle the prisoner overnight until I could follow up with the prisoner, Harold, and my community contact the next day. Harold continued to be a life-giver for the rest of his sentence.

A difficult test

'Nancy' and her two-year-old daughter 'Alice' were parishioners of Saint Francis, West End. Nancy was separated from her husband, who lived in another part of West End with their adopted son Steve. Nancy attended Church regularly, was outgoing, vivacious and a rallying point for many Filipinos. The parties she and her friends, particularly 'Mary', put on were wonderful gatherings of many people from different ethnic backgrounds. People donated money or food for these occasions, and Nancy and Mary delighted in making the tastiest dishes. Noel and I were always invited to the parties, and mostly we attended. If, however, we were unable to attend one of their Saturday night parties, we were gently but firmly berated the next morning at the 8.30 Mass by either Nancy or Mary or both. We would then have to promise to turn up for Sunday lunch, as there was always food left over. The Sunday lunch gatherings were quieter affairs, with less than a dozen people, and often with somebody plucking away on a guitar in the background.

Noel and I employed Nancy to clean the presbytery once a fortnight. She always brought Alice with her, spent the day playing with Alice and, when Alice was resting, did what needed to be done. We saw her regularly and enjoyed her company and that of her friends.

In January 1987 Nancy's friends contacted me and told that she was depressed. I contacted her on several occasions and she told me she was OK. After a few more calls from her friends, I called in to see her. After a period of time she told me that she was depressed, was upset about her interaction with her estranged husband, and did not want to see a doctor (especially a psychiatrist) as she feared she might be put into a mental hospital. I went with her to see a local doctor who listened to her story and promised to work through her problems with her. He made an appointment for her to see a marriage counsellor with the Family Court. Nancy asked me to see her husband, which I did. We talked well together, and I left promising him that I would relate the conversation to Nancy as he had requested.

Over the next few days I phoned Nancy repeatedly, and called in on three occasions, but could not make contact. I was horrified a few days later to receive a phone call to say that Nancy had been murdered: her throat had been slashed and Alice was missing. Her estranged husband 'Pat' was also missing. A few days later, Pat's body was found in the boot of his car in a quarry. He had been shot in the back of the head. A few days later, Alice was found. The murderer had taken her to the home of some of his friends immediately after he had killed her mother. The murderer, 'Tom', was apprehended by the police and charged with the murders. I knew Tom. He had called into the presbytery at West End on two occasions. He was totally infatuated with Nancy and had ordered me to tell her to leave West End and live with him, which I had refused to do.

There were huge difficulties in arranging the funerals, as neither victim had relatives in Australia. The two children, Steve and Alice, had been placed under the Care and Protection of the Department of Children's Services, which was a worry. And the local community was grieving, particularly the Filipino community.

Not long after Tom was arrested, he was transferred to Boggo Road. I dreaded meeting him there, and wondered if I would simply avoid him, ignore him or vent my anger on him. I sought assistance from my God in prayer. I knew I had to treat him with dignity, maybe even forgive him, but I was grieving and I was angry.

A week later, as I was doing my rounds at Boggo Road, I spotted Tom in one of the yards, called him over to the bars, and asked him how he was going. He didn't recognise me, and refused to talk. I thanked God that he had given me the strength to call Tom over and that God had let me off the hook so lightly! A week or so later, Tom spotted me and challenged me: "You don't know me."

"Yes I do. I spoke to you some time ago, and you wouldn't give me the time of day."

"I want you to bring Alice in here to see me."

"There is no way I would bring that little girl into a prison, especially to see you. I am certain that the prison authorities and the police would not allow her anywhere near you."

He turned his back on me and walked away.

The next week he saw me walking past the yard and came over to the fence to talk to me. "I'm depressed. I'm thinking of doing myself in."

I wish you'd done yourself in five weeks ago before you committed the murders, I thought to myself uncharitably, as I listened to him talk about his depression. I told him about the Spanish-speaking chaplain who lived in Brisbane. Tom was keen to see him, so he could converse in his native language. Thereafter my only contact with him was when he wanted to see the Spanish chaplain.

Speaking to Tom was personally one of the hardest things I had to do while I was working in the prisons. My Christian principles were put to the test. As a Christian, and a professional one at that, I struggled to treat Tom with dignity, to forgive and offer him the services which I would offer to any other prisoner.

The 'black hole'

In the late seventies, I had contact with a prisoner who had just been released from Boggo Road, and who told me that underground cells were being built in the prison. I was incredulous, but he convinced me that the story was true. I found it difficult to believe that in the latter half of the twentieth century, we were doing such a moronic thing. In the aftermath of the riots in 1984, the underground cells were closed.

Soon after I began working in the prison system, I heard stories from men who had spent time in the 'black hole'. I remember that one man who had been sentenced for sexual offences was transferred there, not because he had infringed prison regulations, but because prison officers decided he should receive, in addition to his sentence, punishment from them. Six of them entered his underground cell and, after stripping him naked, belted him literally black and blue. When they turned up the next day to administer another dose, they were appalled at the extent of his bruising and left him alone. He told me that his bruises saved his life, or at least further treatment of the same kind. They left him in his cell for a week, until his bruises healed, and then released him back into the mainstream prison.

For a while, our chaplaincy office was located near the entrance to the disused black hole. I was working at my desk one day when a prison officer, whom I had thought to be a reasonable human being, barged in and said, "Do you know where you are?"

"You tell me," I responded, unhappy with his unannounced intrusion.

"This is the dreaded black hole. Come," he commanded, "I'll give you a guided tour."

I downed tools and followed him out into the corridor. At first he kept the lights on and showed me the individual cells with their concrete bunks, heavy iron door and shower on the outside. When he then switched the lights off, in the complete darkness I was unable to see my hand in front of my eyes.

My guide began to enthuse, "We used to have great fun down here. You see, you can't hear down here what's going on in the main prison. The crims down here had no idea what the time was. So we'd feed 'em and put 'em to bed at 4.30pm. Then two hours later, we'd wake 'em up and tell 'em it was morning and feed 'em again. We'd go through a 24-hour routine in one shift. In winter time, we'd turn the air conditioning system onto the coldest setting and freeze 'em. In summer, we'd turn the heating system up high and cook 'em. We had lots of fun with the crims down here."

To our horror, the government announced in November 1987 that the black hole would be reopened. Mr Neal, the Minister for Corrective Services at the time, said the unit would be used to house unmanageable prisoners who committed offences in the jail, such as assaulting prison officers. He said he was also influenced by reports that trouble was expected the following year at World Expo 88, which would be held in Brisbane, "especially from Aboriginal activists."[97]

97 Leading article, *Courier-Mail*, 12 November 1987.

I immediately notified the Federal Human Rights Commission in Sydney and spoke with the Commissioner, Mr Brian Burdekin. He promised to look into the matter and to keep in touch. The very next day the Human Rights Commission condemned the Prisons Department decision to re-open the underground cells at Brisbane's Boggo Road jail. The Commission president, Mr Justice Einfeld, said it demonstrated a total ignorance of the basic principles of human rights, including those in the United Nations Covenant on Civil and Political Rights, to which Australia was a signatory. These absolutely forbade 'cruel and unusual punishment'. Mr Justice Einfeld said the decision to re-open the underground cells was particularly regrettable, coming on the first day of the Muirhead Royal Commission into black deaths in custody. "To even contemplate using sub-standard facilities for Aboriginal prisoners in light of recent tragic events makes a mockery of the Queensland Government's own inquiry into black deaths. It demonstrates either an appalling insensitivity to, or complete disregard of, the problem. While Mr Neal may feel he is administering his portfolio correctly by citing efficiency as the reason for his decision, efficiency alone can never stand as the sole measure of an administrative act. Morality takes precedence." The Commission called on the Queensland Government to announce immediately that the cells would not be reopened for use by any prisoners, black or white.[98]

Our chaplaincy team at Boggo Road met and decided to use our influence within the system to reverse the decision. The Premier of Queensland, Sir Joh Bjelke-Petersen, said the State Government would not back down on its decision to reopen the 'black hole' underground cells. He added: "Any jail is inhumane. We have a good Minister, a good system, good jails."[99]

Our Catholic Prison Ministry Working Party on Prisoners and their Families considered the re-opening of the detention unit at the Brisbane Prison. I made the point at that meeting, that I could not in conscience work in that prison if the black hole was re-opened. There was no way of monitoring what went on in there. According to what I had been told, it had mostly been used for 'square-ups' by prison officers. There were many alternative forms of punishment that could be used instead, such as locking prisoners in their cells or putting them in the cages. The meeting decided on an action plan which Tim, Bernice and myself were charged to implement.

The following day I phoned the bishop and, as he was unavailable, I left a detailed message with his secretary. He phoned me back that afternoon, yelling into the phone: "I have been active. I have tried to phone somebody a few times, but they haven't returned my call." I asked him to whom he had been speaking and what he intended to say to them, but he wouldn't tell me. I also

98   *Courier-Mail*, 14 November 1987.
99   *Courier-Mail*, 16 November 1987.

requested that he convene a meeting of the Heads of Churches about the matter. He again yelled that he had been active. I refused to be intimidated and asked him whom he had been phoning. He refused to tell me saying, "These galahs are so stupid and become more aggressive the more they are attacked. I'll get back to you. I am concerned."

I did not find the conversation satisfactory. I was not comforted by the fact that he was 'talking to somebody about something'. Whilst I was heartened by his concern and the fact he at least had done something, my conscience told me I had to continue to do all I could.

The next day, a letter was sent to all priests in Queensland on Catholic Prison Ministry letterhead, signed by myself. We asked the priests to give the matter their urgent consideration and to bring it to the attention of their parishioners. We outlined our opposition to the re-opening of the black hole and encouraged the priests and their parishioners to contact by letter or by phone the Minister for Corrective Services and the President of the Queensland National Party. We enclosed a sample letter.

Wishing to inform the bishop of our action, I dropped a copy of the letter into his residence. I also contacted two of the regional Bishops in Queensland, alerting them to what we had done. Tim, Bernice and I then phoned those priests whom we thought would be on side and who were working in National Party electorates.

The following Monday morning I was in Boggo Road for my week in the prison. During the morning, while I was making my rounds, I was accosted by an angry prison officer. He had attended Mass in his parish, and was astounded when my letter was read out. His angry outburst attracted the attention of several other prison officers who surrounded me. He had not gone very far in his attack when a senior officer called him away. The others wanted to know what the story was. I told them to ask him, and walked away.

Calls to revoke the decision were coming in thick and fast, from the Federal Government and such groups as the Foundation for Aboriginal and Islander Research Action, the Queensland Civil Liberties Council, the Aboriginal and Islander Catholic Council, the Roman Catholic Chaplain to Aboriginals and Islanders and the Australian Student Christian Movement (Queensland Area Council).

A month or so later, the Premier was replaced by Michael Ahern, who decided that the underground cells would not be used but an above-ground detention unit would be built. This detention unit was built, and what happened inside could be monitored (to some extent) by those who were working or incarcerated nearby.

The Kennedy Review

In late February 1988, the State Government instigated a Prison Review. Mr Jim Kennedy, a local entrepreneur, accepted the appointment as Commissioner of the Review and produced an interim report in May 1988. By August, he produced his final report with eighty recommendations. The Review was conducted thoroughly, and prisoners were encouraged to participate and did so. Once prisoners were convinced there was some hope for action from the Review, the atmosphere in Boggo Road changed from one of violence and hopelessness to one of co-operation: literate prisoners assisted their illiterate brothers to submit their reflections and recommendations.

Ian O'Connor, of the Social Work Department of the University of Queensland, and I submitted our reflections on young offenders to the Review. Within 24 hours of the Commissioner receiving our paper, we were summoned to a meeting. At the meeting we handed him a copy of the numbers of young people in adult prisons. He was incredulous and demanded to know how we had obtained the figures. Of course we could not and did not tell him. I told him that he had the means at his disposal to prove or disprove the figures. (He contacted us a few days later and informed us our figures were accurate). He asked our permission to include segments of our paper in his report, and invited us to sit on a Young Offenders Review Committee which he intended to set up.

Amazingly, the Government began to implement the Review's excellent report and recommendations—resisted, of course, by some of the prison officers. Sister Bernice was appointed to the Review Commission, and later on to the newly established Queensland Corrective Services Commission. Ian O'Connor and I were subsequently appointed to a special advisory sub-committee on young offenders, which submitted its final report in March 1991. Sadly, very few of this report's recommendations were implemented.

Inquiry into Australia's Homeless Children

O NE SATURDAY afternoon in August 1987, I received a phone call from Sydney. It was Jim Fouras, a friend and former State Member of Parliament from Brisbane, who was working as a consultant to the Federal Human Rights and Equal Opportunity Commission. Would I be prepared to accept nomination as a commissioner on the Federal Human Rights Commission of Inquiry into Homeless Children and Young People? He said the inquiry would be a short one—three months, concluding by Christmas.

I told Jim I had been out of the disadvantaged youth and juvenile justice scene for 18 months, and wasn't up to date on recent developments. I was currently involved in the adult prison system, and with the parish of Saint Francis at West End. I added that I could think of at least two or three other people who would be better qualified than myself, who were currently working in the area of homeless and disadvantaged young people. He said that I had been specifically nominated for the Inquiry by two people, although being nominated did not mean that I would automatically be chosen; there were a number of nominations from other parts of Australia. He put the Federal Human Rights Commissioner, Brian Burdekin, on the phone. I asked Brian how long I had to consider. He said 24 hours, at the most, and he would phone me on the morrow.

After discussing the matter with Noel and a few friends, I decided to accept nomination. Noel was prepared to cover my absence in the parish, but I thought I probably wouldn't get the appointment. Three weeks later I was appointed, and very soon afterwards, the Commission decided to conduct a full Inquiry across the nation, in every State and Territory.

I wrote to the bishop to let him know what was happening. His reply was prompt and his congratulations sincere: "My own experience of all that you have done for the homeless and all the reports I get on your work are evidence of how worthy you are of being appointed as a member of such a team."[100]

However, some months later, Noel decided to leave Saint Francis parish, and after 12 months study leave, to return to his work with Aborigines in Kununurra in the Kimberley district of North-Western Australia. I tried hard to find another priest to come and live in the presbytery with me and assist in

---

100 Letter from Archbishop Rush, 28 September, 1987.

the parish on a part-time basis, but to no avail. I knew I could not continue to work in the prisons in a full-time capacity, work for the Inquiry, and meet my pastoral obligations at Saint Francis, so I resigned the parish in January of 1988.

The Church offered me a room in a presbytery, or in a little house in the grounds of Banyo Seminary. Both places were about an hour's drive from Catholic Prison Ministry's office and the main Boggo Road prison, and much further from the other prisons at Wacol and Woodford, which I attended on a weekly basis. I decided to move into a small flat nearby at Mater Hill, with my nephew who was studying at university. I stayed for 12 months, before moving to another smaller flat in West End.

Hopes for the Inquiry

I had high hopes for the Inquiry. I had worked long enough in the area to know that there were many things which could be done. I wanted homeless young people to come forward and speak at the hearings. I knew they could tell us, better than anybody, their sufferings and degradation, and the causes of their predicament. Above all, I knew some of the young people could offer solutions.

I wanted to put my experience in the area of youth homelessness at the disposal of the Inquiry. I also hoped it would be another opportunity for me to put to practical use what I had learnt during the study leave that I had taken in 1980 in Australia and overseas. I knew about the neglect of young people who were wards of the State. The State was neglecting those over whom it had statutory authority, over whom it had either Care and Protection or Care and Control orders. The State had taken these young people from their parents, who were neglecting and abusing them, and in turn was subjecting them to institutional abuse.

I knew the violence inflicted on young people, especially young women who were victims of incest. I had seen the racism which Aboriginal children had suffered at the hands of the authorities. I had witnessed the lack, or the poor quality, of legal representation in the Children's Courts. I knew the limitations of youth refuges and shelters. I knew first-hand, what the worst youth detention centres were like. I knew the damage that underfunded and poorly-led Departments were doing to the lives of vulnerable young people.

I also knew what competent legal representation could achieve. I had seen the multi-disciplinary approach of the Youth Advocacy Centre achieve some significant changes in the lives of young people, influence professionals like social workers and lawyers, and make an impact on the courts, the police and the welfare system. I had also seen prevention of youth homelessness, through community programs such as Bayside Adolescent Boarding Incorporated. Much of the suffering of homeless young people did not need to happen, and families could be assisted to stay together. Local communities could reach out to families in need and their teenage children, and change ignorance into the will and the motivation to make things better for homeless young people. I had seen the work of Zig Zag, the Young Women's Resource Centre, who were assisting young women with a range of issues, especially incest. People around Australia needed to know about these services, and others like them, which were making a difference.

The Terms of Reference

The Inquiry's terms of reference were breathtaking in their scope. Simply put, the members would examine in detail the plight of Australia's homeless children and young people, the causes of their problems and the adequacy of government responses. I knew it would involve a heavy commitment from Brian Burdekin, and from Jan Carter and myself, the two part-time Commissioners. Jan was Director of the Social Policy and Research Centre of the Brotherhood of Saint Laurence in Melbourne. Brian was a former priest with the Church of the Reorganised Latter Day Saints (an offshoot of the Mormon Church), a barrister, and principal ministerial adviser to Mr Lionel Bowen, the then Federal Attorney-General.

At one of our first meetings, Jan warned us of the personal toll an inquiry of this type would take on us all. Jan had worked on an inquiry into the needs of women in Western Australia, and she spoke of the personal costs that the experience had imposed on herself and some of her staff. Certainly, for myself, the Inquiry turned out to be a far bigger commitment than I had anticipated.

The Inquiry conducted public hearings in all States and Territories. Listening to the facts, figures, analyses and stories was overwhelming. I had heard the stories before, but had not realised the extent of the problems. As Australians, we were shamefully ignorant of what was happening to our powerless and voiceless young people. Youth workers and others had been saying such things for a long time. We, as a nation, were able to understand what they were saying, but had barely responded. All these young people were from families, and from neighbourhoods; if we wanted to do something, that was where we should start. Poverty was a major cause of youth homelessness, because it was forcing young people out of their homes. What was emerging was that there could be no knee-jerk reaction: that we had to do to some serious planning, not just posturing or blaming the victims.

"Life sucks, then you die."

The Inquiry conducted formal hearings in Brisbane on 24 November 1988. Maureen O'Regan from Brisbane Youth Service told the Inquiry that two homeless teenage AIDS sufferers were wandering around Fortitude Valley, and that as many as 3,000 children were homeless. Most of Brisbane's young homeless had suffered family breakdowns, abuse and neglect. They had hardly any money, little or no self-esteem, and could be destructive to themselves, peers and property. She said: "There's also no guarantee that once they're in State or foster homes they'll be OK. They live from day to day. They use drugs. They share needles. They are very sexually active and have multiple partners. Their catch-cry is, 'Life sucks, then you die.'"

Most witnesses, including academics, said the main reason children became homeless was due to family break-up and family problems. Ian O'Connor of the Department of Social Work at the University of Queensland said the juvenile justice system was failing because the treatment of children was based on "their deeds, not their needs." Welfare workers said many teenagers could not get their own housing, because people under 18 years of age were not allowed to sign tenancy leases, and there was a shortage of cheap, decent accommodation. Social workers criticised the Federal Government decision to stop unemployment benefits for people under 18.

In Brisbane, as in all other places where the hearings were conducted, several homeless young people presented evidence. Jodie spoke in Brisbane. She was in her late teens, articulate and very determined. She was kicked out of home at 16. The only money she had was from stealing. For a while she had stayed at refuges. She had then started sleeping on beaches and in bus shelters. She had frequently been sexually harassed.

When she and a girlfriend arrived in Brisbane two years previously, they had met two men and stayed in a two-bedroom flat with them and 10 people. In another apartment, a man had jumped into her bed on her first night there and wanted sex. She left. She answered a newspaper advertisement for a shared house and met a man who showed her his bank book and said he could afford to keep her if she had sex with him. She asked him for the taxi fare to get her clothes and never went back. She had also lived with a boyfriend, but moved out because there were too many drugs which often attracted police attention. At the time of the Inquiry, Jodie was living with a friend and struggling to make ends meet. She had a job on a very low salary and had her wages docked for attending the Inquiry.

Listening to such depressing evidence affected all of us. I had heard these stories before and I had worked directly with most of the issues which were put before us. Nevertheless, after listening all day, day after day, I told people that I oscillated between deep depression and suicide. What I found most difficult was that the problem of homeless young people had escalated. In 1977 we could identify, even by name, about 300 homeless young people living rough in inner-city Brisbane. Ten years later, workers were saying the numbers were in the vicinity of 3,000.

Brian made time in our busy Brisbane schedule for us to visit a number of 'lighthouse services'. We spent time at Kedron Lodge, Youth Advocacy Centre, Bayside Adolescent Boarding Incorporated, Youth and Family Services (Logan City), and the Youth Emergency Shelter at Windsor. I was thrilled to be able to catch up with the workers and some of the young people who were currently using the services, and introduce them to Brian and Jan.

This then was the pattern of our hearings: listening to young people, youth workers, academics and parents; visiting some of the local services, and speaking informally with homeless young people and their workers; and occasionally being taken to places where some of the young people squatted or camped out.

After the hearings in Cairns in Northern Queensland, Brian was approached by two Aboriginal men who, with others, had sat through the hearings, but had said nothing. Brian summoned Jan and myself to go on a tour with the men. It was a wet and miserable late afternoon when we climbed into their Kombi van. They took us out to the local garbage dump where many Aboriginal families were living in pathetic shelters. The stench from the dump was all pervading. Because the roads in and near the dump were so boggy as to be impassable, our guides pointed out some barely discernible tracks and told us of the people living down there. They knew that showing us how their people lived would make a deeper impression on us than hearing it described in the hearings.

Meeting Aboriginal young people

Prior to the hearings in Darwin and Alice Springs, I went to Mount Isa in north-western Queensland to examine the situation of young people in this remote mining town. I met with 12 Aboriginal people, including representatives from the Aboriginal and Islander Community Child Care Agency (AIC-CCA) and the Aboriginal Legal Service.

Mount Isa had an Aboriginal population of about 3,000. The extended kinship network was breaking down. Young Aborigines, some as young as 13 years old, were leaving home because of the conditions of their home: domestic violence and alcoholism. They drifted from house to house, from community to community. Some stayed down by the creek, others slept in people's backyards. If taken into care, they were sent to the Mount Isa Youth Shelter. Children coming to court in Mount Isa from outside communities (Dajarra, Boulia, Camooweal, Burketown, Normanton, Mornington Island) stayed in the Marion Street Aboriginal Hostel, which could cater for 10 children, but when I visited, accommodated 18.

Those present at the meeting were critical of the Department of Family Services (DFS). Children from outlying communities were placed on orders of Care and Protection and Care and Control, but the Department offered very little supervision of these orders. Often DFS officers did not know the whereabouts of children they had in care. The offences these children committed were mainly breaking and entering to obtain food. The child's grandmother or aunt could not control them, so they were taken into care. DFS officers, they said, used their powers for small matters, did little good and were a waste of time.

They told me that shelters and institutions were not the answers for their children. Rather, they said, Aboriginal people needed to be given the power, responsibility and resources to look after their children. Many Aboriginal parents had poor parenting skills because they had been raised in dormitories and institutions—and, if they had played up in these places, they had also been sent away to Palm Island as punishment.

Those present were also critical of the police. The Mornington Island police lock-up was atrocious. Sometimes the children were placed in there for the weekend, and the police went off fishing and left the children without food. A child had been flown down from the Island in the police aircraft with an infected hole in his leg. DFS officers delivered him to the Marion Street Shelter, but nobody had offered to obtain medical help.

They said that Aboriginal police in remote communities had little power, and were made to do the dirty work by white police (for example, intervening in domestic arguments). Young people from Mornington Island were spending weekends in the police lock-up in Mount Isa: five had been sent down prior to my visit, with no change of clothing, no food, and no mattresses or blankets; AICCCA had not been notified. They reported an instance of a 15-year-old boy who was recently in the lock-up for three days. He had been given blankets which were in a dirty and disgusting condition—"unsuitable for a dog." He had had to sleep on the bare floor, he had no exercise or recreation and no room to move around. "He was like a monkey in a cage," they said.

They did not know how many children were sent away from Mount Isa or nearby communities to institutions in Townsville or Brisbane. It could be as many as 100 in a year, as many were being sent away from their communities. Most, they said, were sent away for three months, and returned in a worse state. The State welfare authorities did not return those from outlying communities to their homes after attending court in Mount Isa, but left them stranded in the town. They said that most young people were legally represented in Mount Isa, but were not certain what happened in the outlying areas. Some children were sent away from their communities even after being found guilty on minor charges. The magistrates, they said, should know more about Aboriginal culture.

Sometimes police held guns to children's heads, and children were often questioned without an adult being present. An independent person was only called in while a statement was typed out. In Burketown, for example, some children had broken into a school. The police caught the children, put them in the lock-up and gave the keys of the lock-up to the teacher to go in and flog them. "Bad police never get charged," they told me. "Some solicitors seem to do a deal with the cops."

One Aboriginal woman told me there were a lot of rumours about Aboriginal girls being raped in the cells. The young girls mostly said nothing because of shame and fright. She told me she knew of a 17-year-old girl who had been raped recently in the cells.

They said unemployment was very high in Mount Isa, and none of their children had been able to get the Young Homeless Allowance. They said that removing the dole for the under-18s had a big effect, "the worst thing they have ever done," one said. "Some of our kids have done well at school, even completed courses at TAFE, but can't find work. This leads to fights at home and lots of other problems and, in some cases, even suicide."

From Mount Isa I travelled on to Darwin and Alice Springs, and met up with Jan and Brian. With some marginal differences, the depressing picture was similar right around Australia, from Cairns to Broome. The thought often occurred to me that Australia could do a lot towards eradicating homelessness among its children and young people. The problem was not an insurmountable one. The resources were available, but they were misdirected. Australia could have the political will, if only its collective community conscience was activated.

I was reminded of Archbishop Rush's Easter 1988 message. He wrote:

> In our everyday life we should show that we are followers of Christ by the standard of justice we demand and the concern for the poor and under-privileged that we ourselves practise and that we require from the people with whom we are associated. Christ's Passion continues in the suffering of the men and women of our time—in the starving people of the world, in those who remain unemployed in the midst of obscene wealth, of men and women (and children) even in our own city who are without a home. Easter reproaches our insensitivity to other's pain and invites our compassion for the poor, the unemployed and those who are in any way oppressed.[101]

The Report

The final Report was the outcome of two years' extensive research: public hearings in all States and Territories, evidence and written submissions from almost 500 individuals and groups, and a number of detailed studies, including a series of interviews with 100 homeless children. As the title of the Report (*Our Homeless Children*) indicated, we considered the problem of homeless children to be a community problem not just a problem for governments or someone else.

On 22 February 1989, *Our Homeless Children*, the Report of the National Inquiry into Homeless Children, was released in Sydney. In his address, Brian

---

101 From an article written by the author and published in The Catholic Leader, 17 July 1988.

Burdekin made some telling points. The Human Rights Commission had undertaken the Inquiry because homeless children were being denied the basic human rights which Australia was committed to guarantee:

> International instruments incorporated in Federal Law stipulate that children have the right to special protection, to adequate housing, and to protection from abuse, neglect and exploitation. They also, most importantly, have the right to remain with their families wherever possible.

One goal of the Inquiry had been to try to ascertain how many homeless children and young people there were in Australia. While it was impossible to state exact numbers of homeless children, it was clear that the number of homeless young people had been rising, and that the proportion of children among them had been increasing. We concluded that there were between 20,000 and 25,000 homeless children and young people under 18 years of age across Australia, and approximately 8,000 to 9,000 homeless children in the 12-to-15-year age group. This latter group was extremely vulnerable. We emphasised that on the basis of the evidence available, the estimates were conservative and the numbers could be as high as 70,000.

In his address, Brian was scathing about the States' neglect of young people in their care:

> When we commenced this Inquiry we were very disturbed to find that many homeless children were State Wards, that is, children who were supposedly under the Care and Protection of our various State Governments. Many others were former State Wards.
>
> The dereliction of their legal duties by our State Governments is a national disgrace and a scandal. It is a lie for anyone to say that in a nation as wealthy as ours we do not have the resources to help these children. We do. It is simply a question of our priorities. The reality is that in many cases where State Welfare authorities have exercised their power to take over parental responsibilities and take children into care, they have discharged those responsibilities—or rather failed to discharge them—in a way that would have had any parent brought before the courts and charged with neglect. There is very little follow-up assistance for children leaving care, and virtually no programs to prepare them for independence. There is no doubt that this is why many of them have ended up homeless.

Even before the Report was released, extensive media attention to the progress of the Inquiry had alerted the community to the nature and scope of the problem. As a result, a wide range of organisations and individuals said they wanted to address the problem, if not for the first time, then with renewed vigour and a new sense of urgency. The Report was comprehensive and, on the whole, well received by the community and most governments. The Federal Government allocated $120 million to implement some of our recommendations over the following three years.

Recharging the batteries

Burn-out

MY INVOLVEMENT in the Human Rights Inquiry into Homeless Children and Young People thrust me back into the area of juvenile justice and disadvantaged young people. I had hoped that in the wake of the release of the Inquiry's report, my involvement with homeless young people would gradually taper off: a forlorn hope. On 14 June 1989 I found myself writing to the bishop, stating that I did not have the energy to sustain my efforts in both prison chaplaincy and homeless youth ministry. I requested that he give consideration to allow me to pursue full-time ministry in the area of homeless children and young people.

Having received no reply, I wrote again on 4 September 1989, urging the bishop to relieve me of my prison duties by the end of the month, or as soon after that as practicable, and stressing how inundated I was with my work and how my health was suffering.

In October 1989 the bishop appointed me to work among homeless youth. In his letter he hoped "that the many calls made on you because of your expert knowledge will not overburden you and take you away from Brisbane very often." The overburdening had been taking place for too long already, with a breakdown in health taking me out of active ministry and the diocese for a considerable period of time.

In December 1989, the Homeless Children and Young People inquiry reconvened in Canberra to hear the responses from representatives from Federal and State Governments. The night these proceedings concluded, I experienced pain in my right side which persisted throughout the next day. On arriving back in Brisbane I consulted a doctor who suggested I may have colic. The pain persisted and a few days later I was confirmed to have full-blown shingles. The pain was like being pierced with hot needles. I couldn't sleep. I had headaches. Every time I did even a half hour's work I suffered with severe pain and headaches.

My doctor sent me to a specialist who conducted a few tests and told me my immune system was totally run down, and that he was prepared to write to the Archbishop requesting at least three months sick leave.

I tried to undertake some limited work, but as a consequence suffered almost immediately. Rest was the only solution. Jan Carter, the other Commissioner on the Inquiry, had sent me three books on the topic of mid-life crisis. These books were most helpful. One pointed out that men often neglect their feminine side, being more achievement-focused and task-oriented. A suggestion flowing from this was for men to attend to their artistic or feminine side by, for example, painting or writing poetry. One night in 1990, troubled by some news I was hearing on the radio, I began again to write poetry. Soon I was writing poems about interesting people, nature, political comment, and spirituality.

Working on the Inquiry convinced me I would have to learn to use computers. I resolved that I would not use a computer until I had learnt to touch-type. I borrowed a Pitman's 'Learn to Type' book from a niece and, when I felt up to it, practised typing. A 30-minute session was all I could manage until the headaches returned.

Staying in Brisbane meant I was too available. People would drop in or phone. Sometimes I found the conversations draining and subsequently suffered. I took up my doctor's recommendation that I get out of Brisbane. I had planned to visit Noel McMaster, who had returned to his former role as parish priest of Kununurra in the remote Eastern Kimberley region of Western Australia. I phoned Noel and his ready response was: "Come as soon as you can and stay as long as you wish."

I stayed with Noel from May to October that year. I rested, practised my typing, wrote poetry, read books, did the shopping for the house, and joined Noel in some of his pastoral activities, including visits to some of the stations and remote Aboriginal settlements. Staying there for a number of months, I became friends with some of the locals. I would walk across a park to do the shopping for the house. Often there were groups of local Aboriginal people sitting in circles and conversing. On many occasions they would invite me to join them. I felt privileged.

I visited Fr Dan O'Donovan, the parish priest of neighbouring Wyndham, over 70 kilometres away, and often stayed overnight. On my first visit, Dan wanted to introduce me to 'Ferdy' whom I took to be one of Dan's friends. In fact, Ferdy turned out to be an eight-metre-long crocodile. We went down to the mudflats but didn't sight him. (I wondered if he sighted us!) However we did see his widely-spaced claw marks in the mud at low tide.

Occasionally Dan would visit Kununurra for the day. We enjoyed his company, his Irish lilt and often high-spirited conversation. On one occasion the conversation centered on Oscar Romero, the assassinated Archbishop of San Salvador in Central America. Neither Dan nor Noel had seen the excellent movie *Romero*. I offered to obtain it for Dan's next visit.

There were two video shops in Kununurra. I had never been inside a video shop. I entered the first. Once my eyes adjusted to the dim light, I noticed a somewhat swarthy scruffy-bearded man dressed in shorts and blue working man's singlet passionately kissing a young woman behind the counter. Ignoring them, I proceeded to look for the video from the hundreds displayed on the racks. After five minutes I gave up and approached the counter. The man eventually broke off his embrace and asked me what I wanted. The video, *Romero*, I answered. He turned to a computer terminal and again asked the name of the video. Then he asked me to spell it. After announcing each letter he would search for it on the keyboard and belt the letter with a blow of his strong index finger. Having completed the exercise he glared at the screen and announced, "Sorry mate, we don't have that one. The nearest we have is 'Romeo and Juliet'. Will that do?" I politely declined, thanking him for his trouble. The other video shop didn't have *Romero* either.

At the beginning of October I enjoyed my first full night's sleep in 10 months. However, the weather in the tropical north was heating up (34 degrees Celsius in my bedroom at 7am), and Noel and I decided it was time for me to return to Brisbane before all the good work done in the Kimberley was undone by the debilitating heat.

I visited the specialist again soon after my return. He told me I was over the attack of shingles—but that I would have the virus for the rest of my life and, on hearing what kind of work I was returning to, announced that I would likely experience a return of the shingles within two weeks. He suggested I needed more time off—my immune system was in the same state as it was just before my first shingles rash. I approached the Archbishop who readily agreed to my having more time off, as well as some study leave in Palestine/Israel and Switzerland.

I flew to Switzerland and stayed with relatives. I felt the need to do physical work and tried to do as much as I could for my relatives and their friends. Also I spent a month in Ireland at the farm of friends of mine, working in their extensive gardens. The weather was just awful. Before venturing out I would rug up in two pairs of socks, a thick shirt, a track suit and overalls. Finally I put on a thick coat, gloves, beanie and (to complete the picture) 'wellies'. Initially I could only work for 45 minutes before coming inside for a cuppa in the warm kitchen and a rest. Gradually the headaches lessened and I knew I had turned a corner health-wise.

Leo Skelly and Terry Hickling, two classmates of mine from Banyo Seminary, stumbled on the Tantur Ecumenical Institute while visiting Israel and Palestine. When I told Leo I had been granted leave to study the Judeo-Christian underpinnings of justice and peacemaking, he immediately produced Tantur's latest newsletter advertising a summer course on that very topic. While I had never planned to visit the Holy Land, I thought Leo's suggestion was worthwhile and set about enrolling.

The idea of an international ecumenical institute for theological research based in Israel/Palestine was discussed informally by Catholic and observer delegates from other Christian and Orthodox Churches in the early years of Vatican II. The vision began to be concretised after Pope Paul VI's historic visit to Israel/Palestine in 1965 and the purchase of land, which was leased to an ecumenical board. In 1971 Tantur opened its doors.

I loved every bit of the course at Tantur, which was situated between Jerusalem and Bethlehem. I walked to Bethlehem on a number of occasions and, when we had free time, caught a local bus to Jerusalem. A Bedouin camp was also situated nearby. This was the year of the first Gulf War, which meant there were only 14 students instead of the usual 30 or so.

The Tantur experience was very prayerful. The night before an excursion we were given a number of Bible references to look up in preparation for the day ahead. We prayed each day before we ventured out. At most of the sites we visited (for example, Mount Tabor, Gethsemane, the Mount of the Beatitudes) substantial periods of time were allowed for a liturgy of the Word as well as for quiet reflection. We visited Jerusalem on a number of occasions, had field trips to Bethlehem and Masada, and enjoyed six days in Galilee (in Nazareth and Tiberias). Everywhere we went, we were accompanied by one of our lecturers as an enthusiastic guide.

I was impressed with the lecturers. Dr Kenneth Bailey, an Anglican priest and research professor of Middle Eastern New Testament studies, had worked in remote villages in North Africa with Arab Christians. Most of these people were illiterate. He learnt that they often used various forms of poetic construction as an aid to remember the details of important stories or writings. He applied his learnings to the Gospels and discovered examples of what he called 'tight' poetic construction, especially in the parables. I couldn't hear enough of Kenneth Bailey. I loved the unique understanding of Scripture that flowed from his interactions with illiterate Arab Christians in North Africa.

We were also privileged to receive a lecture on Palestinian liberation theology by Father Naim Ateek, a Palestinian priest in the Anglican Church and founder of the Sabeel Ecumenical Liberation Theology Center in Jerusalem. Father Ateek's theology was built on four factors: that he stayed with his people sharing stories of political oppression; that he was an indigenous pastor, one of 'them' which engendered mutual trust; that together they were engaged with the question 'what is the essential message of the Bible?'; and that as a theologian and a pastor he was engaged in a further question 'what is the God of justice and peace saying to us in the midst of this crisis in which we are living?' Since the Lodge days, and especially since I had the privilege of sitting at the feet of Gustavo Gutiérrez in Maastricht in Holland, I had been a student of liberation theology. Listening to Father Naim Ateek was similarly inspiring and stimulating.

The World Council of Churches, Geneva

Father Michael Putney, Seminary lecturer, later Bishop of Townsville and noted scholar, provided me with contacts at the World Council of Churches (WCC) in Geneva as I continued to study my theme of *The Spiritual Underpinnings of Justice and Peace*. I chose the WCC for several reasons. Years before I listened to a recording of some lectures given at the WCC Conference in Sweden. The topic was 'salvation', but in the sense of saving from injustice and oppression. The second reason was that living in Switzerland appealed to me, as it was my mother's country where I still had many relatives. I was welcomed by some of them who lived in Brig in Canton Wallis. At 6 a.m. each Monday morning I would catch the fast train (three stops only) for the two-and-a-half hour journey to Geneva, take a bus to the *pension* where I stayed, and take another bus to WCC arriving there soon after 9am.

I was still struggling with diminished energy levels. My specialist had advised me to break the day into three parts (morning, afternoon and evening) and only work two of the three sessions. He also suggested a short rest in the middle of the day or soon after. Some mornings I would arrive at WCC and feel unwell. I would immediately take the bus back to the *pension*, rest until I felt better, and work the other two sessions.

As I had little to do of an evening, I decided to take lessons in German. A lady who lived nearby was recommended. She spoke no English at all. We hit it off. I had a lesson with her once a week. She gave me homework and corrected it. When she found out I was a Catholic priest, she told me the story of her life over several sessions. Her mother had died when she was a child and her father placed her in an orphanage run by nuns. As she related her story in detail, she would often pause and ask me what I had heard. Sometimes I would interrupt her, telling her I didn't understand the meaning of a particular word she had used. She would point it out in her French/German dictionary and I would then look it up in my German/English dictionary. On other evenings I would be invited to the cinema or a classical music concert by staff from the WCC.

I had two supervisors for my study; one was Father John S. Pobee, an African Anglican priest and author of *Toward an African Theology*; the other, a Catholic priest. I saw them once a week, as they guided my reading and my activities. As John Pobee and I got to know each other, he suggested I try to identify what he called 'moments of grace' in my life. I warmed to this task and within a week had written 20,000 words. He encouraged me to develop this manuscript, which is the genesis of this book.

Taizé

While studying in Geneva, I met up with one of my lecturers from Tantur. He had come to Switzerland with a young man from Palestine, to inform the WCC of the situation in the West Bank and to promote their work of reconciliation between Palestinians and Israelis. He suggested I take a week off to undertake a retreat at Taizé, only about two hours travel by fast train across the border in France. Of course I had heard of Taizé, an ecumenical community founded by Brother Roger that was attracting thousands of young people from across the world, and some older folk like me.

On arrival I was greeted by two young women, surprisingly from Melbourne, Australia. I was billeted in a quiet village about three kilometres from Taizé. A few others my own age were also billeted in the same building. Mostly we walked, in all kinds of weather, back and forth to the activities in Taizé.

On my first morning there, I walked through a light fog into the centre for breakfast. As I was leaving the breakfast tent, three young people from Spain introduced themselves to me. From then on they were always on the lookout for me and we spent much of the free time together, discussing the program and enjoying each other's company.

Every morning one of the Taizé brothers would give a lecture based on Scripture. There were ample opportunities for solitude, discussion and chanting in the huge and simply-furnished auditorium. In the afternoons I was placed in a discussion group with people over the age of thirty-five. In our group were people from Russia, Germany, France and England, while I was the lone Aussie.

One afternoon's discussion was on forgiveness and reconciliation. Our leader was guiding the discussion, working through prepared questions while making time for translations, especially for the Russians. The discussion was slowly progressing when the man from Germany said to the people from Russia: "Were any of your relatives or friends killed by the Germans in the Second World War?" When translated, the question seemed to cause some alarm among the Russians. The German man asked the question again. It was obvious he meant no harm as he seemed a compassionate man. When his question had been translated again, and after some discussion among the Russians, one woman said that her aunt had been killed by the Germans. The man from Germany stood up and moved to the centre of the group. He said: "I am sorry your aunt was killed. Would you kindly forgive me, my people and my country for what we did to your people during the Second World War?" The woman cried out, "Yes." She jumped up and they embraced and cried in the middle of the group.

I wasn't at ease with the Taizé style of chant at the beginning, but decided to let it flow through me and over me. Soon I became more and more relaxed and was able to prayerfully enter into its charm and embrace.

I enjoyed the week. I had another motive for going on retreat. Once again I needed to work out whether I should continue to work with young people who were homeless and disadvantaged. I didn't work out the answer to this prayer, except to relax, be patient and wait upon the will of God.

Homebase

IN THE early 1990s, Brisbane Catholic Education appointed a social worker to research the numbers of homeless students attending secondary colleges in the Archdiocese of Brisbane. I had been consulted by the researcher but was not given access to the final report.

In the mid-1990s, Ray Reynolds, a supervising guidance officer, requested a meeting with me. He gave me a copy of the report. I submitted my comments as well as my recommendations, including that of setting up a community placement boarding program similar to the one I had established in Wynnum-Manly. Ray discussed this model with me in detail. He then sought approval from his superiors to progress it.

Soon after obtaining their approval, Ray and I met with the guidance counsellors from the three Catholic secondary colleges situated on the Gold Coast, an hour's drive south of Brisbane. They talked about the needs of the 'at-risk' students they were encountering, and their struggles to meet their needs. Two of the counsellors had families who were prepared to 'foster' students at a moment's notice. I then presented the community placement boarding model, which we discussed in detail. They accepted the model and were enthusiastic about its possibilities for their vulnerable and at-risk students. Each was prepared to approach their principal.

A meeting with the principals and the counsellors was arranged. Again I presented the model, took questions, and outlined the steps needing to be taken in establishing such a program; the model was accepted.

My next step was to meet with local youth workers at their inter-agency meeting to present the model and to solicit their assistance. They were positive about the model, seeing the need for a preventive and early intervention program on the Gold Coast, and indicated a number of people who could be helpful in the Police Service, Welfare Department and Centrelink.

In March 1996, I approached all the Catholic parishes on the Gold Coast and convened a meeting of their representatives. This meeting was chaired by the Dean of the Gold Coast. All of the parishes agreed to support this initiative through their newsletters and by word of mouth.

Next I arranged meetings with the Parents and Friends groups from each college. One college decided to throw open this meeting to all parents. About 70 parents attended. Again I discussed the need, presented the model, answered clarifying questions and invited parents to consider becoming a boarding family. During question time, some parents expressed difficulty in believing that there were students at risk and in need of emergency accommodation at their school. Thankfully the school counsellor was able to affirm what I had said, and those who were sceptical were convinced of the need.

We announced an information night for prospective boarding families, publicising it though the schools and parishes. At the end of the night we asked participants to commit to training, discussing and agreeing on suitable times and dates. As I wanted the program to be embedded in the local community, I sought suitable trainers from the Gold Coast. It would have been easy for me to import some suitable trainers from Brisbane, but that is not the way of community development practice. For example, after some searching I was able to find a young lawyer, well versed in working with children, to present one of the sessions. He was so moved by the initiative that at the conclusion of his session he handed out his business cards to everyone, telling them that he was on call for them '24-7' should they need his services for any of the at-risk students they were accommodating.

At the end of the training, we requested that each boarding family commit to the program for one year. One final step was to visit their homes for an assessment and contact their referees. Bernadette Wood (one of the counsellors) and myself undertook these not unpleasant tasks. Soon we were ready to begin—our supports were in place, our procedures established.

We needed a name for the program so we conducted a competition among the students from the three schools for a logo and a motto. 'Homebase' was the winner and the motto was *"Never think that you're alone—you'll always have the base as home."*

I had just returned to Brisbane from two days of meetings down the Gold Coast, when I received a phone call from Bernadette. A Year 10 boy, whom we shall call Simon, told her late that day that he couldn't live at home any more. He didn't want to live at home and his mother had told him that she didn't want him at home either. Bernadette contacted one of our boarding families. They were prepared to take him in that night. Bernadette phoned me to return to the Coast to accompany her on a home visit to meet Simon and his mother.

We spent more than an hour with Simon's mother. She told us she had been drinking heavily since she was 13 years old and now was a member of AA. She said her husband had been a very violent person, and that Simon had witnessed him breaking her arm and cracking her skull. When she separated from her husband, she found she couldn't cope with Simon, so she sent him to live with her husband. He wasn't prepared to put up with Simon's behaviour either, and palmed him off to one of Simon's aunts, who had major problems of her own.

Simon looked up to and admired his older brother, who was heavily into drugs and alcohol. This brother confided in him that he was suicidal and swore Simon to secrecy. The older brother did indeed commit suicide; Simon wasn't invited or allowed to participate in the funeral preparations but did attend his brother's funeral. After the funeral his mother moved to the Gold Coast with her children including Simon.

Simon had been attending his new school for just six weeks when we visited his home. During that time he had been suspended on two occasions for selling drugs, and had received detention on a number of occasions for disrupting the class and being disrespectful to his teachers.

In the course of the conversation with Simon's mother, we told her that we had a suitable family who were prepared to accommodate Simon that very night. She was incredulous asking, "Do you mean that somebody is prepared to take in my son?" Later in our conversation with her, she said she would like to give Simon another go at home. I told her that was fine but it wouldn't work unless she and Simon were prepared to seek professional counselling. The school could refer her and Simon to a counsellor who specialised in assisting troubled young people and their parents, and who tailored his charges to their means. She readily agreed to do this.

Next we spoke with Simon. While we had been conversing with his Mum, he had been watching TV in the same room and not missing a word of our conversation.

He asked us if there were really a family who would be prepared to take him in that very night. On receiving an affirmative reply he asked, "Even a little bastard like me?" Soon after this exchange, Simon decided he wanted to give his own home another go.

I offered to drive Simon to school the next day. My reasons for doing so were simply that I didn't think he would go unless I drove him, and also I wanted to have a little chat with him. He was ready and waiting for me when I arrived.

Firstly, I asked him if he had any friends at school. He replied no. He said that the other students were "a whir of faces." I asked him if he thought any of the teachers were OK. At first he said there weren't any, but on being pressed, mentioned the names of two teachers he thought he liked a bit.

I asked him how he was. He said he was depressed. I told him I could understand that, but if he could trust the process I could see light at the end of the tunnel, but didn't expect he could at this stage.

I dropped him off, parked the car and went to Bernadette's office for a chat. I gave her the names of the two teachers Simon thought were OK. She caught up with them and told them that Simon was going through a bad time, to which they added that he was passing that on to them. She requested that they look out for Simon in a pastoral way and try to encourage him.

Next I told her Simon had no friends in the school. I asked her if she knew any student in Year 12 who would be prepared to befriend Simon. She knew of one and promised to contact him. A week or so later she told me she had contacted another student who she described as a 'rough diamond' who was in the same class as Simon. She also told Simon that if he found he wasn't coping in class he could excuse himself and spend some time in her office. Simon availed himself of this offer on a number of occasions.

With all this in place—counselling, support from teachers, friendship from peers—Simon gradually turned his conduct and his behaviour around. Half-way through the year, the sports coach realised that Simon had special talents in a particular sport and leadership qualities, and despite Simon being only in Year 10 made him Captain of the senior team. Simon successfully completed Year 12 and remained living at home.

Miracles do happen

One Friday afternoon a Year 9 student told the school counsellor that she was not going home. She was sick of home. Her father was an alcoholic, she said. He was abusive and violent and she couldn't take it any more. The counsellor listened to her story, told her about Homebase, checked that a boarding family could take her and phoned her mother. Her mother was angry. The counsellor requested she drop in to pick up some clothes. The mother flatly refused, but told the counsellor she would drop a bag full of clothes in the car park of a major shopping centre at 5pm and if the counsellor wasn't there would leave them in the middle of the car park. The counsellor made an appointment to see both parents on the following Monday.

When the parents arrived, they were furious and denied there were problems at home. They vented their anger, so much so that all available time was taken up listening to them. The counsellor made a follow-up appointment with both parents for the following Friday.

At the beginning of the second interview, both parents apologised for their conduct on the previous Monday. In fact, the father went further, to say that his daughter was correct: he was an alcoholic. He had even attended two AA meetings during the week and intended to continue being a regular attender. He had stopped drinking. They said they were happy that their daughter was with a good family and continuing to attend school. They wanted to have contact with her and they wanted her to return home, but when she was ready. The student stayed with the boarding family for a short time. After she returned home she was invited to drop in and stay with the boarding family for a weekend from time to time, which she did with her parents' blessing.

My final story is about 'Ada' who was also a Year 10 student. Ada's mum decided to move to North Queensland. Ada didn't want to go with her, as she liked her school and had some good friends in her class. She applied to be accommodated by a boarding family. This was granted on the proviso that it be only for three months while efforts were made by the school counsellor to reunite her with her mother. These efforts failed. Ada in the meantime had gotten on so well with her boarding parents that she and they requested, and it was agreed, that she stay with them until she completed Year 12.

Ada completed Year 12 successfully, obtained employment, a small flat and commenced part-time study at university. She was so grateful that she offered her services to support other students in the program and to assist in promoting Homebase.

Homebase recorded success rates of 92% in school retention and 80% in family reunification. Many people worked very hard to achieve such brilliant results.

During its lifetime, Homebase experienced great difficulties in accessing financial support to remunerate its families and to support its part-time and then, later on, full-time coordinator. Sadly, despite its success, Homebase had a life-span of only four or five years.

With a villager from the Oecussi enclave, East Timor. Many from this area lost their lives after the Indonesian invasion. Wally visited less than two years after the cessation of hostilities and the withdrawal of Indonesian elements.

Will these scars ever heal?

With the lure of money and drugs
Too stoned to comprehend
I was tricked into the world of
Prostitution, power, corruption and revenge.

Old, Respectable, Wealthy Citizens
I was promised with a malicious grin
Nothing to fear if they hurt you, my dear,
Tell me, as I'll always be near.

Was this a joke or just a flat out lie?
As I took my fear straight to you
You laughed in my face and told me to smile
And to keep my mouth shut if I valued my life.

Unable to do anything without your knowledge
As your overwhelming control soon took hold.
Many a time I tried to run and hide
But always found and made to pay for my crime.

Through bruises, beatings and the like
I was locked in a world of silent misery.
Unable to yell, scream or cry
Just lay there and hope to God I could die.

Other times, I thought my time had come
Driven out of town to the middle of nowhere
So certain I was, I was to be killed
Another dead prostitute, but who cares!

How many times I just turned off
Whether it be through drugs or not
Able to escape from my body and
The piercing pain of bites and punches.

Treated as nothing more
Than an old dirty filthy whore

To be treated as they willed
Thrown, bitten, beaten and God knows what more.

Will I ever, be able to feel real?
Will these scars ever heal?

18 June 1996

Working for Allen

'DIANE', A YOUTH WORKER, worked with 'Theresa'. Theresa had suffered abuse as a child. She was intelligent, a victim and a survivor. Diane met Theresa in the course of her work.

This is how she fell into the clutches of 'Allen' and his thugs. In 1994 Theresa got to know Allen's partner ('Bonney') when they were in the psychiatric unit in the local general hospital. Allen used to visit Bonney and drop off joints. After they were discharged from hospital, Theresa used to visit Bonney to score pot. One day, when Bonney wasn't at home, Allen told her she should work for him. He asked her how much pot she wanted and if she was hungry. She was hungry and he gave her something to drink. They watched a movie together, smoked a few cones and drank a bottle of alcohol. He asked her if she could keep a secret and on telling him she could, he gave her an ounce of pot and $300 in cash. She began working for him as a prostitute that very night.

Theresa told me that Allen hung out at the centre stage of the Mall and at various hotels and clubs which she named. Allen supplied her with a number of regular clients. "Somehow Allen always knew where we were, who we were with and what we were doing," she said.

Allen was involved in selling drugs—both illicit and prescription drugs. He had big black garbage bags full of pot in his house. The prescription drugs he sold were temazapan, benzo's, but mainly anamorph and morphine sulphate. "Allen got us to sell morphine and pot for him," Theresa added.

Theresa was only 18 when Diane met up with her. She was heavily into drugs and prostitution and her life was in danger. She knew what Allen and his gang were doing was morally wrong. She was particularly concerned that Allen was farming out underage girls who were wards of the State for prostitution. He employed a number of girls as prostitutes and paid them with opals.

Diane had come across Allen in her work with homeless young people. He regularly parked his car outside youth hostels trying to ensnare vulnerable young people for his nefarious purposes.

Allen employed a group of mainly Aboriginal boys, often street kids, to break into houses to steal particular objects. Mostly he had buyers already lined up. He paid these boys and the prostitutes with drugs, cash or opals. "Sometimes," Theresa added, "he paid us nothing at all."

One of these boys who lived in one of Allen's houses wanted out. The house was stacked with stolen property. Diane, as his youth worker, explained the consequences of his decision, including arrest, court and certain incarceration in a juvenile detention centre. The lad still wanted to go ahead. Diane, on his behalf, phoned the police who told her they would raid the premises. As the police didn't show up, the boy left the house after three days of sitting around waiting.

Allen was a very violent man and Theresa and the other girls were frightened of him and his henchmen. "We were beaten, strangled, our arms were twisted behind us and he threatened to break our arms. He also threatened us with being raped by park people. One day he pushed a knife into my leg and told me to stop shooting up and disappearing or else."

Diane knew that Theresa's life was in danger. Theresa talked too freely about Allen and his activities. Theresa wanted out of the scene of drugs and prostitution. Diane organised for Theresa to fly to Brisbane and to enter a drug rehabilitation facility. There was a hiccup when Theresa arrived in Brisbane, but a phone call from Diane alerted me. I made a few phone calls and the situation was resolved. Towards the end of her 12 months of rehabilitation Theresa phoned me, inviting me to her graduation ceremony from the rehab centre. That was when I first met Theresa.

Upon discharge from the rehabilitation centre, Theresa rented a flat and was successful in enrolling in science at a Brisbane university. She attended a weekly meeting of people from the rehab centre recovering from addictions.

One day Diane phoned me. Theresa wants to see you, she said. "What about?" I queried. "She'll tell you," was Diane's response.

Theresa, at our meeting, told me about Allen and his thugs; the crime, the violence, the involvement of vulnerable young people. She also told me that Allen often sold drugs in the mall, within a stone's throw of a police station and in full view of the mall's CCTV cameras.

On a number of occasions, Theresa was assigned to pick Allen up from the police station. When he was seated in the car she asked him, "How did that go?" He responded, "It always goes well," and produced a fistful of illegal drugs, joints, foils and tabs from his pockets. He told Theresa that the only reason she didn't have a criminal record was because the police knew she belonged to him.

Theresa was intent on trying to halt Allen's activities. I pointed out the dangers to herself, which she had already considered, and offered to assist her in any way I could.

In August 1996, Theresa and I met with a lawyer who advised us to approach the Criminal Justice Commission (CJC). His partner knew one of the senior investigative police attached to the CJC and advised us to contact him personally, which we did shortly after. He interviewed Theresa in my presence and took down a detailed statement from her, including the names and contact details of three youth workers who were prepared to corroborate her allegations. The interviewing Inspector told us he would spin some of the names and details through the CJC's computers, and assured us he would inform us if the CJC decided to proceed with the complaint. True to his word, two weeks later he phoned both of us to inform us that the investigation would proceed.

On two occasions, some six months or so later, Diane was phoned by detectives from Brisbane asking her if she was prepared to be interviewed. On receiving an affirmative reply, they said they would be in touch. However, they never did make contact with her, nor interview her; nor did they interview the other two youth workers whose contact details they had.

In the meantime, Theresa continued with her studies and attended the rehab meetings. At the same time, youth workers were sending us more information on Allen and his activities. For instance, we found out that Allen was an approved foster-carer whose preference was for the placement of young girls in his home, whom he promptly introduced to drugs and prostitution.

In November 1997, over 12 months later, the CJC wrote to Theresa informing her that "the Commission is unable to productively investigate this matter."

The following month, Theresa and I wrote a detailed response informing the CJC of the evidence we had obtained in the meantime and suggesting that they examine this matter again.

A week later, Theresa received a response from the CJC stating in part that "the Commission does not propose to take any further action in respect of this matter." This letter listed a few minor charges on which Allen had been arraigned—about one a year—and concluded that they could find no evidence of corruption.

Early in January 1998, I happened to notice that an Assistant Commissioner, a friend of mine from the seventies, had been appointed as a Regional Commissioner of Police. We wrote to him and I, on Theresa's behalf, phoned him. He readily agreed to a meeting with us, which took place in my home at West End in Brisbane a month later. He also subsequently interviewed Diane. He was well aware of the danger she was in, and gave her his police and personal mobile phone numbers so she could phone him at any time, day or night.

In June and July of 1998, I met with the Queensland Crime Commissioner and the Minister for Family Services to inform them of our concerns and to solicit their assistance in these matters.

Sadly, the only thing which resulted from our efforts was that Allen was removed from the list of approved foster-carers.

Towards the end of the above saga, Diane phoned again informing me that Theresa wanted to speak to me. At the subsequent meeting, Theresa narrated the abuse she had suffered over the years, and that she was no longer able to "keep the lid on it."

I incurred her wrath by recommending she consider counselling. I told her of Zig Zag, the young women's information and referral centre, student counselling services at the university she was attending, and a number of private counsellors. I set up another meeting with her for the following week. I was so disturbed by what she had told me that I felt the need to put my reflections on paper.

INCEST

Violence,
under the guise of love and sex.

Deception,
disguised as affection.

Innocence violated.
Trust betrayed.

A child,
hurtled into gross torment and confusion,
scarred for life,
carrying guilt, shame and threats.

Alone.
Nobody to turn to
to confide in,
But no one will listen
or believe.

Wounded,
bleeding through every pore,
bereft of feeling;
dead, but still alive,
alive, but dead inside.

Fighting to survive:
for what?
for whom?
    For life.

"I am a nothing,
I am a nobody.
It doesn't matter what I do to anybody.
Nor does it matter what anybody does to me."

A body without spirit,
a spirit entrapped,
yet, apart,
from a worthless body.

"My God! My God!
Why have you forsaken me?"
cries Jesus from within.

"Anyone who so much as scandalises
one of these little ones,
it would be better
if a millstone be tied around his neck
and he be cast into the depths of the sea."
so spoke the gentle Jesus.

W.A.Dethlefs
10/06/1992

I hesitantly shared this poem with Theresa at our next meeting. She pored over it intently, quietly repeating the words, "Yes…. Yes."

It was a battle encouraging her to access counselling. Gradually she put out feelers, and soon she was tentatively interacting with professional services.

Her studies were progressing well; indeed she was accepted to do Honours and, after successfully completing her Honours degree, obtained a grant to pursue her doctorate.

I continued to have monthly contact with her, often sharing lunch in a cafeteria near her laboratory. After a while I sensed she was not travelling well. I felt she was playing around with drugs again. I tried my level best to steer her back to her support group but she wasn't interested. She broke off all contact with me, exited her PhD course without completing it, and disappeared.

Some years later she made contact with Diane, who told me that Theresa had inflicted irreparable damage to herself through drug usage.

I hold her in my heart in prayer.

Working with Brisbane Catholic Education

I N 2003, I COMMENCED part-time work as a Project Officer (Youth Development) for Brisbane Catholic Education (BCE). My job was to research and make recommendations on the nature, extent and needs of marginalised young people in Catholic school communities; the extent and profile of the students for whom current educational provision is irrelevant and who disappear out of Catholic school communities; and the potential for further criminalisation of young people arising from the recent legislation on Education and Training Reforms for the Future.

As David Hutton, the then Executive Director of BCE, told me: "We (Brisbane Catholic Education) wholeheartedly subscribe to the Church's teaching of preferential option for people who are poor. We know we have homeless and marginalised young people in our system. We don't know how many, where they are, what their needs are and which needs are being met and which aren't." This was my goal.

I didn't consider myself to be a researcher; however, I had conducted some small research projects over the years, and had studied research methods at the University of Queensland when I completed two postgraduate subjects in Community Development. I knew that what I didn't know myself, I could find out from friends who had undertaken similar research projects.

Firstly I invited a number of people from within BCE and from the non-government and non-Church sector to form a reference group to guide the work. Busy people generously accepted my invitation to meet where I was living, at the presbytery at Dutton Park, adjacent to the Brisbane headquarters of BCE. We decided to meet at noon for soup and special bread, then commence our meeting at 12.30pm. This arrangement promoted relationships, support and group cohesion. One of our first decisions was that the research should be both qualitative and quantitative. 'Qualitative' meant in this case, that I would try to obtain interviews from a number of homeless students, as well as interviewing some principals, guidance officers, teachers and learning support officers.

Even though I hadn't been asked to conduct research amongst the primary school people, I decided, and permission was readily given, to conduct a pilot survey across a number of primary schools. I wanted to know what the situation was with homeless, marginalised and disengaged primary school students.

I had encountered homeless children of primary school age over the years and knew they existed. I wasn't aware of any research that had been done in this area in Australia.

How would the research define 'homelessness'? There were a number of existing definitions: from the Human Rights and Equal Opportunity Commission Report, *Our Homeless Children*, of which I had been a Commissioner; from the National Youth Coalition for Housing; and from the work of Chamberlain and McKenzie, two nationally-recognised researchers into homelessness. Each definition stressed the instability or transience of shelter, high mobility between places of abode, and people who stayed in any form of temporary accommodation. Having a roof over one's head did not necessarily mean that one was not homeless. I wanted to use a definition that was accepted nationally, so that I could compare the results of my research with the national secondary student research undertaken by Chamberlain and McKenzie.[102]

Out-of-home students is the phrase that I decided to use in the research. It is virtually impossible for a roofless or houseless person to continue to attend school. Although out-of-home students without a roof over their heads may be able to attend school for a short time, most eventually drop out because of the struggle to find a safe place to stay, to feed themselves, to maintain hygiene and do their homework.

Out-of-home encompassed those students who were literally homeless or roofless, those couch surfing, those living in youth shelters or refuges, those children and young people in foster care or group housing, and those living with extended family full-time.

I adopted a description rather than a definition of *marginalised*. I approached school guidance officers, some teachers and some principals and asked them what came to mind when they heard the phrase 'marginalised students'. I used their responses in the survey. This is how I worded this question:

Students may be marginalised for some of the following reasons:

- home life is unstable;
- are subject to neglect;
- are subject to violence (physical, sexual, emotional) at home;
- whose parents have addictions;
- who themselves have mental health problems;
- whose parents have mental health problems;
- who are parentless in the sense that they do not have parents who care for them;

102 Chamberlain, C and MacKenzie, D (2002), *Youth Homelessness 2001*, Melbourne, RMIT.

- who have significant learning difficulties;
- who have severe behavioural problems.

In other words, who are the students you really worry about?

The final group I was asked to research was disengaged students. These were students who were not able to engage actively and confidently with the curriculum. I also asked the schools to provide case studies of what was working and why it was working.

I enjoyed the qualitative work of interviewing out-of-home students, principals, teachers, guidance officers, school chaplains and learning support staff. I had a similar set of questions for each group, including requests for their recommendations on how their school and the BCE system could assist in working with these students.

Speaking with some staff members as well as the out-of-home students was truly a memorable experience. On the day I visited one secondary school the counsellor told me there were 23 out-of-home students at his school on that very day. He told me he could also name another nine who had attended his school that year.

One of the out-of-home students I interviewed was a Year 12 student from Afghanistan. He had left home and country aged 15, as his parents didn't want him to kill anyone or be killed. With a couple of others he found his way to Indonesia, embarked on a boat for Australia, spent nine months in a detention centre (which he hated and said that was the worst thing that had ever happened to him), and was finally released into the community. He knew no-one except his friends, who were in the same predicament as himself. He wanted to complete his education. He told me he was literally homeless, having spent time in 40 different places over an 18-month period of time. Somehow or other, he found his way to the secondary school where I met him. They warmly welcomed him and were able to supply him with stable, permanent accommodation as well as a part-time job. He told me he had lived in the same house for the past six months and was very happy there.

I needed to ask my research questions so we got down to work. The first question I asked him was, "Who supports you in this school?" His immediate response was, "Everybody."

I'd never met a person from Afghanistan before, and wondered if he was exaggerating. So I asked him precisely who. He rattled off a list including the Principal, Deputy Principal, School Counsellors, Vocational Educations teachers and concluded with "all the teachers." At this stage, I was almost certain he was exaggerating.

I asked him how had the Principal supported him. He thought for a moment and then said, "Two weeks ago I had an afternoon appointment with the Immigration Department about my visa. I arranged with the Deputy Principal to have that afternoon off school. The day before the appointment the Principal called me to her office. She knew about the appointment and asked me if she could accompany me as a support. I readily agreed.

"So the next day, accompanied by the Principal who was carrying her brief-case, we were interviewed by the Immigration Officer. The Principal introduced herself and told the Officer that she supported my visa application and, opening her brief case and producing a sheaf of letters, told the official that all the teachers supported my visa application as well by writing individual letters."

I took the title for this report, *Making Room for Us*, from the words of an out-of-home secondary student whom I interviewed:

> *I tell everything to the school counsellor. If it's really important, she'll make room for us: for example, she'll change appointments to fit us in.*
> Laura, Year 12

Making Room for Us

All 32 secondary schools who returned the surveys reported out-of-home students at an average yearly rate of 14 out of 1000 students. All except three of these schools reported having marginalised students at an average yearly rate of 129 out of 1000 students.

As I mentioned earlier, I was keen to see how the figures compared with state and national research for out-of-home students. In their national research on secondary homeless students, Chamberlain and MacKenzie reported that 41 per cent of Catholic schools recorded homeless students in 2001 census week[103]. My research revealed that 100 per cent of Catholic secondary schools in the Archdiocese of Brisbane reported out-of-home students in 2003.

Further, Chamberlain and MacKenzie reported that the rate of out-of-home secondary students for Queensland was 15 per 1000, much higher than the national average of 10 per 1000. *Making Room for Us* research showed that Brisbane Catholic Education secondary schools reported a rate of 14 per 1000 of out-of-home secondary students, much higher than the national average, and consistent with Chamberlain and MacKenzie's figures for Queensland[104].

Of the 38 primary schools which returned the surveys, 26 reported out-of-home students at a yearly rate of 10 students per 1000. Amongst the cohort of 38 primary schools, 35 reported marginalised students at a yearly rate of 69 students per 1000.

When I presented this report to the BCE Leadership Team in January 2004, they were shocked by the figures the surveys produced, especially those for

103 Ibid., *p* 20.
104 Ibid., p 14.

out-of-home primary students. As a result, they requested I conduct further research into the situation of out-of-home, marginalised and disengaged primary students, in the hope that the figures flowing from a wider sample would flatten out. Both primary and secondary responses recommended the provision of enhanced resources, especially in the form of school counsellors.

The Leadership Team immediately responded to this request with 27 new full-time counsellor positions. These new school counsellors were in place by 1 July 2004, that very same year. This meant in practice that schools with a counsellor available for one day per week progressed to three days per week, and some with counsellors employed for three days per week now benefited from having the services of a full-time counsellor on staff.

In 2004 I concentrated my research on primary schools intent on receiving a higher return rate. The survey questions were the same. I was more experienced in working with BCE and now knew my way around. My reference group was in place and its members were keen to continue walking with me on this journey.

Permission was readily given to me to interview some grandparents who were caring for their grandchildren on a full-time basis. Over the years I had from time to time met some of these extraordinary people, and had read articles about their efforts and difficulties. All the grandparents I met deeply impressed me with their dedication, commitment, generosity, unselfishness and love for their grandchildren.

I'll tell you about one set of grandparents, whom I met in their home. They were caring for four grandchildren, three of whom were in primary school and the other, aged three, at home. They were on the pension and received little if any support from the State. Over a cup of tea in their homely kitchen, they spoke about what they were doing. Of course I had my research questions to ask, which they readily answered. Having finished those I asked them if they accessed respite care. No, they answered. "Do you need it?" I further queried. They spoke quietly between themselves for a few moments and then responded, "It would be lovely if, from time to time, someone could watch the grandchildren while we went out together for a cup of coffee." I was able to arrange for this on a regular basis.

Then I asked them if they were able to get away for a holiday. They exchanged knowing glances and told me that over the Christmas holidays they erected a tent and an inflatable pool in the back yard and slept down there with the children for a week.

Of the 109 primary schools surveyed, 104 returned the surveys, and of these 76 reported out-of-home students during the year 2004. This resulted in an average yearly rate of 14 students per 1000 living out of home. I was astounded by these figures. The Leadership Team and I had expected that with a larger sample the figures would 'flatten out', but instead they actually increased. In fact, they were similar to the figures for secondary students.

Of the 104 primary schools responding, 101 reported marginalised students in response to the survey. The average yearly number of marginalised students for BCE schools (2004) totalled 79 students per 1000. In 2003, the average yearly number was 69 students per 1000, a not too dissimilar result.

Implementation

We had recommendations in both reports from survey responses from schools, out-of-home students and grandparents, as well as from the one-on-one interviews. The Leadership Team requested I prioritise these into an implementation report. With the considerable assistance from the (by now expanded) Reference Group, the report was finished by June 2005.

The nine Recommended Key Action Proposals were wide-ranging and involved structural, policy, and practical changes. They included a stand-alone policy to assist out-of-home, marginalised and disengaged students and their families.

I was invited to present the Implementation Report to the Leadership Team. I made my presentation, answered clarifying questions and was about to leave when David Hutton, the Chairman and Executive Director, invited me to stay and for a discussion about the Report and the actions which may flow from it. At the conclusion of the meeting I walked out feeling elated, knowing that all the Recommended Key Action Proposals had been accepted.

I was so excited that I couldn't sleep that night. I phoned my Director's Professional Assistant the next morning, seeking an urgent appointment with the Director to confirm the events and conclusions of the previous day. When I walked into her office later that day she rose from her desk, and extending her hand, congratulated me adding: "You got all you asked for and more." I didn't sleep that night either.

I am glad to say that over the next few years the recommendations were implemented. After further consultation, it was decided that the effort to support and enhance the capacity of teachers, parents and students would occur via a website rather than a hard-copy manual. Eventually the website, *Marginalised Students: Believe in Us* was launched, as was the *Policy on Students who are Disadvantaged and at the Margins*.

School/community partnerships: St Paul's, Woodridge

Denise Ryan, semi-retired principal of a Catholic primary school, had been appointed to examine the needs of St Paul's Primary School, Woodridge. In my research I had found that St Paul's, drawing its students from some of the poorest socio-economic suburbs in Australia, reported out-of-home students at a rate of 25 out of 1000 and marginalised students at a rate of 135 out of 1000. Denise confirmed and enriched these statistics with detailed investigations of the students in each classroom, and through consultation with teachers, parents and student support staff. Her conclusion was that more than 53 per cent of students in that school were marginalised.

Denise had already assembled her Reference Group when I was invited to become a member. She had examined a number of models, for example, full-service schooling. Teachers needed support and families needed support as well. Eventually two new school officers were appointed—one (a teacher) to assist teachers, and the other a community development worker. The Education Faculty at Griffith University was interested, and offered to supply supervision for the community development worker and an evaluation in its third year of operation. BCE generously funded this pilot project for three years.

The project was a huge success, which the Evaluation Report confirmed. Both workers were brilliant, and with the cooperation of teachers, parents and school administration, they achieved results beyond the expectations of the Reference Group. Two unused classrooms were made available for the community centre. Many groups, especially ethnic specific ones, were encouraged to use the centre. The numbers attending Parents and Citizens' meetings increased immensely. What I had expected also happened: the standards of literacy/numeracy rose, as measured nationally by the NAPLAN tests.

Two stories

A girl arrived at school at the beginning of the school year and was enrolled in Year 6. Often she came to school smelly, wearing a dirty uniform. She frequently put her head down on the desk and slept. She was being shunned by some of her classmates. Her teacher tried to discuss her conduct with her, but to no avail. Of course, she was not achieving in class. Out of concern and frus-

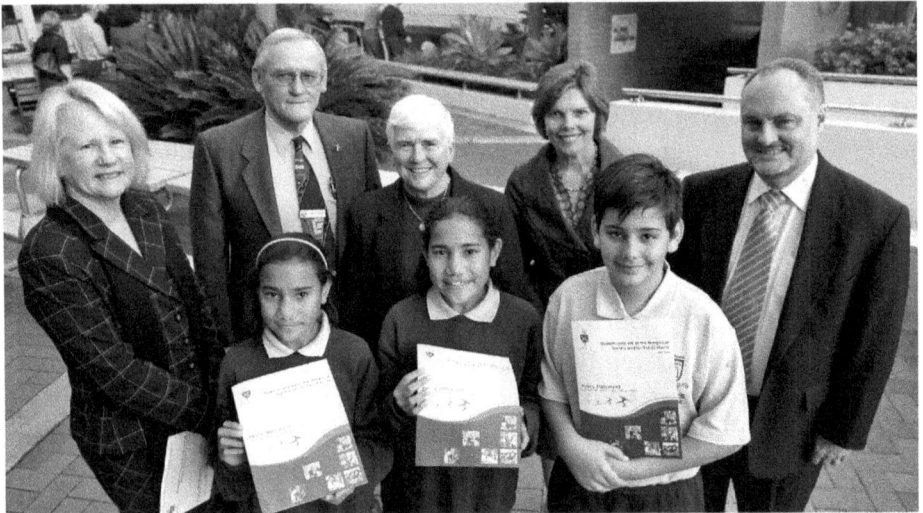

Launch of the policy on students on the margins of society or out-of-home

tration the teacher mentioned this situation to the Student Pastoral Worker who visited the student's family. There she found that the student was running the household, caring for the parents who suffered from mental health problems, and looking after and organising her younger siblings. The Student Pastoral Worker felt she could do nothing more for the parents than was being done by mental health agencies.

What to do? It was decided that what the school could do was to support the student. They arranged for her to call into the nearby convent on her way to school. There, with her own dressing gown and toiletries supplied by the nuns, she could enjoy a hot shower and if she needed to rest could sleep in her own bedroom and then, dressed in a clean uniform washed and ironed by the Sisters, she would go off to school feeling like a million dollars. She blossomed from this arrangement. It came as no surprise that she was soon able to make friends with her peers, and her grades improved out of sight.

A year or so later, a Year 6/7 teacher phoned me, requesting I take a double period with her students. They were just completing a project on homelessness, and she wished me to review it with her students. As some of these students had been, and still were, in out-of-home situations, she requested that I feed into the conversation some statistics, to let them know that this situation happened to other children as well.

I arrived in the classroom armed with a few PowerPoint slides and a whiteboard pen. I began: "I hear you have been doing a project on homelessness. Tell me what you have been doing?" Hands shot up everywhere. The first thing they had been doing, they said, was constructing their own definition of homelessness. The discussion was most interesting and I was able to feed into the conversation some of the statistics from the wider community.

When we seemed to have exhausted this topic, I said: "Thank you very much. I have enjoyed this conversation immensely. I will now be on my way." Hands shot up as some cried out, "But there's more." What else could there be, I asked. We've been studying Maslow's Hierarchy of Needs, was their response. I was astounded and replied: "I don't know a lot about Maslow, so you are going to have to teach me." So these enthusiastic young children told me about their understanding of Maslow's Hierarchy of Needs and how they used it to understand and change their own conduct.

Again I concluded, "Well we have discussed your definition of homelessness and Maslow's Hierarchy of Needs and I have enjoyed every moment of it. I'll say goodbye to you now and thanks for a very interesting morning." Again hands shot up and cries came from around the room, "But there's more!" "What else could there be?" I thought and asked.

"We have been looking at our school community to identify those students who don't feel at home in our school." I told them to tell me more. One girl told me that from time to time new students arrive at the school, and continued: "I say hello to them, offer to show them around the school, invite them to join my group of friends until they find their own group of friends." Another reported that sometimes you see a child unhappy, so you sit with them and offer to take them down to the library to play board games or to the community centre. Another told us that sometimes children have no one to play with, so he invites them to join in with him and his mates. And so the examples flowed.

I was most impressed with what I had heard. I found out later that the idea emanated from the community centre and the project was the responsibility of a social work/community work student who had been on placement at the school.

Adopt-a-Family

In 1999, I was invited by the parish priest to live in the presbytery at Dutton Park, an inner suburb of Brisbane. A few weeks before my first Christmas at St Ita's presbytery, a member of the local St Vincent de Paul Society approached me asking: "We know you work with disadvantaged individuals and families. Our St Vincent de Paul group is prepared to help you out with hampers. How many do you need?" I needed 16, which they readily supplied. This arrangement continued in subsequent years. A few years later when I was working for BCE, I attended a meeting where they discussed their annual collection of tinned food which they donated to the local St Vincent de Paul group. I praised their efforts and informed them of the generosity of the SVDP group in providing me with at least 16 hampers each Christmas.

One of the members suggested that instead of giving their donations for the hampers to SVDP, they should give them to me. I was concerned about SVDP missing out but was assured that an approach would be made to the local SVDP seeking their support.

Two or three people from this group took responsibility for this project. They emailed all managers informing them of the scheme, and suggested they consult their staff to gauge their interest and support. Small work groups were allocated one family, while larger ones were responsible for two or more families. Each work group was supplied with the first names, ages and gender of the members of each family.

In the first few years of its operation I delivered the hampers, with assistance, and witnessed the tears of joy and received the warm hugs from grateful recipients.

I delivered a hamper to one family. The father was in prison and the mother was expecting me. I placed three large cartons on her veranda. "Are these all for me?" she queried. She then asked if she could open them. The first carton contained tinned food. She took out a tin of peaches and said, "My boys will really love this." Then she took out a large jar of peanut paste, again repeating that her boys really loved peanut paste. She asked me if she could open the third box and did so. In it were beautifully wrapped Christmas presents—the top one even had her name on it. "Can I open this one?" she asked. "No." I said, "Two more sleeps 'til Christmas." As she gently placed the gift back in the box I heard her quietly remark, "That will probably be the only gift I receive this Christmas."

I enjoyed both positions I held with Brisbane Catholic Education. At the end of 2011, I decided I needed to slow down considerably, and reluctantly resigned, having received approval from the Archbishop to retire. I don't think I had ever experienced such a consistently supportive environment.

A proud recipient of the Australia Medal

Epilogue

WHAT HAS happened to the young people I worked with in the 1970s and 80s? How have their lives worked out? Have any or many survived? Or have they found peace at last with their Maker away from the troubles, worries and oppression foisted upon them at too young an age? What has become of them?

I continue to have regular contact with a few. I am saddened to report that some of these young people have taken their lives, worn out mentally and emotionally, losing hope at a too-young 17, 18 or 19 years of age. I hold them in my heart in love.

Others have died through 'natural' causes between the ages of 48 and 52. One of these was an accomplished Indigenous artist. She gave me one of her paintings which had taken nearly a year to complete, telling me, "Wally, this says thanks from all of us." Another became a peer leader who worked for better treatment and justice for those who like her had been unjustly incarcerated as children and young people. Some lost their battle with addictions, others have hung on. These too I hold in my heart in love.

Many have won through, making a solid contribution to their local neighbourhood and community. Some have completed study, one became a nurse, another a psychologist, still another a social worker, while several achieved qualifications and are doing or have done solid work with people suffering with major disabilities. I am buoyed up by one who wrote recently, "Wally, you have always been like a father to me. I did not always like what you said to me, telling it like it is. But one thing I will say is that I will always love and respect you."

When I retired at the end of 2011, I phoned a number of these friends, and their responses were heart-warming. One responded with "That's great Wally. Now we'll get to see a lot more of you." Another said, "We'll certainly see a lot more of you now that you are retired, because you are our family and we are your family."

I am still in contact with some released prisoners. We mostly catch up on the telephone and occasionally face-to-face for a cuppa and a chat. Those I am in contact with are going well, positively immersed in the community as they deal with the ups and downs of daily living. Some don't make contact, because they just don't want to be reminded of a horrifying past life. Some have done very well, working for Indigenous Land Rights, lecturing at university, managing a nursing home, or working with homeless and marginalised young people. A number have joined and are still members of twelve-step programs like Alcoholics Anonymous.

What has happened in the Juvenile Justice system and to some of the organisations I was involved in establishing?

The Juvenile Justice Act 1992 replaced the Children's Services Act 1965. Under the new Act, young people who had not been convicted of a criminal offence could no longer be locked away in a juvenile detention centre. Under this Act, restorative justice processes were also introduced in the form of the Youth Justice Conferencing Program, a diversionary program which brought perpetrator and victim together under the guidance of a skilled convenor. The Youth Justice Conferencing Program was a State-wide one which was rolled back under a subsequent government. In mid-2015, the new State government promised to reinstate court-based referrals to Youth Justice Conferencing which had been cut by the previous government. As the Minister said in her Media Release, this would provide "... an opportunity for young people to take responsibility for their criminal behaviour and its effect on victims".[105]

Wilson Youth Hospital, later renamed the Sir Leslie Wilson Youth Detention Centre, was officially decommissioned (and later bulldozed) in February 2001. It was replaced by the Brisbane Youth Detention Centre (BYDC) situated at semi-rural Wacol, between Brisbane and Ipswich. I finished chaplaincy duties there when I officially retired in December 2011. In marked contrast to Wilson, BYDC boasts of full-time schooling, full-time medical staff, a full-size oval and swimming pool, mechanical repair workshop, horticultural area, cultural activities, arts and crafts, music and recording area, and other facilities.[106]

105 See complete statement at http://statements.qld.gov.au/Statement/2015/7/14/ court-programs-to-address-crime-reinstated
106 See more, including photographs, at https://www.qld.gov.au/law/sentencing-pris- ons-and-probation/young-offenders-and-the-justice-system/youth-detention/ about-youth-detention/

Kedron Lodge is functioning well as it continues to befriend, accommodate and assist homeless young people. It offers a living skills program that provides 24-hour, fully supported medium-term accommodation for homeless and disadvantaged young people aged from 15 to 17 years. Staff at the Lodge aim to assist young people in acquiring and maintaining the skills and resources for independent living and to assist them to break the cycle of homelessness.[107]

Brisbane Youth Service continues to support homeless and at-risk young people and their children with a variety of programs including crisis support, housing, health services, parental skill development and specialist services for young women.[108]

The Youth Advocacy Centre (YAC) continues to offer free legal services, youth support, family support and bail support assistance and services to young people generally 10 to 18 years (inclusive) particularly those who are involved in, or are at risk of involvement in, the youth justice and/or the child protection systems, and/or are homeless or at risk of homelessness and live in or around the greater Brisbane region. YAC provides more limited support to those young people under 10 and over 18 years of age, and to young people outside of Brisbane via telephone, website and publications.[109]

Bayside Adolescent Boarding Incorporated (BABI) continues to provide services that are responsive to the needs of children, young people, families and the community by encouraging each person to realise his/her potential. BABI provides a range of professional services that focus on alleviating youth homelessness and promoting the growth and well-being of young people at risk.[110]

The BABI model was duplicated in other areas in the greater Brisbane area. While experiencing normal problems for community organisations they continue to do sterling work with their emphasis on early intervention and prevention work.[111]

* * *

Currently I am a member of the Education Reference Group which is auspiced by the Youth Affairs Network of Queensland. This is a three-year research project funded by the Australian Research Council (ARC) and conducted in Queensland. The final report from this research is titled *Queensland flexischools: Possibilities for an engaging education system* and was completed in 2016.

107 Adapted from the Lodge website: http://www.thelodgeyss.org.au/
108 Adapted from BYS website: http://www.brisyouth.org/
109 Adapted from YAC's website: http://www.yac.net.au/
110 Adapted from BABI's website: http://www.babi.org.au/
111 See for instance, Inala Youth Service (www.iys.org.au) and North West Youth Accommodation (http://www.nwyas.org.au/)

This research demonstrates that many of the young people in flexi-schools would not be in any form of education if such schools did not exist. The report's findings underline the precariousness of many young people's engagement with schooling, especially in rural and remote areas where few alternatives to the mainstream exist.

The research draws on case studies of and visits to flexi-schools across Queensland and interviews with youth workers and other significant personnel, especially teachers. The report identifies both the strengths and weaknesses of the 'flexi-school sector' and draws upon the lessons of the research into these schools to make recommendations to the mainstream schooling sector.[112]

I am also a member of a small group of practitioners working to establish Cygnet, an organisation that aims to transform conflict and adversity by building pathways to peace and community through restorative justice practices.

This poem was written about me and the human rights work I have been involved in. Barbara penned it for and recited it at my 70th birthday party.

One Man

When I was young and in a place
Where no one seemed to care,
One man fought on my behalf
Though others would not dare.

I'd been told I had no rights
For I was "just a kid",
But one man fought on my behalf
And showed me that I did.

They took away my childhood,
My freedom and the sky,
But one man fought on my behalf
When others would not try.

They locked me up in Wilson
But now I have the key
For one man fought on my behalf:
His name is Wally D.

Written by Barbara Lane
(used with permission)

112 See more at the YANQ website, http://www.yanq.org.au/reengagement-in-education.html